Jungle People

JUNGLE

A Kaingáng Tribe

A Caravelle Edition

A DIVISION OF RANDOM HOUSE

PEOPLE

of the Highlands of Brazil

JULES HENRY

WITH A FOREWORD BY RUTH BENEDICT

AND AN ADDED NOTE TO THE READER BY THE AUTHOR

VINTAGE BOOKS

NEW YORK

FIRST VINTAGE EDITION, AUGUST, 1964

VINTAGE BOOKS
are published by ALFRED A. KNOPF, INC.
and RANDOM HOUSE, INC.

Library of Congress Catalog Card Number: 64-22469
First published by J. J. Augustin, New York, 1941.

MANUFACTURED IN THE UNITED STATES OF AMERICA

To

EDUARDO AND DONA FRANCISCA DE LIMA E SILVA HOERHAN

in grateful and affectionate remembrance

Contents

Plates

Foreword

Oꜰ ᴀʟʟ ᴛʜᴇ ᴘʀɪᴍɪᴛɪᴠᴇ ᴛʀɪʙᴇꜱ ᴏꜰ ᴛʜᴇ ᴡᴏʀʟᴅ, we know least about those of South America. It was a continent with the greatest possible diversity of culture—from the high civilization of the Andes with its great political and military kingdoms to the shy hunters and food gatherers of the simplest cultures who had no permanent dwellings, no agriculture, no boats. Old chronicles tell us much about the higher cultures, not only about the kingdom of the Incas, but about the Araucanians of Chile and the Tupinambá of Brazil. But there are only fragmentary and horrified notes on the simplest tribes of the widely scattered Gê peoples, and for very good reason. These people were not only shy, they were desperate and cruel; they not only fled from the Whites into the often impenetrable hinterland, but they killed the invading stranger.

Yet from the point of view of history the simplest peoples of South America are all-important. Many of them have taken over agriculture and social complexities from other cultures, but the so-called Botocudo of Santa Catarina, Brazil—the Kaingáng as they are more properly called by Dr. Henry in this book—were not settled in villages with permanent homes around a central dancing-green; they had no gardens to supplement their food gathering and hunting of the tapir. A reservation had been set up for some years before Dr. Henry's stay among them, but it was no highly regimented affair like United States reservations, and the agency had been chiefly effective in putting a stop to bloodshed both within the tribe and in encounters with Brazilians. The Kaingáng still took every possible opportunity to absent themselves from their little settlement to hunt the tapir, the deer and the peccary. In order to communicate with them it was necessary to speak their language.

xi

Dr. Henry went to Brazil to study the culture of these people who, in a continent occupied over wide areas by tribes whose life was ordered on the basis of much more complex inventions, followed a type of life we often call that of simple savages. The Kaingáng turned out to fit the popular picture of savages in more ways than this. They were savages as Hobbes had pictured them, as he thought they must have been before the organization of the State had brought order among mankind. Even within the little tribe, kin by blood and by marriage, speaking the same dialect, the Kaingáng dealt violent death to one another and kept the memory green, in endless tales identifying every death wound given, down many generations. Little related bands constantly accepted invitations to fiestas when they knew the issue was to be merciless massacre. No man laid aside his deadly weapons. At a sudden signal the hosts fell upon the guests and it was a fight to the death. Outside the small bands—extended families, as Dr. Henry calls them—there were no bonds in Kaingáng society strong enough to prevent this tribal suicide.

It is hard to find another example among primitive tribes of this unstoppable blood feud of the Kaingáng. In other tribes, either blood or intermarriage or reciprocal advantage links people in alliances within which life is safe; there is some way of terminating feud—either a peace chief or a council of elders who intervene to "bury the blood", or a payment which may be made to the bereaved families, or a lex talionis which decrees that scores are evened. None of these provisions existed among the Kaingáng. Yet there was a group which kept the peace and within which not even adultery and incessant quarrels over women issued in bloodshed—the group that "travelled" together, the little party that hunted honey and birds and tapir in the jungle and lay around in each others' arms when the day's work was over. It was only bodily contact that the Kaingáng trusted —not a common language, not blood ties nor compacts among intermarrying families nor common tribal interests. And bodily contact could not guarantee peace in the tribe when the co-travellers were such a tiny fraction of those tribesmen to whom each man owed services. No man could fulfill all the duties expected of him. In half a dozen bands there were fathers-in-law of his, or brothers-in-law or cousins who expected him to help them in the tapir hunt and the honey gathering; when he "travelled" with some other relative, they regarded him as defaulting. Of course, he thought, they were angry; they were ready to kill him. His only recourse was to strike first.

The picture of the Kaingáng is a picture of social tragedy. Within the little band of co-travellers they were gay and self-indulgent and settled their quarrels without violence. But the little band was not co-extensive with their world, and in that outer world they could only kill, and kill those with whom they had social and economic bonds. To the outside observer it is clear that they were cutting their own throats, that no victory could be a real victory. But the Man from Mars would carry back just as devastating a report from the World Wars of the twentieth century on the planet Earth.

The Kaingáng are a fable for our times. They are not, however, as Hobbes thought, an example of Natural Man—man as he must inevitably be without a police force. In their suicidal aggressions they stand almost alone among primitive tribes, and are as truly the victims of an inadequate social order with inadequate sanctions for decent human life as are the victims of World Wars of today. They that slay by the sword shall die by the sword, but what is still more important in the history of any civilization, as the generations pass, the arts of life will be doomed, and brutal and asocial behavior will increase. The civilization will dig its own grave.

Dr. Henry has added to our understanding of society by his picture of a culture which was dying by its own hand. His painstaking investigation puts us in his debt.

RUTH BENEDICT

Columbia University
New York City

A Note to the Reader

On Love and Death

THIS BOOK IS ABOUT LOVE as well as death; it is about loyalty as much as it is about treachery. It tells how even among one of the most primitive cultures in the world an abstract concept like doom—called *lũ* by the Kaingáng—can be formed when a people knows it is doomed. "I shall go dancing to meet my doom *(lũ)*" is the striking phrase that appears in their origin myths. The Kaingáng say, "They are referring to death, and they say that something is killing them.... They refer to their death as *lũ*. My *lũ* kills me and I die. When they are killed and they die they say, 'My *lũ* killed me....' When a person goes to meet the approaching enemy ... [they say,] 'Your *lũ* is looking at you.' "* I know of no other tribal folklore so preoccupied with entrapment and homicide as that of the Kaingáng. Perfidious killing is the artistic theme around which the Kaingáng story teller develops his plot. But though the bloody denouement is always salient, the themes of love and self-sacrifice come through clearly also. Thus just as our movies endlessly blend sex and violent death—where five men die for every woman loved—because our culture is obsessed with love and death, so the Kaingáng stress these elements because they are uppermost for them.

Except for saints, life can be polarized between love and death only if there is no intensity in between; only if everything else has dropped out of life; only if there is nothing else on which to bestow meaning. Thus we can say that man thinks only of love and death when he has nothing else left to him. Put another way, when life is empty man flies from death into love; and when he cannot love he is frightened of death and so turns to love obsessively. Obsession with love and death fills the void left by the departure

---

* The Kaingáng word for death is *tele*. There are many words for kill: *taiñ; katõtügn; katõlup,* are a few. To kill supernaturally is *tädn*.

xv

of significance from life, and significance is driven out of life paradoxically when the effort to survive becomes too much for us. On the other hand throughout history man has sought to give significance to life by elaborating death; thus warfare has often become the most significant manifestation of life. Out of this comes the Dakota Indian father who places his hand lovingly on his son's shoulder and says, "My son, it is time for you to die"; meaning, of course, that it is time for his son to go on the warpath. Where dying has become the most significant element in life, self-love, in the form of seeking glory, competes with love of others. This is what led Leonidas to monopolize the defense of Thermopylae: he wanted the Spartans alone to have the glory of dying in its defense; and this is why *waiḳayu* (self-love) competes with love of women among the Kaingáng.

The Kaingáng were involved absolutely in those they loved. There was a oneness in the relationships among them that could not be given up even to escape death; and it is here that these jungle-dwellers go beyond Buber, for though he does not speak of an I-Thou relationship even unto death, this *is* relationship to the Kaingáng.

And so it turns out that among their friends and relatives the Kaingáng were the most ethical people on earth, though to outsiders they were treacherous killers. It is easy to understand why this had to be, for when the outside world is so threatening, one's own little world has to be made secure.

Everywhere the dialectic of social life tends to force existence into such simple forms; and everywhere the complexity of culture is evidence of the triumph of man over the dialectic of his own society. In this the Kaingáng failed and all their culture has become integrated around its two central themes. Their religion and their divining are elaborations of these, just as their daily life is. Even an arrow lost in the forest will die of loneliness, they say, if it is not found and its spirit will return to kill the man who lost it.

Psychoanalytic Influences in Jungle People

A word is necessary about the writing of *Jungle People.* The first research I undertook as a graduate student was on the austerities of the North American Indians of the Great Plains. Beginning at puberty the males among them underwent self-tortures ranging from starvation and icy plunges to the tortures of the Sun Dance. I tried to gain an understanding of the psychic roots of these by reading Freud and came upon *Beyond the Pleasure Principle,* where I read about the love and death instincts. Though I did not believe in such instincts, I carried with me to Brazil and into the jungle with the Kaingáng the idea of the fateful dichotomy. In the tropical forest I found, purified to its rarest possible form, the Freudian image. *Jungle People* is organized around the ideas of *Beyond the Pleasure Principle,* but not because it is the ideal framework, but because the Kaingáng live it out.

Since, when I was writing *Jungle People* psychoanalysis was barely known in anthropology, it seemed to my professors, as to much of the intellectual world, to be a fad, and I was advised to take the psychoanalytic terminology out of *Jungle People* because its presence would "date" the book. The result of accepting this advice was that the book has not been perceived as the first anthropological monograph written from a psychoanalytic point of view. However, *Jungle People* does not reflect the ideas in *Beyond the Pleasure Principle* only for I use the Kaingáng to examine other principles of psychoanalysis also. For example, the common Kaingáng custom in which father and son marry the same woman is studied in terms of the Oedipus Complex; and this, together with the Kaingáng marriage to the step-sister and step-child, is viewed against the background of theories of incest. The expected psychoanalytic terminology is missing, however, from the discussion. The mechanisms of defense and the fate of narcissistic libido are also studied in *Jungle People,* as one can see in the chapter on "Psychic Structure"; yet because the terms were not used it has not been perceived that I had these issues before me.

Since I considered the use of psychoanalytic theory a success and since the understanding of the fate of the Kaingáng would have been impossible without it, I have had no reason to abandon psychoanalysis as an instrument for the interpretation of culture. It cannot be used alone, however, and psychoanalytic theory without an understanding of socio-economic structure, without a knowledge of perception and learning theories, is like a man without a wife and children.

On Plot and Plotlessness

Jungle People has a plot because the life of the Kaingáng has one. Yet, since behavioral science views life as plotless, *Jungle People* violates an underlying premise. Moreover, in the behavioral sciences, to state that life not only has a plot but must be described as if it did is like spitting in church.

The conception of culture as plotless has a long and respectable history in American anthropology and is supported by all respectable departments. Even Ruth Benedict's *Patterns of Culture* and *The Chrysanthemum and the Sword,* however eloquently they have presented the theme of plot in culture, have not been able to overcome the entrenched respectability of plotlessness. One can understand why this should be, for a determined search for meaning in life confronts us eventually with the fact that many of its meanings are delusive. The search for meaning and plot in culture ultimately compels one to look for them in his own life, and since this may lead to despair, it is better not to search at all. Hence in cultural anthropology "integration" and "function" have been substituted for plot, and anthropology has been made safe.

The search for pattern and meaning does not mean "impressionism." On the contrary, the search is a most exacting one, for the mosaic of a plot can be put together only after the most difficult research. It is immeasurably more difficult to find out, for example, how much suffering is involved in the process of adoption than to discover whether children are adopted by their mothers' or fathers' relatives, by friends or by strangers. While knowledge of the latter is necessary to the exploration of the former, to do only the latter is to settle for mere formalism.

The Existential in Anthropology

There have always been two trends in cultural anthropology: the formalistic and the existential; the preoccupation with parts versus the concern with wholeness; an interest in structure versus a search for meaning; the insistence on plotlessness versus the perception of plot. Since these trends are present in sociology and psychology as well as in anthropology and since *Jungle People* is concerned with the existential, the meaningful, and the whole, I should talk somewhat about the significance of the trend to formalism and plotlessness.

Concern with love and death, with hope, dread, despair, resoluteness, and the striving to be a self—in other words, with the existential elements in life—is demanding. It is much more comfortable to do as many behavioral scientists do: to proceed as if life were just behavior—activity without yearning, hope, or fear.

But comfort is not the only factor making for formalism. Interest in existence requires involvement in other people, and we are turning away from others. As Sartre implies in *No Exit*, for many of us hell is other people. It is better to be uninvolved. On March 27, 1964, *The New York Times* carried on its front page horrifying proof of the fact that we do not want to be involved. The article, "37 Who Saw Murder Didn't Call Police" relates that at three in the morning, 37 people, awakened by the screams of the victim, watched from behind their darkened windows while a man stabbed a woman to death, returning three times to finish the job. Yet nobody called the police until it was all over and the man had fled. They said they didn't "want to get involved." (Of course, they are involved because they will carry their guilty consciences to the grave.)

Involvement in other people requires feeling for them; it exacts worry about their hunger and a wish to share one's food with them; it leads to concern for the death of their dear ones, a sharing of their grief, and even fear of the devils they fear; it involves rage at those who assault them, and even the risk of one's life to protect them. All this brings about mutual dependence, and many, especially in the West, shrink from dependence. Closely related to fear of involvement is the tendency to avoid what is emotionally intense and even to reject one's own intensity as invalid. Along with this goes the rejection of people who are intense.

Anthropological rejection of involvement derives from despair of human relations and one despairs of them because one is in despair of one's self. This is another reason why it has come about that in some quarters of anthropology human issues are a threat, while formalism has become a defense against them.

The third reason for the emphasis on formalism to the exclusion of the existential, is the hankering, in some corners of anthropology, to imitate the worst aspect of sociology—the formalism which has produced mountains of dubious statistical tables and graphs, mathematical models built on phantom experiments conducted from behind one-way screens and so on. It is pathetic that just as the young Turks of sociology are rebelling against this* some young anthropologists should be imitating it. This has occurred because empiricism, once a healthy reaction against arid speculation in sociology, has become prestige sociology. Following natural science, it hoped to establish in sociology the same kinds of truths that the natural sciences had. In its turn, however, empiricism in sociology became arid.† Anthropology must not follow it into the desert.

Flight from the existential is not unique to anthropology and sociology. In psychology it is accomplished through turning to lower animals and in education it has taken the form of flight from children, so that most of the professors in education departments have not spent time in an elementary or high school classroom since their "practise teaching" days. Everywhere the human disciplines run away from the humanity of human beings. Obviously then, human beings will turn away from the human disciplines. I hope *Jungle People* will help prevent it.

J. H.
St. Louis, 1964

* See *The New Sociology*, edited by Irving Louis Horowitz (Oxford, 1964).

† A perfect demonstration of this proposition is *Human Behavior*, by Bernard Berelson and Gary Steiner (Harcourt Brace and World, 1964).

Preface

Tʀɪʙᴇꜱ ꜱᴘᴇᴀᴋɪɴɢ Kᴀɪɴɢᴀ́ɴɢ ᴅɪᴀʟᴇᴄᴛꜱ inhabit the highlands of southeastern South America from the state of São Paulo, Brazil to Argentina. Although no thorough study has previously been made of any of these tribes enough has appeared in print[1] to indicate that they differ in language and culture. The group I studied[2] is localized on the government reservation of Duque de Caxias in the municipality of Dalbergia in the state of Santa Catarina, Brazil. It is one extended family.[3] A handful of fellow tribesmen, probably another extended family, is living on a reservation at Palmas[4] in the state of Santa Catarina, and as late as 1934 a small group of Kaingáng, thought to be tribesmen of those at Duque de Caxias, was reported to be wandering wild and causing damage in the southern part of the state.

Since 1914 when the Kaingáng were pacified and localized at Duque de Caxias epidemics have reduced their number from between three and four hundred to 106,[5] and a number of changes have come over their culture.

[1] A summary of data on the Kaingáng tribes is given in "La civilisation materielle et la vie sociale et religieuse des Že du Brésil meridional et oriental," by Dr. Hermann Ploetz and Dr. A. Metraux, *Revista del Instituto de Etnologia de la Universidad de Tucuman* (Argentina), Tucuman 1930. Volume 1, Entrega 2a, pp. 107-238.

[2] They have also been called Botocudo. This is unfortunate for it confuses this Kaingáng speaking tribe with the linguistically unrelated Botocudo of Minas Geraes, Brazil. Dr. Jose Maria de Paula has published a vocabulary and some remarks on the Kaingáng of Duque de Caxias in "Memoria Sobre os Botocudos do Paraná e Santa Catarina . . ." in *Congreso Internacional de Americanists*, Rio de Janeiro, 1922. 20 Session, Volume 1; pp. 117-137.

[3] This term is explained in the body of the book.

[4] Herbert Baldus has a vocabulary and some remarks on these Indians in *Anthropos*, Volume 30, 1, 2. January-April 1935, p. 191.

[5] 40 children (19 males, 21 females); 9 males and 15 females over thirty; 27 males and 15 females over fifty.

Until 1914 the Kaingáng robbed and killed the Brazilian colonists, but now they live in peace. Under government instruction they have learned to till the soil. Both men and women have adopted the clothes of the whites and the men have cut their hair and discarded their typically male ornament, the lip plug. The young men use fire arms exclusively; one man about sixty uses only bow and arrow; the other men over forty alternate between bow and arrow and gun. Nowadays the Kaingáng attempt houses after the fashion of the poor white farmers of the region—mud walls, thatched roofs and dirt floors—but the Kaingáng often do not get beyond the roof, and even that leaks. Changes are also noticeable in ritual and social life. Some rituals have dropped out and the bloody feuds between the extended families are no longer carried on. Although polygyny is still practised polyandry has been given up.

In spite of change, however, many of the old ways of life are still followed and fundamental attitudes remain the same. The culture is far from dead. Because of their ferocity only the bugreiros—men hired by the colonists to kill the Indians—ever dared approach the Kaingáng before pacification. Since that time the government has steadily resisted all attempts to establish missions among them. Although there is a Catholic church about five miles away from the reservation its effect on the Kaingáng has been practically nil.

I lived on the reservation from December 1932 to January 1934 and my house was in the center of the Kaingáng village.

Although the Kaingáng are now small farmers they still spend about half their time hunting. They are great week-enders. Every Friday some of them plunge into the jungle and turn up on Monday with a few quarters of tapir, deer or wild pig, or some birds. From time to time I joined them on these trips but with the exception of a five week expedition I made with them into the jungle my work was largely limited to wandering about the village, in and out of houses, sitting by fires and talking, working with paid informants, and, of course, treating their ailments.

Frae Mansueto Barcatta de Val Floriana has published a grammar[6] of the language of the Kaingáng of São Paulo but no systematic study of the language of any of the Kaingáng speaking tribes of Santa Catarina had appeared in print prior to my "A Kaingáng Text."[7]

Although today Kaingáng males between 20 and 30 years of age know some Portuguese there was only one whose Portuguese was good enough

[6] "Ensaio de Grammatica Kainjgang," *Revista do Museu Paulista*, Volume X, São Paulo, 1918. Frae Mansueto's grammar suffers from an attempt to impose Indo-European grammatical categories on the Kaingáng language. His "Diccionarios Kainjgang-Portuguez e Portuguez-Kainjgang," *Revista do Museu Paulista*, Volume XII, São Paulo, 1920, is excellent.

[7] *International Journal of American Linguistics*, Volume VIII, 1935, pp. 172-218.

for linguistic purposes. None of the women speak Portuguese. Most of the ethnological data was obtained in the native language, which I learned to speak.[8]

Whatever merits this book may have are due primarily to the training I received from my teachers Franz Boas and Ruth Benedict. The specific suggestions they have made regarding Kaingáng culture have often provided far-reaching insights into its nature. Dr. Margaret Mead's lectures on field methods and her criticism of my manuscript have been of great help in the formulation of my ideas about Kaingáng culture. To Mr. Hans J. Uldall, ace of phoneticians, go my thanks for the excellent preparation that helped make it possible for me to master quickly the peculiarities of the Kaingáng language. The criticisms of my wife, Zunia Henry, have been most valuable.

The field work that supplied the basis for this book was made possible through an appropriation of the Department of Anthropology of Columbia University.

My gratitude is due to my two dear friends, Eduardo de Lima e Silva Hoerhan, and his wife, Dona Francisca whose kindness and solicitude made it possible to carry on under strange and difficult circumstances.

Brazilian officials, particularly Dr. Dulphe Pinheiro Machado, Minister of Labor, Dr. Bezerra Cavalcanti, now deceased, of the Indian Service, and Dr. Roquette-Pinto and Dona Heloise Torres of the National Museum, have also been immeasurably helpful and kind to me.

JULES HENRY

Instituto Politécnico Nacional
Mexico, D. F.

[8] See Appendix IV.

Notes on the Spelling[1] of Kaingáng Words

THE SPELLING OF KAINGÁNG PROPER NAMES is a rough approximation of the true phonetic values. Other Kaingáng words have been more accurately rendered by the following system:

- i   as in English *feet*.
- ï   as in Russian *Bbl*. A sound midway between the vowel in English *feet* and the vowel in English *do*.
- e   as in German *fehle*. Approximately as the vowel in English *rain*.
- ë   as in a Londoner's pronunciation of *third*.
- ê   as in English *fed*.
- a   as in English *father*.
- â   as in English *hat*.
- o   as in German *wohl;* French *eau*.
- ô   as in English *awe*.
- u   as in English *do*.
- û   approximately as in English *sure*.
- w   an *m* that is pronounced with the upper teeth touching the lower lip. In technical parlance a labio-dental *m*.

All other consonants have the same values as in English. The sign ˛ under a vowel as in o̧ represents nasalization as in French *on*. The acute accent indicates word accent. In some cases it has been impossible to indicate accents because of printing difficulties. The large majority of two syllable words, however, accent the last syllable. Three syllable words are more erratic.

[1] A precise phonetic scheme is given in "A Kaingáng Text." See fn. 2, p. xiv.

Jungle People

I

The Forest and Its People

THE KAINGÁNG WERE FOREST NOMADS. For perhaps three hundred years
that was the only life they knew, and they resented it. The forest was not
their original home, for they were driven into it from their farms on the
savannahs to the west by their enemies. They speak with nostalgia of the
time long ago when they lived in little fenced villages and planted corn,
beans and pumpkins. Before the pacification they had no villages and instead of dividing their time between cultivating their crops and hunting in
the forest as they used to do, they wandered forever in the forest and planted
no crops at all.

The forests of Santa Catarina are vast and mighty; they are rich and well
watered, tall and gloomy. Saplings and trees six feet in diameter crowd
close upon one another. Bushes cluster about the trees, and the whole is
woven into one solid mass by the vines that hang from trees, twine about
bushes, and creep along the ground. The forest everywhere grows right
down to the edges of the rivers and looms on both sides like the walls of a
great corridor, silent and lovely, impenetrable except with knife or club.
Flocks of geese, taboo to the Indians, for those landlocked creatures may
not touch these timid and agile waterfowl, skim above the surface of the
rivers, and wherever a lichen-covered cliff rises from the river's edge it
throws their calls echoing back and forth across the water.

I used to joke with the Brazilians telling them that their beautiful state
of Santa Catarina was not a land but a solution, for it is indeed a country
of ten thousand water courses. Innumerable little streams undermine the
earth, and during the rainy season in August and September, when it sometimes rains for a month without cease, when day after day thunder rolls
about the mountain tops and the wind blows and the forest rocks until you

3

imagine it is going to crash solidly on your head, these subterranean streams cast great sections of the earth into the rivers. Then streams that were sluggish and clear become turgid and rushing. Rivers that moved slowly and whose bottoms you could easily see through their few feet of clear water rise almost four feet overnight, and their purling shallows become dangerous rapids, pouring tons of muddy red water down toward the sea. Then all day long the shouts of the Indians—"Storm, go away, I am afraid of you; so stop!"—go up among the camps, rising faintly above the roar of the river, the rush of the rain, and the ceaseless rumble of the thunder.

Water is everywhere in Santa Catarina, and it literally grows on trees, or at least in bamboo, the hollow stems of which are filled with it. You cannot walk far without coming across at least a brook, and the Indians use the streams as short cuts, sometimes walking in the water for half a mile. In nine days a pair of rubber-soled tennis shoes rotted off my feet; by the end of my five-weeks' hunting trip the seams of my waterproof leather boots had rotted. Yet in this land where a hundred thousand terraces bear witness to ages of slow erosion and the winding streams interlace like silver bands, the Kaingáng are without boats or rafts. They have every other technique for crossing a stream that ingenuity and resourcefulness might suggest: they knock down a tree on one side of a stream so that it will fall on the other and form a bridge, and they also build crude bridges. Men who have supernatural power obtained from some water animal may even brave a turbulent stream to carry a line across so that other people may pull themselves across on it. But before they came to Duque de Caxias the Kaingáng knew nothing of navigation, and the one instance in folklore of an attempt at it ended in a fiasco. Of course the Kaingáng were land nomads. It would have been too much work to build a canoe or even a raft just to cross a stream and it was much easier for them to wait until the river went down; for the Kaingáng never felt a pressing need to be anywhere at any particular time. They might just as well have been on one side of the river as on the other.

To know how to walk in the bed of a stream, stepping unerringly from stone to slippery stone, is really a blessing, for a smarting body appreciates the respite from thorns, and the coldness of the water is soothing to one's battered and aching shins. The forest is no place for a pleasant stroll. The gait of the forest rover is unmistakable, for he never just steps; he *places his feet*. Where a thorn may prick, a vine slash, a fallen log batter; where the earth may crumble underfoot or a snake strike from the concealment of a pile of leaves or a low bush overhanging the trail, every move must be a maneuver. When an Indian is scratched or bruised, he stops and removes the cause so that those who follow will not suffer as he did. He gropes for the thorn until he finds it and then carries it far away to dispose of it, or he carefully chops out the root or log until the path is clear; he never leaves a rough edge.

The forest has certain little peculiarities whose marks the Indians recognize when they see one of their number come back from the hunt with a bloody eye or a mass of little cuts on his legs. There is a kind of bamboo that the Indians call *kotkólo* which hangs like a vine from trees and whose mark on the human body is so specific that the Indians can always tell when one of them has fallen foul of it. *Kotkólo* has a surface like sandpaper and a long thorn that curves slightly upward like a tiny scimitar. If you escape the thorn the surface may rasp across your face and leave a stinging welt. There is also a tall strong grass that grows in the open places the Indians love so well and that cuts like a knife. No one dares just walk through it; the feet must swing out like scythes to beat it down.

The Indians are acutely aware of their mountain forests as something with which they have to struggle and which is full of pain for them. The forest is a mass of vines and thorns that cut and trip; it is alive with insects that suck and torment; and they make no bones about saying so. They divide the forest into "clean places," those in which there are no vines, thorns, or bamboo,—they also call them "pretty places"—and "dirty places," where the tangle is so thick that it obscures the light of day.

In the winter these mountain forests are cold and nights are gray with the mist that rises from the watercourses. The temperature often drops below freezing at night, and not even the thickest clothing will keep out the cold and damp. Yet for generations the only clothing the Indians had was a knee-length netlike robe of plant fiber, worn about the waist by the women, and a closely woven shirt of the same material, reaching to the hips, worn by the men in the winter. When they began to raid the Brazilians they stole vests and blankets and it was common to see an Indian naked except for a little belt around his waist to tie up his penis— and a vest. The vest kept the torso warm while it allowed freedom of motion to the arms. The Kaingáng never do anything more with an animal skin than make soup of it, and before they had blankets and vests they simply spread a few fern fronds on the ground at night and lay down on them to sleep, pulling a net-like robe over themselves if they were so fortunate as to possess one.

On winter nights they are miserable and often get up to warm themselves by the fire. One morning in May as I warmed my aching joints by the fire and watched my breath spiral upward, Chukembégn said to me: "Last night I slept all over the place. It was so cold nobody slept." Sometimes they fall asleep sitting by the fire, their arms on their drawn-up knees, their heads sunk forward. The scarcity of blankets brings the young men together in the sleeping parties they love, when a half dozen of them, wrapped in each other's arms, lie under a couple of blankets. Children sleep almost anywhere that they can crawl under a blanket, and any solitary sleeper welcomes warm flesh that will help to shelter him against the cold. If children were not welcome sleeping companions it would go hard with them in families where scarcity of blankets would leave them absolutely unprotected.

The Kaingáng are hungry in winter and early spring. Then the tracks of animals are hard to interpret and the tapir can run far and fast, for it is no longer burdened with its young and the forest is cool. To the Kaingáng the tapir is not only the most important food, it is the very symbol of food. When they have no tapir meat there is very little meat of any kind, for the tapir is most plentiful when the wild fruits and nuts are ripe, and when these are gone the monkeys and birds, the rodents and pigs, the deer and the tapir that have fed on them for months, grow scarce or vanish altogether. Many primitive people who are faced with this seasonal scarcity have developed some technique of preservation, but not so the Kaingáng. They preserve only pine nuts and have nothing to support them in these times of hunger.

Summer, with its warmth, its dryness, and its plenty, brings comfort at last to these people who sew no skins and make no warm clothes against the winter, who have no knowledge of boats or rafts to carry them across the rivers that lie everywhere around them, and who, in a hungry land, preserve no food and make no traps. If necessity were the mother of invention the Kaingáng would have all these things, which would make their life easier. If people systematically adapted themselves to their environment the Kaingáng would not only be dogged and skillful hunters, but they would have the traps and the fishing techniques which they completely lack. The men would not only be untiring, uncomplaining providers, but they would have discovered how to preserve the food they obtain with so much effort, so that in the lean days of winter they would not grow weak and retch and vomit with hunger.

The Kaingáng are powerful and of tough physique.[1] The arms and legs of the full-grown men are thick and muscular, and the women, although shorter and less conspicuously muscular, are strong enough to carry heavy loads. Their hair is straight and black, their dark-brown eyes wide and level, their noses high-bridged and coarse, their lips thick. Their skin color ranges from a deep brown to a golden tan. Sometimes a sick person who has lain a long time by the fire, away from the sun, may be practically white. The men, who are about as tall as the average white European, are graceful in spite of their massiveness. It is a pleasure to see them walk—the tangled forest has never let them learn to run—with their high springing

[1] They have very bad teeth.

step, or balance themselves incredibly on a narrow tree six feet above a stream while hundred-and-fifty-pound loads hang from their heads.

All their lives these people pitted their strength, intelligence, and persistence against the forest, against their ancient enemies the Kangdjá, against the Brazilians, whom they hated and feared, and even against some of their own relatives, of whom they lived in constant terror—eager to avenge murders and sleepless for fear of reprisals. The characteristics of the typical Kaingáng male, tough, resourceful within the limits of his intelligence and experience, dogged and hard to kill, were summed up in one-legged Thuyídn, who died some years ago. In the words of a Kaingáng: "He was not old. In spite of the fact that he had only one leg he used to knock down pine nuts. He would make a loop and climb up.[2] He chopped out honey and killed tapirs. He would run after the dogs. He leaned on a stick in front of him. He had abscesses on the buttocks, back, and hands— he was sick, but he went with them. He was hard to kill. The Brazilians stabbed him in the back and it came out in front. It pierced his lung. Another pierced him below the ribs. He had been shot twice. Once he was cut in the head. He fought. He had seized a knife by the blade and lost two fingers."

There can be no doubt that the Kaingáng bred individuals fit for survival. Certainly men like Thuyídn were born to survive. But for a society to perpetuate itself it must also be able to cope with internal conflicts that might destroy it, and this, Kaingáng society was not able to do. Composed as it was of hundreds of Thuyídns it was nevertheless unable to stay the destruction that certainly would have overtaken it had not the Kaingáng at last established friendly relations with the Brazilians.[3]

As the pattern of Kaingáng culture unfolds in the pages that follow we shall see how this group, excellently suited in their physical and psychological endowments to cope with the rigors of their natural environment, were yet unable to withstand the internal forces that were disrupting their society, and, having no culturally standardized devices to deal with them, were committing social suicide.

[2] Full-grown Santa Catarina pine trees have no limbs within thirty feet of the ground.

[3] In September 1914 the Serviço de Protecção aos Indios accomplished the pacification of the ferocious Kaingáng through the heroism of Eduardo de Lima e Silva Hoerhan.

II

Nomadic Life

THE KAINGÁNG USED TO WANDER about in the forest in small bands searching for food. Even now when they go hunting they rarely stay even a week in one place. They fall asleep without plans for the morrow, and they awaken in the morning without any idea of what they are to do. A few words over the morning fire may decide them to move on, and in ten minutes their possessions will be packed into baskets. The father strides off carrying his weapons in his hands: the indispensable axe and a gun or a massive seven-foot bow and a dozen arrows, while the mother comes plodding behind with the basket full of household possessions and the remaining food, if they are lucky enough to have any, the baby perched atop the load and the brother or sister holding on to her left hand, the right bearing a smoking firebrand for use at the next camp.

The Kaingáng hate to build the frail little shelters they call houses, and they never do so until the rain is on them. I always had to argue with the Indians to help put up my tent. When the clouds piled up in the sky, the air grew sultry, and the sun changed from yellow to dull red, I would say to Chukembégn, "It looks like rain." With a deprecatory glance at the sky he would reply: "No, it's not going to rain—not today. Tomorrow maybe, but today, no." "But look at those clouds." "That's nothing; it will pass." "Yes, the way it passed yesterday. Let's get the tent up, Chukembégn." At last the tent would be put up, sometimes as the first drops fell or in a pouring rain. It was not laziness that made them so slow to put up my tent, for they too could always take advantage of it; but housebuilding is simply an annoyance, and they never raise a shelter even for themselves unless they are forced to. It rains several times a day at the new moon in fall and winter, but though they know this perfectly well, they will not build a house if the sky is clear when they make camp. In the night, when the rain finally does come, they either lie asleep where they are, start up and hurriedly throw together a house from whatever material happens to be lying about, or wander sleepily into the ethnologists tent, where they crowd together sleeping almost on top of one another. If the ethnologist descends from his hammock on such a night he steps on someone's face or kicks an infant in the ribs.

These houses that the Kaingáng are so loath to build are made by tying arched boughs to a high transverse that is supported by two uprights sunk in the ground. Horizontal boughs are laid and tied across the arched ones, and the whole is covered with leaves to within about two feet of the ground. The result is a long shelter open completely on three sides and partly open on the fourth, with a curved roof that forms the rear wall. A man and his wife can put one up in half an hour. When there are many people the house may be doubled so that instead of the arch being like this:

it looks like this:

If people arrive unexpectedly the house can be extended indefinitely by the addition of transverse beams.

On the edge of the long side of the house long logs are laid for the fires; and the Indians sleep in a row with their feet to the fire. Since these houses are not partitioned into family rooms the opportunity for anyone to gratify his curiosity is limited only by the height of the flames and by his good manners. At night when the men have come in and the flames are leaping, the pots bubbling, and the meat roasting, the houses fill with blinding smoke. After supper the fires die down, and it is pitch-dark beyond the faint red glow of the coals. A few hours later it is impossible to see what is going on, and even the Indians cannot tell which dark bulk is Vomblé and which his wife, Kulá. Although everyone is careful to provide a place for himself when camp is made, there is no certainty that he will actually sleep there, for the Kaingáng are nomadic even in their sleep. Although Véye may eat with his wife he may get up to wander over to Chukembégn's fire for a few nuts and to Waipó's for a bit of fruit, and if sleep overtakes him at Waipó's he will sleep there. Perhaps later in the night when the chill and stiffness have crept into his bones he will get up and wander sleepily over to his wife, kicking Klendó in the ear and overturning Amendó's pot in his semi-somnambulism. All of this makes ethnology terribly difficult, for it is hard to be sure that the dark mass you had decided was Yakwá an hour ago isn't Vomblé or just the shadow of the house post now.

Kaingáng camp sites are any shape at all. Level ground is rare and what there is is so irregular that the Indians have to distribute themselves about it in the most economical way possible. But they will never sleep on any kind of slope, and if a particular patch of level ground is just a little too small for a family they may build it up by throwing some dirt on a foundation of leaves. When a woman sits down, lays her firebrand on the ground, piles wood on it, and begins to nurse her baby, it is pretty certain that camp will be made right there. No woman sits down without deliberation, for where she sits she stays, and where she stays she and her husband will sleep. Nothing can dislodge her, and no one will dare to suggest that she move over. It is a matter of complete indifference to her that the spot she has picked out may be such that a large family will have to break up in order to conform to her choice.

After she has nursed her baby, eaten a few nuts, and perhaps put the pot on to boil she gets up and cleans the ground, pushing the surface litter back for a pillow, chopping out the protruding roots, scraping and leveling until it is "clean." Then off she goes for ferns to cover the site, sometimes walking half a mile to get the exact kind she wants. When this is all done the camp looks inviting, but next day, after fifty bare feet have walked, run, fought, or toddled over it and the soup has been spilled, it is untidy and dirty. By the end of a week, if they should stay so long, dirt has piled up around the camp—nut shells, pieces of animal hides, fruit skins, bones, palm-shoot shells, wasp's nests from which the larvae have been taken and eaten, basket splints, and human and animal offal—and the place has a repellent odor.

The Kaingáng are awake an hour before dawn. The young men lie huddled together under their blankets, sometimes five or six of them in a row, chattering and laughing, while the married men shout across from their beds with their wives and someone perhaps lies singing quietly to himself. At last a fire is stirred and a woman or a child goes for water. By dawn the pots are on the fire, and the campers are beginning to shake the stiffness out of their bodies. Perhaps some young woman still lies lazily nursing her child while her young husband sits on her feet to keep them warm. Men begin to take down their bows and bend them against their legs, and arms like wrestlers' swell and bend as the bows are drawn. A famished dog yelps as its owner beats it for stealing food; a woman growls at her child in mild, helpless anger as it defecates in camp. The men circulate around while the women sit quietly nursing their children or eating.

At last a word or a half-suggested idea decides the plan of the hunt, and they are ready to go. They are on their feet or sitting down with their weapons between their legs, stuffing the last bits of food into their mouths, for they will not eat again until long after sundown unless they are lucky enough to find a beehive. Finally, with a last hurried mouthful and a shout to his hollow-bellied dog, the hunter disappears in the forest.

The early sun slants through the trees. The ground is damp; the undergrowth is wet with dew, and the air is chilly. The Indian is strung to the highest pitch, for he must make of his mind a sensitive instrument responsive to the slightest influence around him: to the trembling of a leaf that may reveal a bird, to the faint marks on the trunks of trees that tell where honey is, or to the confused sounds of animal calls that betray the tapir or the monkey. Most birds are just black spots among the foliage for their lovely plumage is their protective coloring, and to the unpracticed eye they are lost among the leaves. A tiny, wax-covered hole—the entrance to a hive—the faint scratches of the claws of a honey-eating animal or his burrow at the base of a tree, or the pecking of the woodpecker, reveal where there is honey. The hunter must be on the alert for all these things, and he must look carefully underfoot for the tracks of animals for on these more than on anything else his life depends. This complete absorption in forest sounds and signals makes conversation almost impossible, and if the hunter talks at all it is in whispers and only about matters immediately at hand. Even if he has to shout a message to some companion it is in a Kaingáng whisper, a high tone of low intensity that floats through the forest like the most delicate topmost notes of a well-trained tenor.

As he plods uphill and down, uphill and down, almost always on a slope, rarely on level ground, the sun mounts higher, sharpening the shadows, intensifying the green. Suddenly there is a rush of wings as some *ururús* fly to another perch. The hunter watches their short, low flight until they stop twenty feet away from their previous resting-place. Then he sets down his iron arrows and barbed ones and selects a couple with nothing but wooden knobs on the end. Now he steps forward carefully, parting the thick foliage as he slips through, although he need not be so careful, for the *ururú* is a stupid bird. Now he stops and lays an arrow across his bow as he prepares to draw. The trees, the bushes, and the vines are thick around him, and a tangle of vines and bushes half hides the birds. With a branch jabbing him in the ribs and another tickling his ear he twists his body awkwardly as he bends his bow, pulling the string with his right hand and pushing the bow away from him with his left. The shoulders and the muscles of the back and chest are called into play when a Kaingáng bends his bow. His whole torso and his two arms suddenly expand like a spring as he draws the string back almost to his ear.

When one of those great bows that the Kaingáng also use for clubs is bent, the strain is so great that a man's whole body tends to quake and shiver. The handling of a Kaingáng bow in the thick foliage where the ground is slippery underfoot and a dozen twigs and branches get in the way, where the light is dim and a mass of vines and leaves half obscure the target, calls for perfect coordination and the control of every muscle. The largest game bird, the jacutinga, appears generally as a black spot high up among the trembling leaves, and the branch on which it stands is almost always between the bird and the hunter. As it fills its maw with berries it turns nervously from side to side—it is a fluctuating spot in uncertain and gloomy surroundings. No wonder that our friend misses his *ururús,* and that the Indians often miss. With a grunt of disgust he goes on, down the hill and across a brook, up the other slope, and then down through a mass of bamboo to a stream. He stands in the water up to his knees, undecided for a moment which way to go. Then he wanders along the stream, stepping with automatic and perfect balance from stone to stone until he finds a place to climb out. His powerful toes hook into the tough damp clay at the water's edge, and he lifts his two hundred pounds by his toes, as self-assured as a ballet dancer, on to the high bank. Now from far up on the side of the hill comes a macaco's whistle, faint and clear, and the hunter beats his way toward it, imitating almost perfectly the monkey's high and penetrating whistle. I never learned to distinguish the macaco's whistle from the Indian's imitation.

As he nears the top of the hill, his breath whistling between his teeth, the monkeys are visible—little black bundles high up in a tree. "The sun is slanting," as he says, for it is growing late, and we have been out all day without a thing to eat. He climbs up past the tree so that he can shoot downhill. The first barbed wooden arrow hisses vainly through the leaves, to land somewhere far off down the hill. A second arrow pierces a monkey and knocks it from its tree. A third and fourth follow the first. The fifth sends the second monkey hurtling, and he falls dead in a tangle of brambles. Five arrows for two monkeys. The heads of the two arrows that found their marks are torn loose from the shaft and will have to be rebound. The three others are lost in the pathless tangle but it is too late to look for them. Next day he returns to search, following his own tracks back through the undergrowth that almost conceals them. The bush is so heavy that he cannot raise his arms or legs until he frees them from the vines that hold them like a net. Round and round he goes, looking about and up in the trees, for perhaps one of his arrows fell among the branches. After each circuit of the area he returns to the tree where the monkeys were and makes note of the trajectories of his arrows, pointing his arm along them. At last he finds two, but where is the third? After almost three hours of constant searching he sees it high in another tree, and up he goes to get it, for if he left it there it would weep and weep until, perhaps, its soul would come and kill him.

All through the morning he climbs the hills. Ticks come upon him in clods like brown mud and he scrapes them off with a knife, but the ones he misses deploy over him until he itches all over from their bites. Early in the afternoon he finds a little hive, and the cool sweet honey quenches his thirst and takes the edge off his hunger. Soon he comes on another, but "dangerous" stinging bees live there; and since he will not stop to make a fire drill and build a fire to smoke them out, he must leave it and return tomorrow or send someone after it. Now the sky clouds over, and it begins to rain. He stands shivering under a fern for a while, but hunger drives him out again. As the afternoon drags on his mood grows blacker and blacker as he searches the ground restlessly for a tapir's track. Nothing less than a tapir will satisfy him. But where are they? Didn't Chukembégn see tracks here yesterday when he was hunting jacutingas? But wait! What's this? Certainly a tapir has been nibbling the shoots of this bush, and there is its track. It seems fresh, too, for it is damp, and the soil appears newly scraped by the tapir's hoof. But in the rain all tracks are damp, and he is not sure that the tapir didn't nibble that bush yesterday. As he goes farther along, however, he comes upon the fresh spoor and then on the place where the tapir moved about, eating red berries that had fallen from a tree.

Now there is no doubt that the track is fresh. Tense and serious, he puts down his axe and arrows, of which he selects two with short shafts and heavy iron heads that look like table knives, round at the point but sharpened to a razor edge. As he moves along following the tapir's track he mimics its curious shrieking whistle. The trail leads through a bamboo network where rotten twigs lie thick upon the ground and the bamboo grows so high and dense that the light is dim; some of the bamboos have toppled over and dried where they have fallen. Hundreds of them lie criss-cross in every direction so that the hunter has to pick his way, twisting and turning his heavy bow so that it will not clatter and jar. He makes noise—no one could avoid it in such a jungle. But the tapir too is noisy, and there is no mistaking when its big, heavy body comes plunging awkwardly through the brush. At last the hunter draws up on the animal that has stopped to wait for him, deceived by his call; but the forest is so thick that he must get close for a shot, and indeed, the heads of his arrows are so heavy that they cannot travel far with great accuracy. But when it does leap from the bow the arrow drives through the tough hide of the tapir right to its vitals. What supreme pleasure that gives to the Indian! What pride is in that smiling brown face!

Back in camp the hunter does not walk around and talk unless he has come back empty-handed, for then he feels he has to say something to explain how it was that he didn't kill. He walks about, telling loudly how he climbed this hill and descended that, how the thorns scratched him and how he saw no tracks. But the successful hunter sits down with the casual remark that "A tapir has been killed," and after a while, or next day, if it is late, the women go and bring it in. Before he sleeps he must mend his broken arrows, and late at night the yellow light of the dry bamboo illumines his puckered face still bent over them, while his wife sleeps with her baby against her breast. The Kaingáng do not sleep much. Even if there is no work to keep them up—no baskets for the men to weave, no arrows for them to mend—they are forever getting up to eat or to warm themselves by the fire. Before the reservation days they were a hunted people, harassed by another tribe, by the Brazilians, and by one another so that wakefulness became highly valued among them.

When the men are in camp they circulate noisily, but the women sit where they are, mingling their high-pitched voices with those of the men, taking an equal part in the conversation if it concerns anything they have any interest in. It is when the men are gone that the women come together for their own particular kind of intimate gossip: love affairs and projected separations; this one's change of heart and that one's scandalous behavior. They sit in a little group making dresses for themselves or sewing for their husbands or brothers, stopping every half hour or so to suckle their babies, who are given the breast whenever they cry, to scold a child who has defecated in a plate, to snatch another from the fire or to rub passionately a little head that has been bruised in falling. A man in the camp is an added spice to a spicy situation, and if a sprained limb or infected foot keeps him at home he becomes the focus for feminine jokes that run eternally in the same channel.

When the young women go out to pick up the fallen fruit or to gather the yellow *tai* fruit that grows in the center of a large spiked plant, they leave their babies with their old mothers or with other women to be suckled and cared for. Sometimes, if they have children who are a little grown, they may take them with them, but the Kaingáng do not feel that a woman should be accompanied by a little child so that its presence may prevent a swift and surreptitious sex encounter. They are generally free to pursue their love affairs secretly in the bush while their husbands are away, and if they cannot do that they spend their time talking about other people's affairs.

There is really very little for the women to do nowadays. Aside from their specifically feminine functions Kaingáng society could exist just as well without them. They "make the bed" and get the firewood, but their husbands help them build the house. The men hunt and also bring in most of the wild honey, for they range the farthest. It is they who climb the trees to chop out the hives that are far above the ground, and it is they who ascend the lofty pines to knock down the all-important nuts. The women stay below to gather up the nuts which their husbands have knocked down; yet very often two men cooperate in the enterprise. The women used to take ages to make robes and shirts and carrying-bands for their babies, but ever since the men began to raid the whites, blankets have largely replaced robes, fiber shirts have given way to vests, and the heavy iron Brazilian pot has become the "real" pot, while the ancient badly made clay one which the women made has become "my no-good pot" and completely disappeared. But there is no substitute for the strong, well-made baskets that the men make with such care. The men are even as good at spinning cord as the women are. The women cook, but Kaingáng cooking is simple and any child could do it. Besides, it is no disgrace for a man to cook or do anything a woman does, and a man often cooks his own supper if he is alone. Even the carrying of burdens is shared by the hard-working men, and I have seen them carrying their babies when the trail was long and burdens heavy.

III

Sexual Relations and Marriage

Even Kaingáng babies learn that the terms connected with sex have an aura of laughter and spice. *Waikó,* to copulate; *waindjï,* to have an affair; *mbâdn,* lover or husband; *plұ,* wife or sweetheart; *ênglânglé,* my co-spouse, are some of the terms which, brought into a conversation, occasion any amount of smirking, tittering and laughing. The sexuality of little boys is stimulated by their mothers by manipulation of the genitals before they can walk. Although little children of two and three are told jocularly to copulate with one another, their attention is directed toward adults. A boy of three has already learnt to say, in answer to the question, "With whom do you copulate," "With Waikome," who may be his grandfather's sister. Babies are jokingly told to copulate with people anywhere from ten to twenty times their age, and a man sixty-five years old will call a toddler of three "my co-husband." Children of all ages are pressed into service to remove ticks, and it is not at all uncommon to see a little girl of five or six hovering over a supine man picking the ticks off his genitals.

A child soon learns to repeat the jokes that go around the campfire and to shout gleefully, "You copulate with your first cousin!" A boy of nine is jokingly taunted with masturbation, told that he has deflowered his fifteen-year-old cousin, or accused of wanting to copulate with a dog. As two dogs copulate the entire camp roars with laughter and a little girl of six cries delightedly, "They are copulating!" The children may see the boisterous open foreplay of the adults and glimpse the sexual act in the dim light of the early morning.

Yet with all of this I never saw or heard of intercourse among children. Jokes about the love affairs of children among themselves are never made by the adults nor by the children. The children receive so much satisfaction

from adults it is hard to see why they should bother with one another.[1]
They are at the beck and call of anyone who wants a warm little body to
caress. As Monyá, age two, wobbles by on fat uncertain legs Kanyahé calls
to him. He slowly overcomes the momentum of his walk, turns about,
smiles and wobbles obediently over to Kanyahé. Children lie like cats
absorbing the delicious stroking of adults. The little children receive an
enormous amount of adult attention and one never sees them caress one
another or lie down together. It is impossible to keep track of children
around the campfire. By choice and from necessity they literally sleep all
over the place. They like to cuddle next to an uncle, aunt or step-mother.
In the winter when there may be only one blanket to shelter a family, the
little ones are driven to crawling under the cover of someone else who welcomes the additional warmth of the little bundle. This wandering around
often culminates in the sexual experience to which the grown-ups are eager
to introduce the child, and he is generally enjoyed first by a person much
older than he. Some married men have nicknames that bear a humorous
reference to their experience in trying to deflower young girls. Yakwá was
called, "You pierced your mother" because he had deflowered a young girl
who had the same name as his mother. Kovi received a nickname because
his first cousin clawed his penis when he tried to deflower her. The growing child's sexual experience is primarily humorous, often illicit, admin-
istered by adults, and apt to be violent in the case of girls.

When the children grow up to be young men and women a strange
dichotomy of behavior is noticeable, which is all the more striking because
the Kaingáng lay no emphasis on such differences. Kaingáng young men
love to sleep together. At night they call to one another, "Come and lie
down here with me, with *me!*" Then there is a shifting and squirming so
that Nggugn or Waipó or Kanyahé can lie down where he is bidden. In
camp one sees young men caressing. Married and unmarried young men
lie cheek by jowl, arms around one another, legs slung across bodies, for all
the world like lovers in our own society. Sometimes they lie caressing that
way in little knots of three or four. Women never do these things. I have
never seen any signs of complete homosexual relations among the men or
women. I have sat night after night talking to knots of young men, and I
have seen them caressing one another in an absolutely open fashion in the
broad light of day. But I never saw them make an overt sexual gesture. In
other cultures and even in our own one may see young men continually

---

[1] This whole situation contrasts strikingly with what I observed among the Pilagá Indians
(MSS in preparation). There the children receive slight attention from the adults. Sexual inter-
course begins at about 5 years and most of the sexual play of the children is perfectly open.
Everyone talks and jokes about the sexual affairs of the children.

reaching for each other's genitals, but the Kaingáng, although they stand around holding their own penises, do not hold other men's.

In the whole mass of Kaingáng folklore there is one hundred-word story of a homosexual relationship between two men and another that tells of a male supernatural that was killed by a man because it sodomized him by trickery. I never heard a remark that alluded in any way to homosexuality. The men like to congregate together, and when the women are in camp they leave them and sit around in groups, weaving baskets or just talking. Sometimes a woman may join them because her husband is there, but even when the men are away the women rarely come together as the men do. They just visit. Like the indiscriminate playing of the children, these caressings, sleeping parties, and gossipings do not follow relationship lines. Whatever may be the specific obligations of cousins or brothers-in-law, they are completely lost sight of in these ephemeral, wholly casual masculine contacts. The basis for man's loyalty to man has roots in the many warm bodily contacts between them. The violent, annihilating conflicts among men in Kaingáng society were all among those who had never shared the languid exchange of caresses on a hot afternoon under the green arched shelter of a house nor lain together night after night under a blanket against the cold. The very transient, unfixated nature of these contacts leaves no grounds for jealousy. The relationships built on these hours of lying together with anyone at all bear fruit in the softening of conflicts that are so characteristic of the Kaingáng. Indeed, there is a patterned friendship between men that has woven this contact into its very warp and woof, and that is the friendship of hunting companions. Men who have hunted together day after day, raided the Brazilians together, slept together beside the same fire, under the same blanket, wrapped in each other's arms, hold this relationship above their kinship with their brothers. The consequences for the general integration of Kaingáng society are immeasurable.

The elaborate laws of sexual avoidance that chart the behavior of men and women in many primitive societies, dividing the entire community into the touchables and the untouchables, are undreamt of among the Kaingáng. Little boys and girls play together in rough and tumble. Brothers and sisters, brothers- and sisters-in-law and cousins, sleep next to one another, cross legs, or embrace one another. The corollaries to this are the marriages and love affairs among almost all classes of relatives. Only marriages between parents and children and between full brothers and sisters are avoided. Marriages between half brothers and sisters are rare.

A complete lack of emphasis on temperamental differences between the sexes permits to boys and girls, men and women, the same jocular and often violent sexual aggressiveness. The term for intercourse may have either a masculine or a feminine object. The vulgar English terms can take only feminine objects, and thus reveal in the very grammatical form of our vulgarisms the feeling that the male is the active and aggressive partner. But among the Kaingáng if Chukembégn picks up his hundred and fifty pound wife by the ears and thumps her down with tears of pain starting from her eyes, she may get up immediately and pound him as the tears trickle down her laughing face, and he roars with delight. Sexual approaches range all the way from the unobtrusive contact of bare legs beside the evening fires to open, ribald, and aggressive onslaughts by both men and women.

Although I never put it to the test, I have a strong feeling that the widowed Kundídn, like many of her sex, was stronger than I. Her amorous pinches, punches, and pushes were a trial to me. Kundídn's aggressiveness stopped only at direct snatches at the sexual organs.

Anggló, who was having a passionate affair with Kanyahé, was not averse to pressing another suit on the side. While she did not square off in the boxerlike manner of Kundídn, she was aggressive enough in her own mild way. She did not pinch so hard nor call so loud, but if there were no one around, her quiet "I should like to talk to you and see the inside of your house" would set me thinking how I could best avoid her without hurting her feelings. But I might have spared myself worry on that score, for in this society, which lays no stress on man's aggressiveness as against woman's passivity, a woman who makes advances feels no vindictive anger at a repulse. In our society a woman who temporarily steps out of her culturally decreed role of the attacked to become the attacker feels shame that quickly becomes resentment against the desired object if she is rebuffed. The shame that she feels at reversing her part in the drama of the sexes is forgotten if she obtains her desire and turns to anger if she does not. But the Kaingáng women are able to make the same jocular approaches day after day without a change of attitude.

When a husband goes away his wife becomes fair game for anyone who is interested, and she is generally willing prey for the enterprising hunter. I must often have served all unwittingly as a chaperon to some man's wife while he was away hunting, but although my naive presence may have seriously handicaped the pair I was left to chaperon, it did not always inhibit them entirely. One day while Chukembégn, his wife Chantágn, Kanggúin, and I were on a hillside feasting on wasp's larvae, the bark of the dogs in pursuit of a tapir came faintly from the distance. Chukembégn seized his gun and was away in a flash, leaving his wife, Kanggúin, and me alone. When he had gone Kanggúin began to boast of his love affairs and to remark how curious it was that he never married. On the way back to camp he kept singing all the way, stopping every once in a while to say:

"Chantágn, listen to this. Chantágn, listen to this." Singing is a favorite way of showing off among the Kaingáng, as among ourselves. Sometime later after Chukembégn had had a fight with his wife he complained bitterly that Kanggúin had said to her: " 'if you were my wife I would not treat you that way.' Whenever anyone has a fight with his wife Kanggúin always talks that way to her. He wants a wife, but no one will live with him!"

Nanmblá has two wives. Although his wives compete for him they are not totally at a loss if they have to sleep without him. When I was at his brother-in-law's house one day while he was away, Nanmblá's wife Wainlúin was there watching with amused appreciation while Padnmbá cast a knife at a log. Nothing passed between them but their boisterous laughter, but when Padnmbá at last went away Wainlúin leaned against the housepost and gazed after him. When he had gone fifty paces down the path he turned around, flashed a smile, and disappeared down the slope. I never heard what happened between Wainlúin and Padnmbá after that, but I did hear of a quarrel that Nanmblá had with both his wives because they had relations with other men. One day I saw Vomblé caressing his son's mother-in-law. Another time Chukembégn told me that he and a few others were on the side of a hill when a little way's off they saw Padnmbá making love to Waikukló's wife in the bushes. Soon she got up and ran off but Chukembégn and his companions called out laughingly "You don't have to run; we saw you." A complete account of all the sexual intrigues would fill a long but rather repetitious chapter.

The amorous history of every young man or woman is one of the favorite themes of conversation among the young people. "First Koktá had an affair with Yonggó, then with Kanggúin and then with me. Then she went around with Kanyahé but he left her and took up with Yu'ó." "I went around for a while with Koktá. . . ." "Oh, no you didn't. She used to go around with Kundágn but now she's going to change to Kanyahé." They enumerate, expand, correct without end and with unflagging interest.

I never heard them discuss these affairs in front of the principals' spouses, but Amendó's presence did not prevent them from joking about her unmarried daughter's relations with Padnmbá and Ndíli. "Layongndá [her daughter] is lying with Ndíli. She has gone off with her lover Ndíli to get nuts." Amendó sat listening and laughing while she nursed her little bastard of five months.

The Kaingáng preoccupation with sex expresses itself also in the belief that death is often caused by intercourse with a supernatural monster or with a ghost. Both men and women may wake up in the morning sick and bleeding or insane because they have spent the night with the supernatural, who has lured or forced them into intercourse. Unlike their neighbors in

Paraná the Kaingáng have no love magic. They are, in general, a very practical and aggressive people and not given to the use of charms. They view all people but little children as spontaneously, vigorously and indiscriminately sexual, and act accordingly.

The young man who, urged at last by his desire for a woman to cook and keep house for him, and the young woman who, impelled by her wish to have someone who will constantly care for her, at last settle down with a spouse, have this background of philandering, jesting and frequently adulterous sexual experience that will color married life into old age. Kaingáng men and women are not advised by their parents to be faithful to one another. The only case I heard of is that of Amendó who was one of the wives of Wanyekí. When she and her sisters married him her mother said to her: "Live with him. If they leave him, you remain with him." And she always did.[2]

In our society the traditional, the ideal stabilizer of marriage is love—an exclusive sex interest in one person. The Kaingáng have no tradition, no background for the development of such an interest. Marriage in other primitive societies is sometimes stabilized by a large payment for the bride, but in Kaingáng society there is no such payment. If a woman leaves her husband she can always find a relative who will take care of her. Her brother or her cousin or her sister will always take her in, and although she lacks the full security that marriage gave her she need not starve, for there are any number of men who will accept her as an added responsibility without complaint, even boasting a little that they took care of her and that she called them *yûgn*.[3] Besides having this dependable bulwark to her security a woman's own aggressiveness makes it far easier for her to get another husband than for a woman in a similar position in our society. When a woman is left without a husband the liaisons which she has established surreptitiously serve her in good stead, for then one of her lovers may become her new husband.[4]

Chukembégn had been having some trouble with his wife, Chantágn. When he left her for a few days to go hunting he told his hunting companions that he was going to leave his wife. News got back to the post before he returned. One day Chantágn, who had previously amused herself by casual approaches to me, called me. I came out of my house and sat down where anyone who happened to be around could see us. "What do

---

[2] See p. 30. These people have been long dead.

[3] See Appendix II, p. 177. Such a woman can partially earn her keep by gathering fruit and wood, helping with the cooking and the children, and clearing the ground for camp sites. If she has lovers they will contribute to the family larder.

[4] Sometimes, though rarely, former husbands may become lovers, but this does not occur where the woman herself has rejected them as husbands.

you want?" said I. "Chukembégn is going to leave me." "Oh, no, he isn't." "Yes, he is. He said so up the river and they are talking about it." "But he is not going to leave you." "How do you know?" "He told me." "What did he tell you?" "He told me that he loves you." I used the strongest term that the language has to offer, a term that I heard used only in folktales. "But he *is* going to leave me. Julio, if he leaves me, will you marry me?" "No," said I; "I never marry anyone." And there the matter rested.[5]

A man separated from his wife may live with someone else and share his fire. At the worst he can cook his own meals and spread his own bed, for no shame attaches to a man who does a woman's work. But after a woman has borne three children a marriage does not break up. The woman needs the man to take care of her children, and Kaingáng men are fond fathers. There is no end to the fondling and delousing a child gets from its father and other men. He makes toys for it and takes it hunting for company. Nowadays they are as much interested in having their little girls decked out in brand new calico dresses as American mothers are in getting their children permanent waves. Even in death parents do not relinquish their children, for, they say, a child who dies before the age of about twelve returns to its mother's womb and is reborn. The corpse of a grown-up is placed on the funeral pyre, pounded on the chest and told to go away, and summarily burnt. But, I was told, a little child is placed in a grave, covered with wholesome herbs and begged to return. Its mother puts a little honey and meat aside for it, puts her baby's carrying-band on her head and walks about crying, "Come here, come here! Come and eat the meat and honey I have put aside for you. If you stay in some other camp one will be angry with you! Come back! Come back!"

Except for the somewhat aberrant Chukembégn there is not a single case of a marriage dissolved after three children had been born. Chukembégn was a child of about nine when the Kaingáng settled on the reservation, and he grew up in close contact with the agent. He married Tendó but left her after she had borne him three children. His present wife, Chantágn, "led him away by the hand." Now he rarely goes near Tendó, but she is still regarded as his wife. Two years after leaving her he still buys cloth for her to make dresses for herself and her children. Yet idle tongues will wag, and one day when Chukembégn, Klendó, and I were hunting together, Chukembégn burst out: "It is not true that I ignore her. I got medicine and bought a chicken for her when she was ill!" Klendó observed mildly that he had never said that Chukembégn had not taken care of her. Then Chukembégn, turning to me, blurted in Portuguese: "This man has

[5] I mention this, and other cases in which I myself have been one of the actors, not because they are the only instances of the kind that I have, but because they are usually the most complete.

been saying that I have not been taking care of that woman, but I have!"
Tendó had not married again and the community refused to admit that
Chukembégn's obligations to her were ended.

Indeed I have no way of telling what would happen if a woman in such
a position remarried, for Kaingáng society has no other such case to offer
in more than a hundred and fifty years of its history.[6] Unless a woman is
separated from her husband under the conditions of vendetta, a couple
with several children stays together till death. Although the case of Chukembégn and Tendó is isolated it emphasizes the Kaingáng attitude toward
marriages of long standing that have produced several children. The breaking up of Tendó's household left the society confused as to just how it
should treat Chukembégn for there were no parallel instances. So they
simply continued to insist that he owed some kind of support to Tendó,
even though he planted his field with Chantágn, seldom went to visit
Tendó, and that only when absolutely necessary, and maintained the most
tenuous relations with her family.

But separations before many children are born are legion. Young people
frequently pass through one or two marriages before they finally settle
down. The relationship between the sexes is informal, and there is no
marriage ceremony. In its early stages the only thing that distinguishes a
marriage from a protracted affair is the announcement by the principals
that they are married. There is no term for marriage. The Kaingáng use
the term *nê,* to sit, to express the husband-wife relationship. "He sat with
her" means "he married her." Sometimes people do not know whether a
couple who have separated have ever been "married." Even before marriage a man and woman may go hunting together, and unless her family
takes it upon itself to "send her to him" or the man and woman themselves
decide to set up a household, the relationship between the two remains un-
changed. The man may even hunt with his sweetheart's relatives and contribute to the household's food supply without yet having the status of a
husband. When one of the woman's brothers or sisters or parents see that
she is pregnant they may "send her to" her most constant lover, but no
stigma attaches to an extramarital birth. Mothers are just as passionately
attached to their illegitimate[7] children as they are to their legitimate and
all the children have equal chances in life. Illegitimacy, so often the pivotal
point of some of the most dramatic episodes in our own and in primitive
societies, is completely lacking in drama among the Kaingáng.

Though the Kaingáng know that unfaithfulness and brittleness are inevitable conditions of marriage among them, its implied permanence and

[6] My genealogies go back about two hundred years and include five hundred individuals
of all ages. The fact that a woman has one or two children is no obstacle to her remarriage.

[7] I use this term simply to indicate children born out of wedlock.

the actual security it affords make them seek it eagerly, and in spite of the lightness with which they seem to take it no marriage can be broken without some kind of mild stir and an early effort on the part of the principals to form another alliance, while their relatives try to patch up the old one. When Chantágn only felt that she *might* lose her husband she was already at my door asking whether I would be her next. However, unstable it may be, particularly in the beginning, marriage nevertheless is one of the ideal pillars of security on which the Kaingáng personality seeks ever to support itself. They have built their society on warm personal attachments, and anyone without such attachments makes them uneasy and perplexed. No one is spoken of more sadly than a mature person who is alone. "For a long time," said Vomblé sadly, "my father wandered around all over without a wife. At last when his brother died he married his wives." The women who did not try to interest me in themselves or in their children besought me to marry someone else—anyone—and one day even Yokó, a matron who was generally too shy to speak much to me, quizzed me uncomprehendingly on my bachelorhood and advised me to marry—not so that I could have someone to cook for me and mend my clothes, but just in order to be married. "Why? Why?" she kept repeating, "why do you live thus without a wife? Get a wife." "Whom shall I marry?" said I. "Marry anybody. Why go around unmarried?" Even the children found it hard to believe that I was single and they used to question me interminably: "Have you a wife in your country?" "Have you a sweetheart in your country?" "Will you marry her when you go back?" "Do you intend to marry?"

Once a couple are married they do not drop the liaisons formed before marriage. Their long training in philandering and the absence of an ideal of faithfulness have not suited them to the stability that marriage implies. Furthermore the absence of binding legal forms or big property stakes, as well as the knowledge that a meal can always be found at one's father's or brother's fire, that one's mother or sister-in-law is ready to cook the food and spread the bed, makes marriage brittle and its rupture not sharply felt. Yet, in an utterly contradictory manner, the Kaingáng believe that a man and woman, once they are "sitting together," belong to each other, and they use the same word to designate this possession as they use for the exclusive possession of material objects. This theoretical possessiveness comes into constant conflict with the actual sharing in which the young people have taken part all their lives. The young man who for years before his marriage has dallied with the wife of anyone from his father to his second cousin, who has day in and day out enjoyed adultery with an equally delighted adulteress, decides suddenly, once he is married, that his possession should be exclusive. "I left my wife," Yuvén said to me, "because she took Kanyahé and Kundágn as lovers. She sleeps with everyone. All the women are that way. When their husbands go away they sleep with others. That is why I want to marry a Brazilian woman."

The conflict between the sharing that is experienced and absolutely exclusive possession, which is simply and unqualifiedly theory, is far more fundamental in Kaingáng society than it is in our own. Adultery in Kaingáng society is not a circumstance of some marriages but a condition of practically all. Yet, although husband and wife live in constant suspicion of each other's loyalty, it rarely becomes desperate. Husbands do not as a rule follow their wives about, nor wives their husbands, although if there are good grounds for suspicion a husband may beat his wife or a wife her husband. He often leaves her for days at a time even when he knows that there are enterprising men still in camp and no one to chaperon her. This attitude really saves the culture from becoming a nightmare. In a society in which everyone believes that everybody else is engaged in seducing his neighbor's wife, suspicion backed by intense jealousy would drive people to desperation. But when Waipó leaves his wife to go across the river to make manioc all she has to say to him is a laughing, "You're going over there where everyone is living in very close quarters," and with a rough caress he is gone. One evening when Chukembégn and I were coming from the manioc mill I said to him, "Now that you've left your wife alone she may sleep with someone else." "I don't care; let her," said he. There is something more than mere bravado in this statement. It expresses the typical determination not to see what is not forced on one.

Since hunting is the most vital occupation, it might be supposed that a good hunter would be the most desirable husband. It might be felt also that since the Kaingáng used to be perpetually at war with the Brazilians, with the Kangdjá, and with their vendetta enemies, they would place a high premium on ferocity, daring, bravery, enterprise, and intelligence and that these traits would influence a woman in the choice of a husband. Nevertheless a number of attitudes combined to render all these qualities almost completely inoperative.

Although hunting is the very basis of their economy the Kaingáng, curiously enough, do not recognize differences in hunting skill. If a man returns empty-handed from the hunt he and his wife may share their relatives' food without shame. In all the time I was among the Kaingáng I never heard an unsuccessful hunter spoken of with scorn nor saw one overcome with shame, and although she may scold him roundly, no wife ever leaves her husband for coming home without meat.

Just as they assume that all men are practically equals in hunting skill the Kaingáng assume that all men are brave. Special emphasis is laid on this trait, therefore, only in exceptional cases. This holds also for intelligence, for the Kaingáng have a strong tendency to think of wisdom and courage together. Today no one among them could be classed as outstanding in accordance with the fundamental feelings of Kaingáng society as it existed twenty years ago, for localization on the reservation, with its automatic suppression of feuds and raids on the Brazilians, has almost eliminated the necessity for making important decisions that call for the exercise of judgment and aggressiveness and has made considerations of ferocity and daring irrelevant. For an example of a really vital personality in Kaingáng society we must turn to the culture of twenty years ago when attacks on Brazilian settlements and pack trains raised daring and enterprise to the first importance and when dangers of surprise or the planning of a vendetta massacre enhanced the value of shrewdness, aggressiveness, ferocity, and wakefulness. Vomblé's father Kuthúgn, whom the Brazilians called Thunder Storm because he had a voice like thunder, was a dominating figure. Even the Indian agent spoke of him with profound respect, singling him out above all the others. When Vomblé sings his praises we can understand that it is not merely glorification of his own father. In one of his long feud stories Vomblé has Yatí, an old woman, say to an arrogant young man: "You think that you are men. If Kuthúgn heard what you were saying about him he would be angry. He is *waikayú*,[8] and therefore my in-laws listen to his counsel and go with him. That is why my in-laws give their women to him." Even the young man's brother reproved him for his arrogance, saying: "When I was young I used to go about with Kuthúgn and I have seen how wonderfully agile and vigorous he is. And he is exactly that way now. His relatives tell how he kills Brazilians. See his property beside him!" Kuthúgn's property was not a measure of his importance as a wealthy man but a sign that he had made many raids on the Brazilians. The equation of *waikayú* and wisdom is borne out by other remarks of Vomblé about his father: "He was a thinker. He always spoke to people when there was anger. He was like a captain. If the people did not do the right thing he always spoke to them. Therefore he killed many Brazilians."

This, then, was the ideal man: swift as lightning in the handling of his weapons and the shifting of his massive body, enterprising and daring in raids, shrewd in judgment—*waikayú*. Kuthúgn was all of fifty years old when Yatí made this judgment of him. The great warriors among the Kaingáng were not the young men but the middle-aged—the men between fifty and sixty. The *këlú*, the young men between fifteen and thirty-five could marry and have children, they could go on raids, and they might kill,

---

[8] The literal meaning of *waikayú* is "self-love." Any daring, ferocious, quarrelsome, enduring person is *waikayú*. These characteristics are directly related to a Kaingáng's opinion of himself and the good impression which he has tried to make on others, and which he dares not jeopardize.

but they were never the equals in accomplishment of the men of middle age and over. So positive judgments were not made of young men. They were just *ķëlǘ*, who had yet to make many attacks on the Brazilians and who had yet to bathe their spoon-shaped lance blades in the blood of a vendetta enemy. We can understand now why a man's *waiḳayú* did not influence a young woman in the choice of a husband, for all men were assumed to be *waiḳayú* and only the warriors of middle age or over could be adjudged as outstanding.

If the absence of emphasis on hunting skill, the knowledge that relatives will always feed them, and the lack of expectation of great deeds from *ķëlǘ* effectually muffled all estimates of young men, the concentration of vital effort in the hands of males and the scarcity of women with a number of brothers eliminated the necessity for judging of *tëtágn*,[9] young women. After all, what could they do? What techniques did they have that men had not? Only the increasingly unimportant techniques of textile weaving and pottery. The most important occupations, hunting and basketry, were masculine. As for brothers-in-law, they were good to have, and polygyny that did not provide them was to be avoided, but the small and scattered populations made it impossible to demand brothers-in-law as one of the conditions of marriage. Marriage among the young people was and still is, therefore, largely a matter of chance. It is the crystallizing-out of informal sexual relations, which may be due solely to their own initiative, when the couple feel that their needs will be satisfied by the relationship or when they may be instigated by some one of their relatives who sees that they are lovers and decides that they ought to live together.

If human beings followed our ideas of consistency the ethnologist's task of investigation and understanding would be simple. If the Kaingáng were eager to marry off the daughters for whom they have such a difficult time in providing, it would be perfectly understandable. But the Kaingáng see parents as so attached to their daughters, so full of misgivings at the fate that might await them at the hands of their husbands, that they sometimes have fits of anger when they are approached by a go-between. They are sometimes pictured as clinging to a daughter so strongly that they must be asked to "let her alone." Not the parents, but some other member of the family, a brother or an uncle, is often the one who is concerned because a son or daughter is without a spouse. With certain reservations, the following conversation is typical of a dozen others that I recorded.

When Tondúin became interested in marrying off his cousin's son Vomblé, he went to the latter's father and said, "I am going to ask Kemblén

---

[9] *të*, woman. *tágn*, fat (noun or adjective), said of animals; hence desirable; also, new or fresh, said of tracks or weapons.

for one of his children." Kemblén was Tondúin's younger brother. "For whom are you going to ask him for one?" "For [your son] Vomblé. He is full-grown, but he has no wife. I have been waiting for someone or other to send a daughter to him, but they never do; so I am going to send one of Kemblén's daughters to him." Then Vomblé's father said, "What shall I do? He is full-grown; yet no one sends a child to him. If you tell Kemblén he may be angry. But tell him." When Tondúin told Kemblén he sat in silence and at last said: "I shall never send her to some këlú who will beat her when I am dead and gone. Send her to some one of your affinal relatives who treats you well. Then he will give you food and ignore me, eating it alone. He will not give any to me." "That is what he said," remarked Vomblé, as he told it to me; "he was a fool." But in the teeth of Kemblén's anger his brother sent Kulá to Vomblé, and he married her. If a young couple do not decide to take matters into their own hands they may continue as lovers indefinitely. At last someone may take enough interest in their affairs to assume the task of go-between. Then in the face of opposition they cheerfully settle down—at least for a while—and continue their relations with the various parties as if the waters had never been troubled.

The culture has so little immediate stake in marriage that it exercises itself very little about it. There are no dramatic stories of girls who were betrothed to boys they did not like, of sudden passion interrupting a prearranged marriage, of flight by night and lonely wandering in the forest away from enraged parents or from potential in-laws who felt themselves cheated of the prize for which they had already paid dearly. There are no ramifying laws of incest for the violation of which the culture might administer a swift and violent punishment. The assumed personal equality of all young people, the dead level of economic conditions, the lack of accumulated property, and the fact that there are no class lines make all planning for a first marriage unnecessary. The relatives of the young man do not have to save up over a long period of time to pay for the bride, nor do they have to sit awake at night for fear that she might be suddenly raped, toppling at one blow the complicated structure of preparation and throwing the community into an uproar. Kaingáng marriage, except when it becomes the temporary concern of some go-between, is the immediate affair only of the principals. And even the go-between has no stake in the marriage. It is true that he (or she) automatically becomes the in-law of the young man, but this is not particularly important in a society of myriad relationships; and if the young man refuses the young woman who is "sent" to him the matter is forgotten.

Polygyny comes about in Kaingáng society in the same informal, almost accidental manner as monogamic unions. In Kaingáng ideology one of the primary causes of polygyny is that "There are no other men." Like Wan-yekí,[10] the first husband of Amendó, a man may acquire two or more wives because there "are no other men around." But although this was true in the case of Wanyekí who lived far away from other people, it is necessary to remember that it is easier to give this as a blanket explanation than to bother about the numerous causes of a man's taking two or more wives. Among the young men on the reservation today there are several young bachelors; Nanmblá, however, has two wives.

Kuthúgn, old Thunder Storm, on the other hand, went around without a wife for years until his older brother died, leaving two wives, and Kuthúgn married them. But the Kaingáng do not impose or bestow on men the duty or the privilege of marrying their dead brothers' wives, nor do they compel widows to marry their brothers-in-law. Since the Kaingáng have no lien on spouses, since spouses are not conceived of as belonging to one group that has bought them or whose entire pattern of affinal exchanges is based on their permanent attachment to it, and since, furthermore, no group has given a man or woman in marriage in exchange for one received from a different group, there is no mechanism to compel a widow or widower to accept any particular new spouse. The ideology of mourning and the isolation of the widowed shows a complete lack of interest in these things.

A widowed person is dangerous, for the ghost of the departed clings to its last earthly vestiges in the hair of the surviving spouse that touched its own while living and under the nails where the dirt from food cooked or killed for the one now dead still lies. It follows its spouse about wherever it goes, for it is loath to give up its earthly attachments. It is a menace not only to the surviving spouse but to the whole community, for no one knows whom it may select as desirable to keep it company in the land of souls. So the widowed must be got out of camp for two weeks or two months, until the attachment of the ghost is enfeebled. Then, at the end of this time of fasting from the foods that he killed for his wife or that she cooked for her husband, the spouse is brought back with hair and nails cut off and is thus freed from the dirt that was so close a link to the ghost. Before the Kaingáng came to the reservation the return of the surviving spouse was the occasion for an elaborate ritual. With head covered with feathers as a disguise to fool the ghost, with wholesome herbs strewn in the path, to the noise of frantic singing and rattling to frighten the ghost away the widowed person came back and soon began his sex life anew. When the ghost of her husband had been frightened away contact with the woman was safe, for Kaingáng ghosts do not suffer from sexual jealousy after the first few weeks but oscillate eerily between the land of the dead and the dwellings of the living, harassed by a loneliness that urges them from time to time to

[10] He and Amendo died in about 1905.

snatch away some human being to bear them company. If the ghost longs to renew intercourse and return at night for this purpose, it is the old spouse who suffers, never the new partner. No woman remains a widow because men are afraid to marry her. The Kaingáng are forever daring the supernatural anyway.

The children belong to their parents, if one can speak of "belonging" in a society in which children are not valued as property. What we so strongly idealize the Kaingáng actually feel, for to them children are like highly charged emotional batteries. They are valued for their potentialities as emotionally satisfying living things, like most other pets.[11] There is no idea expressed that when they grow up they will feed and protect their parents,[12] for in nomadic days the latter knew only too well the whims that urged and the necessities that compelled their children to wander away from them. They themselves had felt the desire to go north or west or east to see the country or to attack the Brazilians, and they too had left their own parents to follow the camps of their wives' relatives. But when children are left fatherless it often devolves upon the father's family to take care of them, for they feel that responsibility, and it is in this way that it comes about that a widow often marries someone of her husband's kin. She goes where her children are, and it is there, in the midst of her husband's close kin, that she begins her sex life anew and often finds her new husband.

It is a similar factor of residence that brings it about that in the majority of cases the co-spouses in a polygynous or polyandrous marriage are either siblings or first cousins. For in the closer relationship that springs up among the members of the families related by marriage the most obvious choice is a person whom one sees all the time and with whom, therefore, one delights to have an affair. Since this choice rests almost wholly with the widow and since it is conditioned by a large number of accidental factors, principally what men are available at the moment, her new husband is as likely to be older than her dead husband as younger. Even when he is past middle age a man is still a vigorous hunter, and even if he is an old man, he can depend on someone to help toward the support of his household. His wife may philander as she will, but she is still his wife, and if he catches or suspects her he may beat her or even put a club through her chest.

If we were to believe Yatí as quoted by Thunder Storm's son, we could say that Thunder Storm acquired his third wife because he was an outstanding figure. But I am inclined to doubt this. His third wife was

[11] The Kaingáng, like many South American peoples, keep pet monkeys, pigs, quatí and hawks. Only the latter are used—for their feathers. Dogs are not pets; emotionally they belong rather in the category of unrelated human beings.

[12] It is true, nevertheless, that the parents could generally depend to some extent on their children's help, particularly before marriage.

Angneló, the sister of Kangndádn. Kangndádn had married Thunder Storm's sister and the two men had become almost inseparable. Though they are dead their relationship is perpetuated today in the relationship of their sons. But it was only after Kangndádn had married Thunder Storm's sister that Thunder Storm married Angneló. It is not at all rare among the Kaingáng that when a man marries another man's sister, her brother marries her husband's sister. The constant companionship of the two men, thrown together by the first marriage, brings this about in an informal way. Chukembégn, who deserted his wife Tendó and three children, was "led away" from her by his brother-in-law's sister, a young woman whom he saw day after day in his sister's house.

There is still another way in which polygyny may come about and that is if a wife calls another woman to "work with her." The husband, ostensibly, has no hand in the matter at all. The woman who does this gains a helper and companion, one who will nurse her children when she is away, who will accompany her on fruit-gathering expeditions, who will relieve her of the heavy loads of meat she has to transport and who will care for her when she is ill. At the same time, however, she assumes in herself an ability to share which experience may prove to be non-existent. But the Kaingáng tell me, the first wife may become so jealous of the second that her continual anger at last drives the second wife out, even after she has borne as many as two children. First wives never leave in such a situation. Thus it comes about that a second wife in a polygynous marriage shifts about a good deal. If she is heckled by the first wife she begins to look more seriously on her lovers, and when she slips out of one marriage she slips as easily into another.

Polygyny is not always an entirely pleasant experience for a man, for although it is good to have a second wife during the several months after childbirth when intercourse with the mother is stopped, and two wives lighten each other's and their husband's burdens and bring in more food, a man must put up with their quarreling between themselves and the insults of either one who feels herself slighted.

Every marriage system is organized around some system of ideas no matter how unformulated they may be. Our own culture continually balances the ideal of love against the desire for property. The ideas that serve as the basis for the contraction of marriage carry within them the criteria by which all individuals are judged. We value people insofar as they are lovable or rich and powerful. Our ideas of what we consider a desirable sex companion are pretty clearly formulated and furnish the subject of many a conversation. But the Kaingáng are not educated to an ideal of love, and they have not formulated success in life in terms of wealth or prestige. Even raiding the Brazilians has given them little property, and the little they have they do not keep for themselves, but distribute among their relatives. My greatest trouble with them was that they could never understand "what you want with all that stuff" that I kept for trading, nor with the wood I accumulated against the rainy season. And they have carried the same attitudes into their marital relations.

Several wives are not a mark of prestige but the result of special events. Love as the nucleus of sexual relations implies loyalty in our culture, for loyalty is an essential part of love. Even where marriage lacks the essence but preserves the ideal it may still have a certain amount of loyalty left in it if other factors such as security and power make loyalty expedient, and early education has conditioned spouses to be loyal when they do not love. But the Kaingáng have never been educated to sexual loyalty, their *ethos* is not built on the twin columns of wealth and power, and no one starves among them as long as there is an ungnawed piece of tapir hide or a pine nut in camp. So in their informal, almost casual marriages they are not loyal to one another in the special sexual way in which we think of marriage loyalty—as an exclusive sex interest in one person. And because they are not fixated in their sexual interests and because there are no social forms and few economic considerations to stabilize marriage, it is extremely brittle until several children are born. Even then the stability that marriage achieves does not fix sexual interest.

The Kaingáng are a people with no sense of social form. As an artist with a fine feeling for form will communicate that sensitivity, that sense and realization of an "inner harmony," as one artist put it to me, to everything he does, a people with a feeling for or an interest in social form will do most of the things that are important to them in a highly stylized way.[13] If they are particularly interested in following lines of kinship or some other rules of organization almost everything will be done in accordance with their feelings of fitness as determined by these rules, and not a hunting party or a husking bee will be undertaken without its having been planned along the lines of this organization. If their interest runs to dancing and ceremonious display instead, they will manage to bring in dancing and ceremony on every occasion. But the Kaingáng have no interest in social forms of any kind. They have no pattern that will exclude one kind of relationship while permitting another. So their sexual relations show the same formlessness, excluding only parents and blood siblings and admitting every kind of marriage known to anthropology. The Kaingáng are not only monogamous and polygynous; but they were polyandrous too and they also established what I shall call "joint marriages" in which several men lived together with several women in mutual cohabitation. These last two types will be discussed in the following chapter.

13 This refers, of course, to societies which are more highly structuralized.

IV

Polyandry and Joint Marriages

THE KAINGÁNG ARE RIDDEN by hunger and swayed by the strength of their libidinal ties, and they have in some degree overcome the one by building on the other. Food and sex have become so closely interwoven in the Kaingáng mind that they even use the same term for eating as they do for coitus. In human relationships the overt, articulate emphasis is always upon food, and the strongest bond that one man can have with another is that he suffered hunger with him. When the soul of the deceased is sped on its way the dead man's relative, tormented by the fear that he might be taken along by the ghost, shouts as he pounds the dead body on the chest: "Leave me and go! You and I suffered great hunger together; so leave me and go!" Now, since men are the principal sources of food supply, talk of marriage centers primarily on their value as providers for the girls and their parents and brothers and sisters. When a man speaks of his marriage he does not discuss the qualities of his wife nor the material advantage to him of the alliance, but of feeding his wife and her relatives. "First I married Kulú," said Vomblé. "Then I left her and married Kulá. My father's brother sent her to me. At the same time Wanenggló sent his sister Waikíli to me, but I sent her to my brother Ndíli. When she left him he married Kulú. I lived only with Kulá. I went hunting with Waikíli but sent her to Ndíli. Two women have many children, and my wives had no families that were capable of giving me food. Yet I had to feed my children. I was hungry. My father [Thunder Storm] had three wives, but they had brothers who could give him food. I have to give things to Kulá's brothers and sisters, but they could give nothing because they were so small. Waikíli had only one brother."

Through her marriage Kulá's family gained Vomblé as an ally in the quest for food. Even before marriage a girl's sexual interests are beneficial to her family, for her lovers come with presents of food, and they are welcome at her parents' fireside. The food a lover brings is not payment for favors he has received but a gift in expectation of favors still to come. Even after her marriage a woman's amorous intrigues are of considerable advantage to those around her—even to her own husband, for every time she attracts a man she has added a hunter to the band. Wherever his mistress is, there the lover stays, and unless her husband gets wind of the affair and flies into a rage the lover may very likely follow the camp almost indefinitely. His presence is welcome, of course, for another gun or bow and another knife and axe mean so much more meat and honey. Thus even adultery plays a constructive role in Kaingáng society, for it keeps within the band men who might otherwise go elsewhere in search of satisfaction, and it often culminated in polyandrous marriage, which has been one of the strongest integrating forces in Kaingáng society.

The story is told of Kuvén who was the lover of both Kanggá and her mother. Now as Kanggá's father grew old and it became difficult for him to get meat, he felt more and more the necessity of having someone to help him hunt for his large family. As long as Kuvén remained he could depend on him, but when it seemed that the young man was becoming interested in Yemái, a woman who was no relative of his and whom, therefore, Kuvén might follow far away to her relatives, Kanggá's father said to his wife and daughter: "Call Kuvén; if he marries Yemái he will leave me and go away. Let him get food for your children when I die. If he marries another woman he will throw your children away." So Kanggá's mother called Kuvén and said to her daughter: "Marry him. I am going to live with you and him." So Kuvén married both mother and daughter, and when Kanggá's father died Kuvén took care of the latter's children.

The Kaingáng have no system of clans or moieties[1] to impose social obligations on them. Their kinship system is not the crystallization of inescapable obligations that is found in many other primitive societies but principally a device for grouping people in large age classes. Their mode of life also made the maintenance of complex systems of obligations and loyalties extremely difficult, for they wandered from place to place in little groups of two to twenty adults. Even the biological family had little permanence as a cooperating unit, for children wandered away from their parents when they grew up and brothers separated to go with their in-laws or to travel with childhood playmates and hunting companions in search of adventure. Under the influence of the conflicting obligations of blood and marriage the composition of the small group of adults was forever changing. The dependence of the men on one another, and even their fundamental reali-

[1] See Appendix II, p. 175.

zation of this dependence, is not enough to stabilize any relationship among them even today, for there are any number of men with whom an individual may join forces, and if he hunts with his father today he may go away with his wife's father tomorrow and with his sister's husband the day after. Nothing compels him to fix his allegiance.

Nevertheless the Kaingáng had achieved a certain degree of social cohesion, and one of the ways in which they managed it was by building permanent cooperating units around their sex interests. It is in this way that social integration, although explicitly expressed in terms of the economically important men, often actually revolved about the women. As in the case of Kanggá and her mother, the women often became the nuclei of polyandrous and also of joint marriages, which often changed their male composition frequently. Thus by her mere existence the woman held together a complex household, which disintegrated when she died. A general lack of formal rules for marriage permitted the easy building up of large *ménages* by gradual additions of men and women. A household might begin with either a monogamous or a polygynous marriage; as time passed another man might be added to the household and become the co-husband; perhaps another wife was added and then another man. Through the years the family would expand and contract or simply change as the wives or husbands died or were killed off in feuds or the raids of the bugreiros.

The Indians told me of the marriages of Wanyekí.[2] Together with his wife Tendó, his sister and his hunting companion Chu, he wandered about, far away from other members of the tribe. This was nothing unusual for the Kaingáng, who sometimes did not see one another for years. When Chu's wife died Wanyekí's wife cooked and made a sleeping-place for him, simply, as the Kaingáng put it, "because he had no wife," and he became her co-husband. So Chu was saved for Wanyekí and his little isolated band and did not wander away in search of another wife. But as time passed Tendó, the wife, died, and Wanyekí and Chu were left alone. Until his nieces, his sister's daughters, grew to adolescence, Wanyekí had no wife. Then one day his sister said to him: "Wanyekí, live with them. There are no other women. They are in the same position as you—there are no men. So go around with them. There is no one else for you to marry. So marry them." Chu had died in the meanwhile, so Wanyekí, who already had had two wives married these three girls, who were much younger than he. This kind of relationship is not difficult for a Kaingáng girl, for far from wishing to retain her hold on the recreations of her childhood she looks forward to the sexual experiences that she has been urged to seek ever since she was a baby in arms.

Wanyekí lived alone with his three wives, his sister's daughters, until

[2] See footnote p. 30.

they each bore him a child. Then he joined forces with two men whom he
had left long ago, and he once more became monogamous, for two of
his wives left him to live with these men. Wanyekí did not object. Even
though his wives took their sons with them the children remained attached
to their father and were frequently in his camp. If Wanyekí had objected
there would have been two courses open to him. He could have beaten his
wives, in which case they would have left him anyway, or he could have
quarreled with the men. In the latter case he would have lost the companionship of the angry men, who would certainly have left him. Actually
Wanyekí lived for many years on friendly terms with them, and they continued to make love to his remaining wife Amendó even though they now
had wives of their own.

Soon after this Wanyekí was joined by two other men, who became the
co-husbands of Amendó, and when Wanyekí's son Véye by his first and
now long-dead wife grew to manhood he too shared his father's wife. So
father and son, instead of glowering at each other across the fire out of
their jealous desire for the same woman, cohabited with her in peace,
strengthening the precarious bonds of Kaingáng society. The solution
would not be the same in every case, for in another such household
Kangndádn beat his son and drove him out for daring to copulate with his
second wife. But Wanyekí and Véye shot game for each other and for their
robust wife while she bore her four husbands nine lusty children and one
weakling who died.

Judging from her numerous love affairs it could never be said that
Amendó was unable to cope with the sexual demands of her husbands, but,
as the Kaingáng put it, she had a great deal of work to do cooking and
fetching water for four hungry men and her children; so she called
Nggevén, one of her husbands' nieces, to be her co-wife. Amendó had
nothing to fear from the younger woman, for they had four husbands to
share between them and Amendó was active in seeking enjoyment outside
the bonds of matrimony. So without jealousy or disruption Nggevén moved
into this household. She did not have the ignominious position[3] of the
second wife that is so common in primitive societies, nor did Amendó ever
attempt to drive her out. This closely-knit cooperating unit held together
through the years until Nggevén had borne the four husbands ten children.
Then Wanyekí and one of his co-husbands died. But although two of the
oldest members of the household were dead, although Wanyekí, the husband of Amendó's youth, was dead, the remaining husbands stayed by her
and hunted for her. But soon only Véye was left, for the Brazilians killed

[3] The position of the first wife is superior to that of the second only in one respect: in a
case of jealous conflict the first wife never leaves.

Amendó and the other husbands and Nggevén married her young son-in-law and went away.

In relationships like these the violent hostility between an aging father and his son, both striving for the same woman, is resolved through the son's marriage to his step-mother. This has happened over and over again in Kaingáng society, and it is one of the few instances in which a people have been able to settle this ancient conflict peaceably. Instead of being violently possessive like the typical male in our society and like not a few in his own, Wanyekí was willing to share his wives. First he relinquished two of them and then he permitted his son and other men to come and share his remaining wife. This brought peace and security not only to him but also to the men who escaped conflict through his behavior, to the innumerable sympathizers who would have taken sides in the concomitant quarreling, and to the women who escaped the beatings that an angry husband might have given them. Wanyekí possessed a foresight that Yuvén[4] lacked. Yuvén, young, jealous and possessive, drove out his two co-husbands, but as he grew older and his family multiplied he was compelled to accept Kuvén as the husband of both his wife and daughter, for only in that way did he feel that his wife and children would be adequately cared for.

Yakwá is another violent possessive man who got into difficulties because he was unwilling to share his wife. Although he is about sixty years old he is as vigorous as any young man. His powerful muscles bulge beneath his skin and he is tireless in the hunt. No one is faster than he at clearing land for planting. For a nomad, unused to the ways of white civilization, he is an unusually energetic farmer. His violent rages were a trial to me. His wife was not at all like him. She was given to thieving, it is true, but my battles with her were always more or less genial. She was a persistent but gentle thief. She must have been about fifty years old, wonderfully well preserved, and her skin was a beautiful golden tan. There was no doubt that Anggló wanted a kind of love-making that her husband could not give her. So she turned to her son-in-law Kanyahé. Years before she and Yakwá had had a daughter, an only child, who had married Kanyahé but died a few years before I came to the reservation. Kanyahé was about thirty years old. He too was powerfully built, and for energy in the hunt he could match Yakwá. He kept a large household supplied with meat when no one else had any. His sexuality was aggressive and open, and he carried on his affairs almost under the noses of the husbands.

His affair with Anggló made the older man desperate. When Anggló came home he fought with her, not daring to mention the subject of the

4 Kanggá's father. See p. 36.

quarrel, but always pretending to rage about some irrelevant matter. One night there was a terrific uproar in their house. Both Yakwá and Angglό were yelling at the tops of their voices. But never a word about the real subject of the quarrel. Instead Yakwá was berating her for working somewhere else instead of helping him. Angglό in a towering rage struck her husband. There was no limit to her daring. Once she slept in the forest two nights with Kanyahé and came back early in the morning and lay down among the Indians who were making manioc at their mill. The Indians told me that when her husband saw her he kicked her twice in the belly. But, Angglό said to her cousin: "He may kill me, but I will not leave Kanyahé. I don't want Yakwá. I want something new." Angglό's passion for Kanyahé was a fine show that nearly everyone enjoyed.

Under the influence of her love affair Angglό's desire for a child became heightened to a passionate intensity. First she asked her cousin Koktá to ask me for something to "make her blood come out." Once before Koktá's husband had come to me for medicine, because his wife had a "pain in the belly." I had given him a phial of castor oil. It turned out, however, that the pain was a menstrual cramp, and the dose of castor oil precipitated the flow. Since the Kaingáng think that "women menstruate in order to have children" an association between castor oil and childbearing was easily made. I explained to Koktá that she was mistaken in thinking that castor oil had anything to do with menstruation and she at last gave up trying to persuade me to give her some for Angglό. But Angglό was not satisfied, and several days later when there was no one around she came up to me shyly and begged me for "medicine to make my blood come out. My blood is all choked up inside of me." Of course I could do nothing for her. As we stood there arguing her sister's husband walked by unconcernedly. Next day he said to me, "I know what she asked you for, she asked you for a medicine to make her have children. She asked me too, but I wouldn't give it to her because she won't sleep with her husband and he won't let anyone else do it; so she can't have intercourse anyway."

There was no limit to the enjoyment that the people derived from this struggle between three human beings, which might have been so easily settled if Yakwá and Kanyahé had become co-husbands of Angglό. Once when most of us were up the river at a weeding bee on Yuplú's farm a group of people around me began to talk about how Yakwá pursued his wife. Yakwá was not far off; so they talked quietly, without a change of expression or a smile that would have indicated the spicy nature of the conversation. A few days before, in the dead of night, Yakwá, who had come looking for his wife, had come where many Indians were gathered to help the agent weed his corn. He had wandered around among the sleepers like some wild animal, and some of them even thought he was one.

Later in the day Kanyahé took it into his head to make fun of me. "You're always walking around making love," he shouted. "No I'm not," I yelled back. We had a large audience. "You make love everywhere," Kanyahé bellowed; "everybody sees you!" "You lie, you're the one who makes love." "You bet I do," he roared. This was my cue to see how far he was willing to walk on thin ice, and I retaliated: "No one has to see you. It is the talk of everyone, how much you walk about taking women." This was too much even for Kanyahé. He dropped the subject immediately without another word and turned to weeding. Through it all Yakwá stood, his powerful hands on the handle of his scythe, a broad smile on his face, completely enjoying the show.

This affair throws into bold relief the fate that awaits the principals in a conflict whose solution is prevented by a possessive husband. The jealous husband pursues his wife to the point where his behavior causes much smiling behind polite hands. His endless quarrels with her culminate in blows and often in dissolution of the marriage. Yakwá's threat to kill Kanyahé would never have been carried out because murder in Kaingáng society must have a background of vendetta,[5] but it illustrates well the complete break between the two men.

Another drama enacted by a mother and a son-in-law, illustrates the ever-ripening character of this relationship. Just as they have resolved the struggle between a man and his son for the same woman through the son's marriage to his stepmother, the Kaingáng have arrested the conflict between a woman and her daughter for the same man by the man's marrying his mother-in-law too.[6] Instead of surrounding the mother-in-law with disrupting taboos that send the son-in-law flying when he hears her coming or keeping him cooling his heels outside as long as his mother-in-law, whose face he may not see, is in the house, the Kaingáng have developed the relationship between a man and his mother-in-law to the point where he sometimes marries her and becomes the second father of her children. Such was the relationship between Kuvén and Kanngá's mother and between the captive Nyepá and his mother-in-law, Kuichó. Yakwá has no one to take care of him if his wife Angglló chooses to remain at the post while he goes hunting with me and the Indians. But if his widowed mother-in-law, whose household he never left as long as she was alive, went along, his food was cooked when he came back after a long day's range in the forest just as if she had been his wife and there were always fresh fern leaves for him to stretch his body on. At night he slept beside the old woman or at her feet across the campfire. When he moved camp it was she who carried his few belongings, and when she needed a basket it was he who made it for her. When her family gathered around her it was she who gave him food. An Indian told me that when the old woman died[7] he did not say to her, as the Kaingáng usually say to the dead, "Leave me and go away," so that her soul would not take him along, but instead: "Do not leave me. When I am sick I shall ask your protection."

The relationship between co-husbands in polyandrous and joint marriage was one of the strongest in the society. Children might leave their parents, brothers might separate to follow their affinal relatives, brothers-in-law and parents and their sons-in-law might rarely see one another or might interrupt long-standing relationships casually, but co-husbands who had grown to maturity did not part. The strongest loyalties in such marriages were not between the husbands and their wife or wives but among the men. However strongly the men and women may be linked together in a common household the charm of casual intrigues is too great for them to forego. Although Amendó had four husbands she still had time for swift rendezvous in the forest, and many children called Wanyekí and his co-husbands yûgn[8] "because he had intercourse with their mother."

The motive that lead a man to accept a co-husband was always the same, his own and his family's security. The more independent and the more possessive avoided it as long as they could. Many could avoid it all their lives, but others, driven by old age and the lack of young sons to take care of them or forced by a crippling injury, at last accepted co-husbands. And it was generally only because there were no marriageable women around that a man consented to become a co-husband. Young co-husbands separated as soon as a likely young woman appeared on the scene and that was why polyandry among young men was so unstable. Older men preferred the comfortable security of joint households, so that even if they encountered a marriageable woman they preferred to absorb her into a joint household rather than venture the precarious independence of a separate ménage. When one of my informants, Klendó, was a young man he asked his half-brother to come and live with him and his wife, but after a while the half-brother, having acquired a wife of his own, established his own household. The young men shifted around, but when they had matured in polyandry and had learned the value of such a relationship they did not change. A nice realization of their mutual dependence prompted father and son to live peacefully together with the same wife, and impelled a man to share his wife with his brother or even with a distant relative. Father-in-law and son-in-law also became co-husbands, forming a firm cooperating unit which guaranteed food to the older man and his wife and children and which gave the younger man an additional claim on his wife's relatives.

[7] She died during the grippe epidemic in 1933.

[8] The term a person uses for his father and all men very much older than he.

Their rigorous environment and lack of a close social structure that would automatically provide the aging hunter with helpers or the widow who has children with a husband make the problem of food supply terribly pressing for these people. It was for this reason that Ketédn made my next-door neighbor, Kuthúgn, a member of his household when the latter was still a boy. "When I am dead," said Ketédn, "you will take care of my wife and children." Events showed that Ketédn had acted with foresight—perhaps because of his supernatural power—for he was killed by the Brazilians, and now Kuthúgn was living next door to me with Ketédn's wife who was so much older than he.

A widow who is no longer young has a hard time of it with her small children. Dependent on relatives, she wanders from household to household. At night she sleeps alone with her little child. There is no one to take care of her. Her brother or cousin or brother-in-law give her food when they have it. They share what they have as a matter of course, but when there is little food their children come first and the widow may get only short rations. Kundídn is such a widow. One day she eats at her cousin's house, the next at her brother's, the next at the house of another cousin. When she is sick her cousin Angglé sometimes comes to sit beside her, but if Angglé is away at some secret rendezvous with her lover, or off hunting with her brother, Kundídn often lies alone and miserable. None of the young men would marry a woman of forty with a goiter. But when she is well Kundídn is vigorous and aggressive. She works longer days in the fields than the younger women, she goes out frequently to look for honey, she is an aggressive and determined suitor and she had almost chopped off Véye's leg when the latter deliberately drowned her brother. Whenever I had to pass her house I made a wide circle because I knew that Kundídn would attempt to seduce me in her violent and jocular manner if she caught sight of me. At last she offered me her wild, thin little daughter, Tombá, aged about eleven. "Take her and bring her up," she said. "When she is grown, marry her, and she will keep house for you."

These forms of marriage and the custom of occasional adoption with an eye to the consummation of a future sex relationship are only crystallizations from an almost amorphous social life. Nevertheless, however imperfectly defined, informal, and even casual their sexual arrangements may be, the Kaingáng have made them the center of some kind of relationship that has a permanent value for this society. The casual relationships among young people in our own society that are the outgrowth of passion often serve no other function than to satisfy an overwhelming desire for sexual experience and companionship. Once the couple has drifted apart they have no claims on each other. They are strangers and can never depend on one another for anything. But among the Kaingáng, who literally have their backs to the wall of existence, who have been hunted by the Brazilians and their enemies, the Kangdjá for two hundred years or more, and who have been torn asunder by bloody vendettas, ties created by passion are never really broken. A boy's sweetheart is *plὴ* and a girl's is *mbâdn*. These are terms that they never fully relinquish, and the sense of status implied by these expressions is never quite lost. Although the terms as they are used between sweethearts have not the same significance as between husband and wife, they do indicate that there is an attachment which cannot be entirely broken and which may even be recognized by a woman's children after she has at last married someone else. When Nenggachá[9] was about to be killed by Kenggó, Anggló, the latter's wife dashed between her husband and his victim and grasped the lance that would have killed Nenggachá. He was her mother's lover, the Kaingáng say, and therefore she protected him from her husband.

The feeling that once a man and a woman have been lovers there has been established a relationship which, however tenuous its bonds and obligations may be, never fully loses its significance, is expressed in the Kaingáng use of terms of relationship. In line with their almost complete lack of feeling for social structure, the Kaingáng entertain contradictory ideas about their relationship terms. They have theories about these terms which they never put into practice in anything like a consistent way. Yet some of these unpracticed theories demonstrate a feeling about relationships that has an actual though subtle significance. The Kaingáng feel that the term *yὐgn* which means "father," but in a broader sense, "any man much older than I," denotes also a paternal relationship. The fact that they use it for men who have been their mothers' lovers is important once we have come to understand the attitude of the Kaingáng toward their love affairs. The man who has been their mother's lover is in some way associated with their father, and they owe him a certain allegiance that will become active in situations of conflict.

The Kaingáng are such enterprising lovers that one would imagine that a woman would call many of the men around her *mbâdn* and that a man would refer to most of the women as *plὴ*. And this is true within certain limits. In making a detailed analysis for the ethnologist an informant carefully distinguishes between the women with whom he has had an affair and those with whom he has not. The number of the latter in a man's own age-group is small and might be even smaller if he were more careful to include not only those women with whom he has been on constantly friendly terms but also those with whom he has had little contact in the last few years. In generalized thinking, however, a woman speaks of all the men of her group[10] as *mbâdn* and a man calls all the women *plὴ*. Thus the

---

[9] See p. 118. All these people are dead now.

[10] Her own extended family. See p. 50 for exact definition of this term.

terms *eklą,* "my offspring," and *éng yí,* "my child," which every man or woman applies to individuals who are very much younger than he, come to have a significance that is intimately related to the entire sexual life of the Kaingáng. A mature man who has lead the normal philandering life of the average Kaingáng suspects that not a few of the children who have other putative fathers are really his. At any rate, since he had intercourse with their mothers he bears to them such relationship as springs from all such contacts. Just as their mothers are forever his *plą* these children are his *klą.* The fact that whole groups[11] of a hundred or more people are referred to as the *klą* of so-and-so, a very old man, reflects not only the adult Kaingáng practice of calling all very young people *klą* but also the deep-rooted feeling of having an actual role in their procreation.

"Klendó's daughter, Pathó, is my child," said Vomblé. "How do you know," said I, "since Klendó also lay with her mother?" "Well, when two men lie with a woman they just call her child their child." But not only do men feel that their mistress's children are their children, but people whose mothers have had intercourse with the same man, whether as lover or husband, regard one another as siblings. The result of this socio-sexual outlook is to draw ever more closely together this small, closely inbred group of people. To the clearly defined and explicitly expressed ties of blood, which already connect them intimately, are added the subtler ties of sex, which, however unimportant they may seem at the moment, nevertheless endure in some measure and are capable of playing their part in life's crises. When Véye was sick with the grippe it was not his wife or his wife's sister's husband or some other relative who came to me to get medicine and food for him, but Kulá, his lover, a strong, aggressive woman a good fifteen years older than he and the wife of my best informant. When he at last died she mourned the longest—even longer than his wife.

The Kaingáng present, therefore, the picture of a society whose very structurelessness permitted the building of stable cooperating units around sex interests. Intrigues that frequently might have been the cause of trouble were often stabilized into lasting polyandrous and joint households, and even when they were not, they nevertheless established ties that were never completely dissolved. But although polyandrous and joint marriages were most valuable to their principals, most Kaingáng men and women are possessive enough to want to keep their spouses to themselves, with the result that 60 percent of the marriages are monogamous.[12] Usually when a man marries he looks forward to gaining as allies in the struggle for food

---

[11] These are the extended families. See p. 50.

[12] An analysis of 308 marriages taken from genealogies that represent about 100 years of Kaingáng history past and present, yields the following percentages: 60 percent monogamous, 18 percent polygynous, 14 percent polyandrous and 8 percent joint.

at least some of his wife's brothers or male cousins. In a group of a few hundred individuals that has had little contact with the outside world for hundreds of years, however, everyone must be related to everyone else in a variety of ways, and no one has any choice but to marry among the people he sees every day and who are his first or second cousins. The moment he marries, a Kaingáng is supposed to shift his attention from various loyalties which he has developed around the bonds of common residence or descent to a specialized loyalty to some of his wife's kin. But Kaingáng society is so closely inbred that this shift often cannot really mean very much. One of my informants had married his mother's half-sister, with the result that he came to view all of his mother's brothers as his in-laws and owed them his special allegiance. This did not involve any particular adjustment for him, for he had always wandered around with them anyway. It would be utterly impossible for anyone in such a society to keep tab on all his theoretical loyalties. The Kaingáng have set up for themselves an ideal pattern of affinal relations through which not even the most intellectual Kaingáng can possibly pick his way to clarity.

Far from being embarrassed by this system which says that a man must be solicitous of every one of his wife's relatives down to her second cousins, who may be legion, the Kaingáng go through life supremely indifferent to it. When the ethnologist comes along with his passion for clarity he discovers that Klendó has completely ignored the relatives of his second wife, while Vomblé never hunted for his wives' sisters and brothers at all but devoted himself completely to the husbands of his sisters and cousins. Every once in a while the body of impracticable theory is invoked to excuse a murder that had been years in the planning, or to rail at an affinal relative from whom less has been received than was expected, but on the whole the Kaingáng are quite willing to allow one another to choose what in-laws they shall associate with. Then these become a man's only affinal relatives, and he is unable to see that anyone else is, no matter how much the ethnologist, with his theoretical interest in social structure, may insist that the logic of the theory has been violated. With indignation in his voice my best informant denied that his wife's brothers and sisters were his in-laws. What, call those people in-laws, who never gave him anything? He should say not. At first they were too young to give him anything, and even now that they were grown up they ignored him.

Whoever lived alone with his wife or wives, that is to say more than three-quarters of the adult males, was really without any man on whom he could absolutely depend to keep him from starvation at all times. His own chosen in-laws with whom he went around day after day might leave him at any moment because they felt that they ought to give some attention to some other of their in-laws for whom they had shot nothing in a long time or who had invited them to go on a marauding expedition against the Brazilians. His own brothers had similar obligations. The entire adult male population was torn by half a dozen crosscurrents of loyalties that pulled them from one end of the forest to the other. From year to year, throughout their lives, the Kaingáng wandered about, looking for one another, until a man's life became a record of partings, searchings, and encounters. Through all this parents were separated from children, brothers were parted, relatives by marriage drifted apart for years, only to join forces again and continue a severed relationship. Husbands were even parted from their wives, and only matured co-husbands were inseparable.

V

Disruptive Forces in Kaingáng Society

THE VERY FORMLESSNESS OF KAINGÁNG society makes us wonder what gave
it coherence. There were no territorial boundaries to limit the range of the
hunter, there was no chief or government to impose its will on the people,
there were no binding marriage forms and incest restrictions were minimal.
Marriage was brittle, and even the polyandrous and joint households, by
far the most stable units in the society, included only 20 percent of the
married population. Men were torn between the ties of blood and the ties
of marriage; they spent their years fluctuating between groups of both
kinds and haunted by a sense of insecurity.

The mechanism of kinship did not enforce cooperation among specific
individuals, and there was no large unit of specific outline that might
accomplish coordination of effort in some other way. The cooperation
among in-laws might be broken almost without reproach, and the ties that
bound children to their parents or to one another yielded to the strain of
affinal relationships or to stronger bonds that grew up between men and
their hunting companions. Yet, with all this, Kaingáng society could have
held together, however haphazardly its bonds are slung, for the Kaingáng
have a strong sense of being one people against other people. After all, they
are all related to one another by blood, and they are all *"our"* people" or
"our" living things" to one another, as opposed to all other "living things"
that have no possessive pronoun to bring them within the group. They felt
the need for renewing ever and again their informal contacts, and whoever
let the years pass as he lived in isolation wandering thoughtlessly in a distant part of the forest risked a quarrel when he met again the people he
had neglected. The very lack of fixity of relationships and the multitude of
ways of forming them left the Kaingáng with no device for controlling a

conflict. Once a feud arose there was nothing, neither dominating ties of blood nor the voice of chieftainship or government, to stop or limit it. Where the demands of kin by marriage conflicted with the claims of blood and where the call of a hunting companion whose bed one had shared clamored above the voices of blood and affinity the individual was pulled in a dozen directions, by a dozen magnets. Feuds spread, cleaving the society asunder like a deadly axe, blighting its life like the plague. Thus it came about that the very forces of integration carried the seeds of disruption within them. A man's link with his wife's people pulled him from his siblings; his bond with his sister's husband tore him from his wife's people; and his relationships with his hunting companions drew him from all.

The Kaingáng are divided into extended families ranging in numbers from 50 to 300 individuals. These families are made up of the descendants of two or more men who have intermarried and whose children have intermarried. Thus each family is closely inbred, and almost every member can trace his genealogy[1] to one of the two or more male ancestors. These ancestral males are real personalities, and the data on them is usually rather full, but there is always a point beyond which memory cannot go, and it is impossible to learn anything about any of their parents or siblings. Marriages with other extended families occurred, but marriages within the families far outnumber marriages between the families. This endogamy was brought about not by a specific taboo on marrying outside but by the hostility between the families which made them distrust one another and which kept them apart. When members of different families did marry it almost always caused a split in the ranks of one or both of the intermarrying groups. In such a case brother might be aligned against brother to the death. Those who shifted from one family to another either through marriage or through having been captured as youngsters were looked on as blood relatives of their new associates and hence as enemies to their former friends and were given no quarter in case of attack by members of the family to which they once belonged.

The Kaingáng call members of their own extended family "my own people," and the warm personal relationships that have been described in the preceding chapters exist only among one's "own people." For hundreds of years there have been several Kaingáng extended families and they have lived in a state of perpetual feud with one another. Whole lineages have been destroyed, and others, overcome by panic, have wandered away into the endless forests, never to be heard of again. Sometimes two extended families have come together and have been able to live in peace, but gen-

---

[1] The Kaingáng are minutely interested in their own genealogies, and they know who their father's father's father's son's wife's sister's daughter's husband is down to the last detail of all his names, what he died of, and how many children he had.

erally whoever went contrary to the behavior of the rest of his "own people" and threw in his lot with "another group of people" was lost, for he had joined forces with those whose hate and fear were directed against the ones with whom he had ties. He became a wanderer divorced from his own blood, sleepless at night for fear that they might come to kill him, anxious in the day lest his new companions slay him. If he survived, his children bore the weight of his deed, for they might never return to their father's people. They were ķőinggëgn utpá, "different men," to them, even though they were first cousins by blood. They had never shared their women or caressed their men. They were shut out of the circle of warm arms and bodies that mean security to the Kaingáng, and they were killed on sight or hunted down like wild animals. In Kaingáng terminology "a different group of our people" is a synonym for thûgn, enemy. The hated Brazilians and "our different people" are both thûgn, enemies, "something no good," and severed from the ties of blood in behavior if not in fact.

The Feuds

Today Kaingáng memory does not go further back than the murder of Nduichá with anything like exactness. But it transports us to this death more than a century ago with a precision that is almost mathematical. The complicated genealogies of the people whose descendants are alive today check rigorously. When the Kaingáng discuss such killings as Nduichá's they seem to be fitting together the parts of a machine the intricate workings of which they know precisely. Their absorbed interest in the history of their own destruction has impressed on their minds with flawless clarity the multitudinous cross-workings of the feuds. They remember not only the genealogy of everyone but even details of weather, conversation, and facial expression and the precise spot in which an arrow or a lance struck.

In order to understand the feud conditions under which Nduichá was murdered we must take advantage of these memories and try to picture the composition of Kaingáng society at the time. When our story opens three groups of people are living together: the children of Mumbégn,[2] the children of Kanggúin, and the children of Vomblé. Mumbégn had three wives who bore him many children, but for the present our story is concerned only with three of his offspring: Kumbló, and his sister, and their half-brother, Wanyekí,[3] the son of Mumbégn by another wife. Mumbégn himself had died, and one of his wives, the mother of Kumbló, had married Koví, "a different man," one for whom memory provides no blood tie. For

[2] His real name was Kuvén, but I have called him Mumbégn in order not to confuse him with his son Kuvén, who was killed later. These three men are the ancestors of the extended family with which I lived.

[3] See pp. 37-38.

many years Vomblé, Kanggúin, and Mumbégn had lived harmoniously together. Together they had exterminated another group of "different men," and far from wanting to shed each other's blood, they had saved each other from destruction. One of Kanggúin's sons had married a daughter of Mumbégn, and their daughter in turn had married a son of Vomblé, so that the ties of companionship were strengthened by the bonds

GENEALOGY I

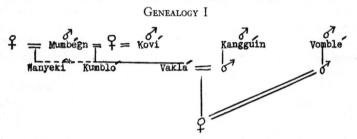

of marriage. But the marriage of Mumbégn's widow to Koví (the "different man") was destined to split this compact group, for true to the character of "different men," which Kaingáng history has repeated time out of mind, Koví slew Nduichá, a hunting companion of his new wife's people.

No Indian knows how Koví came to kill Nduichá, but many think they know. They say that because Nduichá lay with one of Koví's wives and ridiculed him, Koví slew him with an axe as Nduichá bent over to cut him a piece of meat from a tapir that he had killed. But if the Kaingáng killed one another for adultery they would all have been dead long ago, for their life is the very essence of adultery. The children of Vomblé and their hunting companions have intrigued with each other's wives and husbands for two hundred years with never a murder among them. It is true that the Kaingáng often told me that murders occurred because one man lay with the wife of another, but whenever I was able to trace them back I always found that each was just one in a long series of vendetta murders whose origins are forgotten. And here exact genealogical records help us to bridge the gap between two episodes of the same history where Kaingáng memory begins to falter, for years before this murder Vomblé, Kanggúin and Kuvén, the hunting companions of Nduichá, had joined in the midnight slaughter of Koví's brothers-in-law, and their deaths were still unavenged. Thus the murder of Nduichá, although perhaps provoked by his relationship with Koví's wife, would never have occurred had not Nduichá and Koví been destined to be enemies because of a pre-existing feud.

But having killed Nduichá, Koví had started himself and his group on a path of blood from which they could never turn. With the bitter logic that has characterized Kaingáng murderers as far as the living can re-

* Dotted line indicates step-sibling relationship.

member, they reasoned that unless they killed all of Nduichá's group his relatives and hunting companions would kill them. With a single murder the murderer enters a locked system. He must kill and kill again, he must plan whole massacres lest a single survivor remain to avenge his kin. Kaingáng murderers are like the characters of a Greek tragedy in the grip of a natural law whose processes once started can never be stayed. So when Koví killed Nduichá he at once plotted the murder of all of Nduichá's relatives and hunting companions. But although he and his accomplice succeeded in killing and wounding several, among them Kumbló's own brother-in-law, they themselves soon became the hunted. All of the adult males of Nduichá's group, an entire well-knit family, banded together and tracked them through the forest day after day until they scattered in panic, throwing away their possessions to lighten their flight.

Perhaps the most tragic figure in this drama was Kumbló, for he was related by marriage and association to both camps. To make things worse a half-brother, Wanyekí, had been the hunting companion of the murdered men, and Kumbló never dared to face him again. But he could never rest with the murderers with whom he had thrown in his lot, for how did he know that they did not suspect him?

These seeds of disruption bore their inevitable fruit, and Koví himself was slain by Kumbló's brother Kuvén. They say that Kumbló, Kuvén, and their hunting companion "found out" that Koví wanted to kill them; but in an atmosphere of distrust and terror, where people do not sleep at night and an almost paranoid fear oppresses the mind, it is not necessary to "find out" anything. When fear swells beyond control, and they can stand it no longer, the Kaingáng strike and they often "find out" afterward. With characteristic cunning they plotted the death of Koví, for centuries of feud have made the Kaingáng masters of deadly shrewdness. Kumbló took Koví's bow from him, saying, "Kuvén asked me to get your bow, for his is broken." So the foolish Koví handed over his bow, leaving himself incapable of fighting at a distance. At night they slept near Koví and early in the morning they attacked, killing him, their stepfather, and wounding Patklé, their own brother-in-law.[4] Quaintly contradictory to my informant's

GENEALOGY II

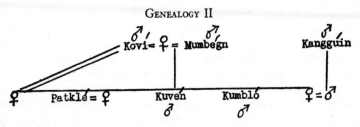

"they found out" is his remark, "He [Koví] killed Nduichá and they had not avenged him; so they killed Koví"! They wanted to avenge Nduichá, and "they found out" that Koví wanted to kill them. Thus where murder is planned, murder is suspected, and whoever wants to kill his neighbor fears that his neighbor wants to kill him too. When Yakwá says to me, "My cousin wants to kill me," I know that he wants to kill his cousin, who slaughtered his pigs for rooting up his corn; and when he says, "Eduardo [the Agent] is angry with me," I realize that he is angry with the Agent for not having given him a shirt. Yakwá's state of mind is a pale reflection of the Kaingáng habit of projecting their own hate and fear into the minds of those whom they themselves hate and fear. Yet one cannot always be sure that it is just a projection, for in these feuds currents of danger may radiate from any number of points of conflict, and there is often good and sufficient cause for any fear. If Kumbló and Koví feared each other there were grounds for it in Kumbló's association with the dead and wounded men.

With Koví dead, Patklé was in a position analogous to Kumbló's: he had married Kumbló's sister, and one of his own sisters had married Koví. Besides this, Patklé himself had been wounded. When he met Koví's murderers again he was in a quandary, for although they had killed his brother-in-law they were also his brothers-in-law. But if Patklé was confused, Koví's brother Wainló saw his duty clearly; and he said to Patklé: "Call Kuvén and live with him. I am going away. A long time from now I shall return and kill him."

Now Kuvén had intrigued with Patklé's wife, but Patklé had never tried to put a stop to it. Better to have him intriguing with his wife than wandering around in the forest unwatched. So when Kuvén went away one day Patklé sent his wife after him, saying: "Follow your *mbâdn* and then come back to me. He wants to kill me, and probably that is why he is going away." So she went after Kuvén and brought him back.

This is the darker picture of woman's role in Kaingáng culture, for if she is the nucleus of compact cells of economic security she is also bait for the murderer's trap. The role of the women in the feuds is generally passive. They follow their men wherever they go unless they are captured, and even then they sometimes manage to escape; only rarely do they use their better judgment to prevent murder, or intervene to save their mother's lover. Actively and aggressively sexual though they are and holding, by virtue of this, really a key position in Kaingáng life, they seem nevertheless to have been generally content not to take anything like a vital part in the determination of action. Perhaps these women feared lest were they to intervene to halt a murder, their husbands should turn against them, knowing all too well that the men they sought to protect were their partners in adultery.

So Patklé's wife brought Kuvén back, and one day as he wandered about in the forest he was killed by Wainló, who had secretly returned and was lying in wait for him. With the murder of his brother, Kumbló became even more frightened and enraged. He blamed his own sister for luring Kuvén and him to their death. But Wainló too was miserable, for he was utterly alone. He stole back to live with Patklé but never dared sleep at the same fire with him for fear that Kumbló would come and kill him. He would sleep in some hidden place and his wife would come to him in secret at night. At last in desperation he went away, leaving his wife and children with Patklé and saying, "If Kumbló does not kill you but comes to live with you, let him bring them [the children] up." This brings to a close the first episode in the story of the killing of Nduichá. His murderers fled, but they came to distrust one another, with the inevitable result at last of more murders and disruption. Throughout the years the companions of Nduichá were content to let his murderers escape, but at last they hunted them down and killed four women and captured two, one of whom they had wounded. They also captured six boys, three of them sons of Kumbló.

Since Kaingáng economy is built primarily on the occupations of men, a large cooperating male population is a necessary condition of its survival. If the male population is scattered and reduced by feuds, the economic support is destroyed, and if the women are killed the loss of men cannot be compensated. Had the Brazilians known how efficiently the Kaingáng were destroying themselves, they might never have bothered to hire bands of murderers but could have depended on the Kaingáng to do away with themselves. The Brazilians killed many women and children, the death rate that they inflicted on women being about twice that of the men; but since the intratribal Kaingáng feuds also reduced the men, the women were dying off only about 25 percent faster. The population was scattered in two different ways by internal conflict: first through the escape of murderers and second through the sudden flight of whole families terrified by murders. But it was not only internal conflict that scattered the Kaingáng but also aggression from without, for their usual way of protecting themselves was to scatter in all directions when there was danger of attack. They ran away from their ancient enemies the Kangdjá, from the Brazilians, and from each other. Whenever they attacked the Brazilians and feared pursuit they scattered. When the Kangdjá hunted them they scattered, and they themselves say that the reason that they now live so widely separated is "because Koví killed Nduichá." The Kaingáng have no idea of coming together and forming a solid unit against an outside aggressor. For them there was safety only in wakefulness and flight. Whoever pursues them constantly has them at his mercy, for they become panicstricken and never turn to face their pursuers until they are brought to bay like hunted animals.

The killing of the women and children by Nduichá's avengers brought an inevitable retaliation in the slaughter of men, women, and children by Kumbló's family. They stole upon a camp late at night, intending to kill the sleepers with clubs, but suddenly they remembered that the captured children were among them and that in the darkness they might be killed. So they waited until someone rose and stepped out of a house. When his cries aroused the camp the attacking party pursued each individual, killing them, men, women and children, like cornered rats. Those who escaped wandered about, sick and half starved, until they at last met with other members of their family. Since Kumbló's half-brother Wanyekí[5] had by this time become firmly bound to the children of Vomblé and Kanggúin, it did not seem strange to them that they should ask him to go in pursuit of his brother and kill him. Because of some trifling quarrel, however, Wanyekí never undertook the massacre, and before long he died. When his sons grew to manhood their relationship with their father's brother's family had become so obscured that they regarded them as "different people." Kumbló and his children were, to them, simply the murderers of members of their family, and they nursed a desire to kill them all until at last they pursued and slaughtered them. Kumbló and a few of his group escaped, but soon afterward the Brazilians killed Kumbló and the rest of his family, so that their extermination was complete.

Before this happened Patklé's entire line was annihilated, and the story of this massacre, which took place about 1885, is full of refinements of treachery and dissimulation. As the years passed the grandsons of Vomblé, Kanggúin and Mumbégn grew to manhood. There had been a series of intermarriages between the children of Patklé and the grandchildren of his ancient enemy Vomblé, who was now long dead. But Patklé never trusted his in-laws and was forever wandering away and returning. At last Kanyahé,[6] a son of Vomblé, who still remembered the murder of Nduichá, the wounding of his own father, and the whole series of murders and counter murders that had followed them, resolved to kill Patklé and his line. The fact that two of Patklé's daughters were his wives did not deter him. The killing was to be done in traditional Kaingáng style: they were to be invited to a festa, made to drink, and then slaughtered. Although the Kaingáng associate festas with quarreling and murder they never refused an invitation to one even though they knew their lives were in danger. One might imagine that at a festa where large sections of the tribe come together to enjoy themselves the bonds of kinship would be renewed and strengthened and old attachments of man for man would draw new warmth from the general good feeling.

Although this was true of some Kaingáng festas they were as often the

[5] See Genealogy I.
[6] Died of old age shortly before the Kaingáng came to the reservation.

scene of violent quarreling and disruption as they were of friendliness and solidarity. The men and women got drunk, and the men boasted to their children of their invulnerability and their deeds of blood. The men "told their *waikayú*," walking about, shaking their clubs or lances, slashing at the air, crying out the deeds they had done and the murders they would yet commit. As the beer and excitement mounted to their heads they turned on their neighbors and quarreled with them because they suspected them of adultery with their wives or because they themselves had had affairs with their neighbors' wives and themselves felt suspected and hated. Courage, daring, suspicion and ferocity were screwed to the sticking-point, and even among friends the atmosphere might become so charged with conflict that half the men would engage in brawls. Kaingáng folklore abounds in tales of festa massacres, and the expression, "Let us make beer for him," has such a sinister connotation that it needs no explanation.

Kanyahé decided to "make beer for Patklé" and his family and sent one of his nephews to invite them. Kanyahé and his group were afraid of Patklé, for his history gave them no reason to trust him. The statement of one of Patklé's daughters made after the death of her father and brothers, that her father wanted to kill Kanyahé's group, showed that Kanyahé had good grounds for fear. With the background of mutual distrust of the characters in this drama, we are in a position to understand their hypocritical behavior.

Kuthúgn [Thunder Storm] came to invite the group of Patklé, and when Yuplú, Patklé's son, saw him, he said, "Who is it?"

K. "It is I!"

Y. "Have you still the name I once knew you by?"

K. "Yes."

Y. "Is it really, then, the truth?"

K. "Yes, it is I."

Then Yuplú caressed Kuthúgn—the very token by which the Kaingáng understand security.

Y. "I have been thinking about you. Whenever someone died I thought of you. Did you think about seeing me, too?"

K. "Yes. I do just that. I have remembered you. I had almost forgotten you, and now, at last, I see you."

Then Yuplú called his wife and told her to give meat to Kuthúgn, a second token of security.

Y. "Kuthúgn, eat this and then talk with me."

When Kuthúgn had eaten, proving by his acceptance of the food that there was no evil in his mind, Yuplú spoke to him again. "Kuthúgn, where is your dog?" Kµthúgn had had a dog that was a fine tapir hunter, and he and Yuplú had hunted together with it.

K. "My dog died recently. It got sick and died."

Y. "What a pity! That big dog that used to bè so good for tapirs! That big dog that I used to hunt with; that big dog that I have been thinking about, is dead!"

This "friendly" conversation continued with first one and then another of Patklé's sons joining in to tell how much they wished to see various members of Kanyahé's family. For days they hunted and talked together until Kuthúgn returned and another messenger went out from Kanyahé's camp to continue the friendly overtures. At last part of Patklé's family arrived at the festa. But since only some came, the rest remaining away in fear, they were permitted to dance and drink until nightfall, and nothing happened; for their hosts wanted to wait until they had them all in the trap. In some way Yuplú had found out that the women were saying that he intended to kill Kanyahé's group, and in the evening, when he was resting after his day of dancing, he addressed the enemy group, saying: "My *plu̧* [the women of his enemies] are lying, and when you hear their lie you will kill me. I saw you and came to look for you, but when the women lie you will kill me." Yet he slept where he was and left the following day, but before he went Kuthúgn said, "I am going to make beer and invite you again."

At last the entire group of Patklé arrived and joined in the festa. Each of the people of Kanyahé placed himself next to an individual of the other band, and as they drank they watched one another in mutual suspicion. Waimbégn[7] said to Kiyitá[8]: "Do not look at me while you sing. I am going to sing with you. Do not look at my eyes!" Kiyitá became enraged and said: "I go around with men, and when I hold a festa with them I do not look at them. It seems to me that you were going to talk to me and that you called my name, but you said that I see your eyes!" At last when Patklé and his sons were drunk the group of Kanyahé turned on them as they danced and drank and killed Patklé and four of his sons and wounded a fifth. When the wounded man recovered and ran away with another who had been spared, most of the women and all of the children escaped with them. They were not heard of again until they were localized on a reservation in Palmas in 1915. Not long after this those who massacred Patklé and his sons completed their task of avenging the murders of Nduichá and his companion by slaughtering the children of Kumbló.

The history of this feud may be summed up in the following way:

First. Peaceful living together of the sons of Mumbégn, the sons of Vomblé, and the sons of Kanggúin.

Second. Murder of Nduichá by Koví, "a different man," wounding of

<hr>

[7] Patklé's son.

[8] Kanyahé's group.

Vomblé, killing of his wife, wounding of Kanggúin and killing of his son, followed by the flight of some of the sons of Mumbégn together with their relatives by marriage and their hunting companions.

Third. Suspicion, followed by murder, breaks out among the murderers of Nduichá *et al*.

Fourth. Final disruption of the forces of the murderers (i.e. separation of Kumbló and Patklé).

Fifth. Slaughter of the women of Kumbló's group by Nduichá's group.

Sixth. Slaughter of men, women, and children of Nduichá's group by Kumbló's group.

Seventh. Massacre of Patklé and his sons by their relatives by marriage.

Eighth. Massacre of Kumbló and his sons by the children of Kumbló's half-brother Wanyekí.

It is easy to see from this summary what the history of the Kaingáng vendettas has been: murder, followed by flight of the killers; then conflict within the ranks of the murderers themselves, with ensuing murder and splitting of the group. The murderers are hunted down by the relatives and companions of the dead men and women until not one is left. No society can stand such conflict, and the history of the Kaingáng shows clearly that they have been diminishing in numbers. Even they themselves are perfectly aware of the fact that their population has dwindled and that they have been split up into smaller and smaller groups because of the feuds.

Many societies must have gone to pieces and disappeared under the influence of disruptive forces within. In the course of the development of social forms those that fostered severe conflicts must ultimately have destroyed the societies in which they developed. The result would obviously be the gradual weeding out of such societies, and we would have left only such as could maintain themselves by satisfactorily reconciling the disintegrating forces within them. But from time to time in some societies situations develop that are incapable of adjustment, and that of the Kaingáng is one of these. In its otiose social theories and a curious system of body paints Kaingáng society shows traces of what may once have been a more complex social system. Their history goes back to a time when they lived in villages and cultivated the soil, but even then there were feuds. It is impossible to tell at present whether the development of the feuds brought about the destruction of a more complex social life or whether the contradictory social theories that we hear of today were ever more than notions picked up from contact with other cultures and never fully understood. But even in those very early times the Kaingáng were busily killing their affinal relatives and raiding the villages of "other" groups of their "own people."

Analysis

The most striking single feature of Kaingáng disintegration is the contrast between the warm, highly affective relationships within the "families" and the uninhibited ferocity of the behavior of the members toward all outsiders. Within their own circle of relatives and companions the Kaingáng will endure a high degree of personal discomfort to avoid a quarrel, but toward "other" groups of their "own people" their overwhelming desire is to shed blood. The result of the nervous insistence on the preservation of internal peace is that serious quarrels scarcely arise, and when they do they are swiftly forgotten or their effects muted. In quarrels over adultery within the extended family the entire brunt of the squabble is usually shifted on to the shoulders of the defaulting spouse, with the result that amity among the men—the very cornerstone of Kaingáng society—is preserved. But adultery by "other men" was fuel to the smoldering flames of long-cherished hate and always precipitated murder. The sexual aggressiveness of man against man never finds full expression within the family, spending itself, at the most, in secret intrigues and surreptitious "home-breaking." But with "other men" it broke out into the frank "taking away" of their women—the deliberate asking for wives who were never refused.

The taking away of wives was a kind of dangerous play indulged in by groups of "other men" when they met. The deadly consequences of such open preempting of sexual rights were known, but they never acted as deterrents. The taking away of women created an atmosphere of fearfulness that formed a perfect medium for the development of states of mind leading to murder. When the children of Wanenggló met with the children of Yokégn the children of Wanenggló took away their wives; but when they had "led them away," the children of Wanenggló feared that their victims wished to kill them to regain their wives and to wipe out the shame of the experience. The children of Yokégn really were secretly enraged and eager to kill their wives' new husbands. The two families dwelt in fear of each other, and it soon became a question only of who would be clever enough to strike the first blow. It turned out that Yokégn was the slyest and in a single night he destroyed Wanenggló and all his children. But nothing like this ever happens within the extended family, where peaceful relations have been the rule for generations.

Another aspect of this same insistence on preserving peace within the family at any cost is the reluctance to look for trouble. The Kaingáng are utterly unwilling to face a situation pregnant with conflict unless it is thrust under their noses. That is why husbands do not follow their wives around but are content to leave them in camp alone for weeks while they go hunting, and that is why when things are stolen no one prowls around to find who took them. Unless he is confronted with his stolen property a Kaingáng is content to murmur in secret rather than precipitate a quarrel by accusing the thief and demanding the return of the property. The same attitude leads them to make concessions rather than to back their demands with vigorous self-assertion. An aggressive individual can usually obtain his ends simply by asserting his wishes with vigor and insistence—provided he is driven to that extreme. But generally people get what they want if they ask for it, and it is only the aggressive people who ask. The rest take what they get and complain in secret if they are dissatisfied. The Kaingáng avoid any internal quarrel and run with headlong fury into an external one. They are by no means a passive, acquiescent people, but they cannot oppose self-assertion within the extended family.

One day while Chukembégn was out hunting, a few families arrived in camp, and one of them moved into Chukembégn's camp. He and his wife took this eviction without comment and simply moved into my tent. "Why do you let him put you out?" said I. "It's your camp, isn't it?" "Ah," he replied, "if I put him out there would be the deuce of a quarrel." If two self-assertive people happen to desire the same thing the Kaingáng are utterly confused, for generally that kind of situation does not arise. Before I went hunting up the river my cook asked me to get him a deer skin. As we drew near our destination a deer suddenly slipped into the river with that wild and quiet grace that is their special gift. All the Indians were caught unprepared, and before they could fire I slipped a cartridge into my rifle and shot the deer, breaking its leg. The swift current swept it downstream, and it was picked up by Ndíli and killed. In the old days the Kaingáng never used skins for anything, but now that they can sell them to the Brazilians for a few cents the Indians are eager to have them. The old pattern of gain through self-assertion still holds, and the person who gets the skin is the one who asks for it. The practice among the white Brazilians is to give the skin to the owner of the dogs that brought the animal to bay, but the Kaingáng rarely follow the Brazilians in this. Now both Ndíli and I wanted the skin, and Ndíli was a violent and aggressive person. In the past I had always given away the skins of the animals my dogs had flushed, but here was one skin I wanted. At last Chukembégn came over to me and said, "Why don't you give him that skin? He wants it." I refused to surrender. Had I not already given deer skins to Ndíli? Why shouldn't he give me this one? At last he yielded me the skin, only to steal it later.

The most striking feature of the dispute was Chukembégn's failure to understand why I should cling to the skin in the face of the obvious fact that Ndíli wanted it so badly. Another time I wanted to give the skin of a deer my dogs had flushed to the cripple they called Dung, for I felt that since he had clubbed the deer he should have the skin. But when I went to hand it to him, Ndíli said, "I want the skin," to which Dung replied, "He wants it; so give it to him." The willingness to yield to aggressiveness, coupled with the indifference to trouble unless it faces one squarely, operates to reduce enormously the number and severity of conflicts within the extended family.

The obsessive interest of the Kaingáng in destruction and murder was all externalized against the "other people," and it was this ability to externalize their obsession that was in part responsible for whatever coherence and security the families preserved. The overpowering urge toward destruction that manifests itself still in the wanton gashing of trees and the killing of the tiniest bird that happens to perch on a limb where stick or stone may reach it is never directed inward against the family but always outward. The function of the feuds, therefore, was twofold, for they served both to gratify the need to destroy and to direct it away from the extended family; and this duality contributed to their perpetuation.

The overwhelming bulk of Kaingáng folklore is murder stories—murder committed in every imaginable way and on all relatives except sons. Stories begin with murders committed for no reason and rehearse over and over again the whole wearisome theme of treachery and retaliation. The interest in the feuds has suffocated any other mythological theme, and instead of the elaborate variations on widespread mythological elements that are so common among many primitive peoples we find that when these elements actually do appear in Kaingáng folklore they are bare, fossilized, neglected plots which the literary imagination has never developed. The one elaborate art form that the Kaingáng have, their folklore, is overwhelmingly concerned with their own destruction.

Perhaps the best proof of the obsessive nature of this trait lies in a split within an extended family which occurred after the Kaingáng were localized on the reservation and which culminated in the murder of Thechá. For years the Kaingáng had committed no murder. Their vendetta enemies had been killed or driven far away, and now the group that had lived in harmony for generations was isolated from the dangers of attack and settled peacefully on the reservation. But Thechá took to saying that he wasn't afraid of anyone, and he was angry at everyone; so "since he was angry with them they became angry with him." They decided to kill him, and one of the plotters was his own first cousin, his father's sister's son, Koví. Now Thechá was a most unusual Kaingáng, for he could not swim. That simplified matters, and one day when he was crossing the river with a number of people—"nine people and five women," as one informant put it—"the canoe tipped over." Nobody tipped it, for such baldness of statement would offend Kaingáng good taste, but "the canoe tipped over" and

Thechá went to the bottom. "He stayed there six days and when they brought him up he was dead!" Thechá paid the penalty for being too *waikayú,* but it must be borne in mind that this is the first time in two hundred years that such a murder has occurred within the extended family on any grounds whatever.

It was this same obsession with murder that led Yakwá to say to me one night, "Koví wants to kill me," because he wanted to kill Koví. The Kaingáng have a long tradition of slaughter, and twenty years have passed since they murdered their last Brazilian. When they can they vent their urge to destruction on dogs and on trees, but they occasionally need a human object. The last one was Thechá—the next may be Koví.

VI

The Supernatural

Death

WHEN WAIKOMÉ'S BABY FELL ILL, she sat all day gazing at it in desperation. "Will you give me some medicine for it?" said Ndíli, its father, to me. "What is the matter with it?" I asked. "I don't know; it's just hot, hot," he replied, and his face and voice were utterly despairing. "If I don't know what's the matter with it, I can't give you anything," I said, and Ndíli walked away. When I returned to camp, Waikomé was keening. Tears streamed down her face, and her voice rose in a loud rhythmic wail as she spoke of her dead relatives. "I long to see my father who always gave me food. I have been forgetting my mother. Will I see her again?" These formulae are recited on every occasion of mourning, and it does not matter who the dead or dying person is. As the baby grew worse and seemed to lapse into a coma, Waikomé completely lost control of herself. Her face became terribly distorted with fear and grief, and she tried to make the poor little thing on her lap suckle. She rubbed her hand over its face and attempted to pry the rigid jaws apart with her finger so that she could pour her milk between the lips. Again and again she tried to force this symbol of life into the child's mouth, but in vain. The more susceptible women around her keened too, and finally Ndíli began to weep and to keen loudly. As Ndíli's emotion became more intense he turned in anger on the people sitting around in sympathetic silence: "Why did you and Julio bring me here into the forest? If we had stayed at the post my baby would never have fallen ill!"

No one uttered a word in reply. They were utterly helpless. Waikomé, beside herself, could think of nothing to offer her baby but her breast, with which she had nourished three other children and which to her was a source of life and healing. Ndíli handed her some "medicine," a pounded herb mixed with water, and she tried to force that between the child's lips; but it only trickled down its chin. Some of the women sought to help her by heating their hands over the fire and laying them on the baby.

When it seemed that the child must surely die, Waipó left camp to call the others of our hunting party, for when the ghost-souls are about they may take away the living; and the Kaingáng feel the need for each other's protection and "live piled up."

When I climbed into my hammock that night, there had been a lull in the weeping, but I was awakened several hours before dawn by the frantic keening of Waikomé. One by one, others joined her, and I knew then that the baby was dead. As I watched, the emotion gradually grew more intense; and some went to join the group mourning around the child. There was no play-acting here, no singling out of those whom relationship obliged to weep from those who could just look on. Those who were not affected kept aloof and performed their daily tasks, but those who felt an identification with the bereaved parents mourned with them. Ndíli's second cousin sat with his arm around him and wept, but Ndíli's brother seemed entirely untouched and soon went off to get honey. At last, late in the morning, the parents took up their little bundle and went away, and the sound of their keening came back to us through the forest.

That day no one went hunting even though there was no meat in camp. Toward noon Waipó said to me, his voice intense with fear: "You'd better pack your things, because we're going away from here right away. We thought we would stay and kill another tapir, but the baby died; and now we have to move." Who knows what might have happened if they had remained? The ghost-soul of the baby might have taken someone along with it or the ghost-soul which had killed it might kill again. It really does the Kaingáng no good to flee from the ghost-soul, for although it has a tendency to lurk about the place where the bones of its dead body are buried, it also is nomadic like the Kaingáng and may dog their footsteps wherever they go.

If we think of death among ourselves and the demonstrations that accompany it among the less inhibited members of our own society; if we disregard for a moment the wild surroundings, the rhythmic keening, the fear of the ghost-soul, and even, perhaps, the useless medicine that was forced between the choking child's lips (although, Heaven knows, that too might be easily duplicated in our society), we cannot but see a striking resemblance between the grief of Waikomé and Ndíli and the members of their group and similar displays in our own society. Among ourselves, anger is generally thrust into the background and often disappears entirely when grief is sincere, but among the Kaingáng it pervades the entire scene and manifests itself in an irritability that may easily become anger. It is difficult to talk to many of the Kaingáng on these occasions because they are so easily enraged, and the ethnologist had best hold his tongue and try to appear as small as possible. In death the Kaingáng feel a threat to their security. As they put it, "We are afraid of the ghost-souls; so we come together and live piled up." As in the feuds, no one knows when the deaths will cease. The presence of death lays bare the very fiber of the Kaingáng personality, for it is in terms of this emotional amalgam in which anger and fear are indistinguishably fused that we must understand all of their behavior in times of stress.

In 1918 when the first wave of the grippe struck the Kaingáng, killing them in such numbers that their bodies lay about unburied until the dogs ate them, Thunder Storm rose up in his rage and fear and beat the air and trees with a club. "When disease came," said his son to me, "my father beat the trees because he was afraid of the supernatural beings (*nggïyúdn*). He said, 'If I see you, I'll kill you. You are *waiḳayú*[1] and kill us all the time. So if I see you come to me, I'll kill you! The Brazilians kill my relatives; so out of revenge I destroy them when I see them! When I see them, I kill them, and I'll do the same to you—when I see you, I'll kill you!' He spoke thus as he beat the trees." Nothing could express this side of the Kaingáng character and world-view better. Here is condensed the Kaingáng frantic fear and anger at the forces of death, the equation of the supernatural with any other enemy, and the identification of the situation created by death with the vendetta tradition and revenge.

The Kaingáng not only fight with death; they also fly from it. That is why Waipó told me that we must move on when Ndíli's baby died, and that is why old Kakthí moved out of her house when the grippe descended again in 1933. "Why has she left her house?" said I to her son-in-law. "She is afraid of our sickness. She said, 'If I stay there, I'll get sick'; so she went away. She is in the forest to get away from it. She went to another place so our sickness would not see her." Poor Kakthí fled in vain, for she soon fell ill and died. "Her [dead] husband called her, and that is why she died. Our ghost-souls led her off, and that is why she died. Her husband's ghost-soul led her away, and that is why she died. She lay there telling about it, and then she died. The supernatural beings and her husband's soul led her away. He [her husband] led her away so that he might go with her."

The ghost-soul loves and pities the living whom it has deserted, but the latter fear and abhor the ghost-soul. The ghost-soul longs for those it has left behind, but they remain cold to its longing. "One pities one's children and therefore goes with them [i.e. takes them] when one dies. One loves [literally, lives in] one's children, and dies and goes with one's children, and one [i.e. the child] dies." The dead pity those they have left alone with

[1] Vicious, aggressive.

no one to care for them. They have left behind parts of themselves, for their children are those "in whom they live." But to the pity, love, and longing of the ghost-soul, the children return a cry of "Mother, leave me and go!" as she lies on the funeral pyre. The Kaingáng oscillate between a feeling of attachment for the dead and a desire never to see them again. Over and over again, their keening formulae repeat, "I desire to see my people," but the fear of seeing them is so great that some deny that they ever even dream of the dead: "I do not wish to get sick; that is why I never see my dead relatives," said Klendó.

The longing of the ghost-soul and its promise of good hunting is no more of an inducement to the Kaingáng to forsake this world than the glories of Paradise are to us. "A year[2] after my father died," said Vomblé, "I saw his soul. My brother was about to die, and probably my father came to call him. My father was about to talk to me. He said, 'I come to call you.' 'I don't want to go with you. My children are not here.' [Kulá, his wife, was away with her father.] 'But come with me to see my place. Leave your children and come with me.' 'No! Go! I won't go with you. Your ghost-soul went. I am not a ghost-soul. When you died, your ghost-soul went away and your children suffered. So I won't leave my children. If I die, all my children will go with me. But you left your children and things and went. I'll go to see your place and then come back, but I won't go with you. You live in a bad land. Your soul eats slugs that live in dead wood. My land is good. Women and game are plentiful. I will die when I am old. As I am now, I will not die. When I am old and weak, I will die.' When the others heard me talking, they shook me and told me why I was talking." This story expresses other things besides Vomblé's desire to live and his resentment against his father's ghost-soul. While Vomblé does not wish to be his father's companion in the other world, he declares that when he himself dies, he will take his children with him so that they will not suffer through his absence. The feeling of resentment at having been deserted by the dead runs through these accounts of experiences with the ghost-soul and integrates with the Kaingáng attitude toward social obligations.

There is another way in which Kaingáng life expresses itself in the emotional and imaginative streams that are loosed at death. The dead pass out of the embraces of the living, they are shut out of their lives in precisely the same way as members of other extended families; and they constantly threaten them with death. Their status is veritably that of "different things." When a man's ghost-soul came to call his sister, saying, "I have come to call you and your husband," she became angry with him and replied, "No! You are a different thing, and yet you come to me. They

[2] Literally—"one period of no pine nuts."

killed you. When they killed you, I wandered around suffering, but you come to call me!" When the ghost-soul at last went away, she was "all green. She stood there without saying anything. He [her husband] said to her, 'Why are you green?' But she said nothing. She sat down holding on to a post. Then he asked if she was sick—if she had a pain in the belly. But she did not talk. Wanengglò [her husband] asked her whether she had seen a ghost-soul. Probably she saw a ghost-soul. But she did not say anything." Like vendetta enemies, the ghost-souls are "other things"—it is the only category the Kaingáng have for those who dwell outside the limits of the extended families—and for people in this category they know only one emotion, fear-anger.

When the Kaingáng are drunk, their malevolent and fearsome impulses rise to the surface, and the memory of death plays its part in this. Festa time, when the beer troughs are brimming with the steaming, sourish, honey beer, is a special occasion for remembering the dead. It is also the occasion when recollections of adultery unpunished or of slights unrequited surge into consciousness. While some dance, sing, or brawl, others sit around the edge of the dance circle with their heads in their hands and tears streaming down their faces, and their sobs and high rhythmic keening mingle with the noise of quarreling and disordered singing. When they have done with their hour or so of weeping, they rise and fill their baskets or gourds with beer and join in the festa. No recollection of the dead can occur without unleashing fear, and fear cannot be liberated without the eruption of anger, so the memory of the dead only adds to the disruptive forces that are set in motion by the beer. The more one knows about the Kaingáng, the more one is struck by the extent to which the very roots of their being have been undermined and torn by impulses to violence. This is all the more amazing when we remember what affectionate people they seem to be—how much they love to multiply a hundredfold all kinds of personal attachments. Nevertheless, when drunkenness uncovers the Kaingáng personality, it does not bubble over in rivulets of tenderness, but pours out in torrents of violence. The only outlet is murder, and that is why festas, if not actually the scene of murders, used to be almost always the forerunners of raids on the Brazilians or on vendetta enemies. The Kaingáng themselves understand, in a way, what the festa meant to them, for they say, "We had festas in order to go to attack the Brazilians." Of course not every festa is characterized by violence, but many are.[3]

[3] Although the Kaingáng held an old-time beer festa at my request the aboriginal beer troughs have been superseded by jugs of sugar cane whiskey, and the tumultuous singing by the music of an accordion played by a white man. These changes, however, have not curbed the essential temper of the Indians, and fights still occur at festas.

The Supernatural Monsters

Of all the supernatural beings, Yóin is the most terrific. His head, which is very large at the top and crowned with a mop of hair which some say is red and others think is woolly like a Negro's, has a groove down the middle. That is why little Thegnmbégn, who had an almost imperceptible depression in the middle of his head, was jokingly called Yóin. Yóin's eyes are white and are provided with red lids. His head is always shaking. He has great jaws, and his neck is thick and long. His body is broad and thick, and his belly flashes like a giant firefly as he flies through the sky at night. His buttocks are very narrow and widely separated, and his penis is long and his testicles large. When he walks on the ground he is like a man, but in the air his arms are pressed to his sides and his legs are tight together. He roams about, devouring men, women, and children, and his hands and mouth are red with the blood he has rubbed on them. He carries a little knife with him, and when he seizes a victim, he thrusts his bloody hand up through the anus, cuts out the heart and intestines, and devours them. "Yóin kills people because he is a different thing and never calls men 'my people'."

Then there is "Kuchágn which never dies. It kills people by crushing them, and its mouth is red with the blood of the people it eats. Its arms and ears are like those of a man, but it has a beard like a tiger. Its hard bristles stand out all over it in isolated clumps, and it walks on all fours and makes a noise like a pig. They think it is a pig and they go to look for it, but they never see it. One never sees its body."

"Kanggúin saw Kuchágn leaning on a rock. It said to him, 'Why have you come here?' 'I came to look for howler monkeys.' Then he lost consciousness. When he regained consciousness, Kuchágn was there. When Kanggúin saw it, he went away. His sister was coming along in the meanwhile shouting for directions, but he did not answer. Then at last Kanggúin cried to her. So she came to him. He was yellow. Then she said, 'Brother, why are you yellow?' 'I am sick. I have a pain in the abdomen, I am sick.' Blood came out of the corners of his mouth, and he said, 'I am sick; so do not feed me.' Late at night, Kuchágn came to Kanggúin and seized him. It sat on him. Then Kanggúin sat up and threw it on his father, and Kuchágn seized the father. When the father felt sick, he threw it on Kanggúin again. Kanggúin became all black. He was rotten from the chest down. His father was rotten and full of blood. Kanggúin stood up and cried, '*Hïi!*' He burst open next day. He was so rotten he was full of holes, but he was alive. His sister asked him, and he said: 'There is a different thing that stands on all fours. Its hair is scattered over its body in clumps. Its mouth is red. I saw it and I am dying. A different thing has killed us.' "

Wangdjó is also a monster. Some say it is like a tapir, some that it is like a horse; still others think that its nose, eyes, hair, arms, legs, and buttocks are like those of an Indian. "There is no meat on it," and "its backbone sticks up." Its belly flashes as it flies through the trees, and smoke, ashes, and flame pour from its mouth and nostrils.

Like Kuchágn, Yunggí is piglike, and it kills people by shooting them. Véin was another supernatural. He was good-looking. He looked just like a man; he was smooth and had no body hair at all. He walked on the earth like a human being and never flew through the air. He had red eyelids and an enormous penis, and his testicles were as large as those of a horse. His sexual desire kept pace with his corporeal endowments, for he wished to copulate with women constantly. In folklore he suffers death twice: once when he sodomizes Padnmbá, who kills him for it by throwing bees' sugar into his mouth, and on another occasion when, after eating several communities of people,[4] he is killed by a shaman.

This pantheon is rather a nightmare, but the Kaingáng are not so consistent in their thinking as they are in their dreaming. They call all supernatural beings, whether good or bad, *nggïyúdn* and confuse the malevolent with the benign, with the result that occasionally Yóin and Véin appear in benevolent roles. For a long time, for example, Yóin was a man's hunting companion and used to tell him where to find tapirs, and once Yóin told another man where he could find howler monkeys. But advantageous contacts with Yóin and Véin are rare, they are predominantly frightful characters to the Kaingáng.

As malevolent personalities Yóin and Véin are apt to be confused, at least in name, with any evil-working supernatural. "One night," said Klendó, "I died. A tapir that was an *nggïyúdn* that was a woman came and led me off and I went around with her. Then I came back and recovered. Next day they asked me about it, and I became well. Yóin did this to me. She wanted me to copulate with her, but I would not. I was young and that is why she wanted to take me away."

Spirits of the Natural World

The ghost-soul is called *kuplêng*,[5] but together with the monsters and the spirits of the natural world, it is also called *nggïyúdn*. The spirits of the natural world dwell everywhere—in trees, under the water, in rocks, and in cliffs. They inhabit the sun and the moon and the stars, and animate the wind and the storm. There are the spirits of the tapir, the deer, the squirrel, the snake, and all other animals and insects. These spirits may appear to humans in their natural form or in the shape of human beings.

[4] This act is attributed by some to Yóin.

[5] Plural, *anggaplêng*.

A monkey may address a man from a treetop, or "the tapir that is a super-natural being that is a man" [or woman] may suddenly appear to a hunter. Water's Talking, the *nggïyúdn* of the waters, is an alligatorlike monster whose principal occupation is to seduce women when they come to fetch water. Spirits may confer supernatural powers, but encounters with them are just as often disastrous as they are beneficial. "A man sees an animal in the forest, and it says to him, 'Why do you come? You frightened me.' 'I come hunting.' 'You will not see any animals. Go away! Go back!' Then he goes away, and when he returns to camp, he tells the people and dies." Characteristically enough, when a Kaingáng meets the supernatural, the attitude is one of mutual distrust; the Indian fears the spirit, and the spirit fears him. Sometimes the spirit invites the Indian to visit his house, but the Indian is usually afraid for his life and goes away.

Snake said to Kemblén,[6] "Come and look at my house." So he went there and saw the tremendous number of offspring the snake had. They were like human children. "My children are here," said the snake; "take one of them." But Kemblén was frightened and said nothing. "Do not tell about having seen me," admonished Snake. But Kemblén told of his ex-perience, and Snake became angry and bit him. That is how Kemblén lost his hand. "If he had not told, he would not have been bitten." The spirits tolerate a refusal to visit them or even to adopt one of their children, but they cannot endure anyone's telling about having seen them. Whoever reveals his experience with a spirit dies or falls sick, and if he has already received power from that spirit he loses it. But sometimes encounters with spirits are useful.

My informant Vomblé, for example, met Bee, who appeared to him in the form of a man. "He said to me: 'Live with me in my house. If you live with me, you will not be hungry. In my house it is warm even when it is cold. I am going to place some food aside for you.' I asked him, 'Where is your house?' and he said, 'It is here.' His honey was in the hollow of a tree. It was the door of his house. But I became afraid that I would be killed; so I said, 'I am going away. Later I will come back to you.' And I went away. But Bee said to me, 'When you go, you may be hungry;' so he showed me where there were honey and jacutingas, saying: 'Shoot some. Then go beyond and you will see howler monkeys on a pine tree. Shoot them all. Some may go away.' So next day I looked at the hive and told Angnelo[7] to cut it out. 'That is what Bee showed me,' said I. She chopped the tree down. It was a big hive, but I did not eat any of the honey because I was afraid since I had seen a *nggïyúdn*. I also shot the jacutingas. I saw another hive. I met my father, and when I was walking along with

[6] See p. 77.
[7] His step-mother. Deceased.

him, he asked me whether I had seen any honey. 'Yes,' said I, 'it is the one that Bee told about; so I came this way to look and saw it. I also shot the jacutingas he told me about.' My father chopped out the hive—there was a great deal of honey in it, but I ate none of it. I told him about the howler monkeys, and next day we went to look for them. After that I saw no more of Bee."

Since Vomblé told about his meeting with Bee he never saw the spirit again. It is not characteristic for people having these experiences to abstain from the fruits of their good fortune, and as far as I have been able to discover, this abstinence on the part of Vomblé was a matter of personal choice. Vomblé is not a shaman, and the economic benefits he received from the supernatural were only temporary. Yet one visitation yielded him something of permanent value, for it rendered him immune to all sickness. Once he was so sick that he became unconscious. While he lay there, he saw Moon. "He came down. He was like a cord—white. He came down with his wife, Star. Moon had a potsherd and there was medicine in it. He said to me, 'What is killing you?' 'I have a head- and chest-ache. My body is sick and I cannot stand.' Moon kneaded me and felt of me. He poured medicine over my body and head, and I recovered. I fell asleep. Moon was a little man. Now I am never sick."[8]

One of the ways in which mortals may establish permanent and friendly relations with the spirits is to adopt one of their children. One of Amendó's children [the Amendó of many husbands] was a bee child. She took one of the spirit's children and placed it in her womb, and ever after that she was able to find beehives easily. Another story tells how a man adopted a child of the monkey spirit. It looked like a human being and remained devoted to him like his own child. It deflected the arrows of his enemies, and when they tried to knock trees down on top of his house to crush him, it caused the trees to fall on the attackers. Sometimes men take the children of spirits and put them into their wives' wombs, from which they later emerge in the form of human children. Even if a spirit is adopted in its animal form and even if it never confers power of any kind, it is loved like a pet, and its death is avenged like the death of a human being. A highly affective relationship with the supernatural is the only kind of friendly relationship that is intelligible to the Kaingáng. Another kind of friendly tie with a spirit is phrased in terms of the hunting-companion relationship. Having a guardian spirit involves "going around with it" and "living with" it, just as one does with a hunting companion or in one's extended family. When the Kaingáng describe a shaman's relation to his guardian spirit or spirits, they say that "he saw it *all the time.*"

[8] Vomblé is one of the most resistant of the Kaingáng and was one of the few who did not fall ill during the influenza epidemic in 1933.

The characteristic North American guardian spirit experience in which an individual sees his benefactor once only and receives a token from him is unknown to the Kaingáng, to whom the only earnest of security is continuous, unbroken contact. All lasting relations with the spirits are expressed systematically in the habitual mode—"all the time." The Kaingáng do not say that the spirit did so and so. They say it "would [i.e. regularly] do so and so." So Ketédn,[9] who could walk dry through a downpour, "used to see *nggïyúdn*. He saw Yóin and used to go out with him and shoot tapirs. Yóin would say: '*Yúgn*, there is a tapir,' and Ketédn would shoot it." Although "living with" the spirits does not involve intermarriage and sharing of wives, as it may on the human level, it does imply the sharing of food. A quarter must be left for the spirit that has shown one where to kill a tapir, and honey must be shared with one's supernatural benefactor. Kakthí[10] "saw Snake, who told her to get honey, and she always shared it with him." Such a division of food is not conceived as a sacrifice or as a payment for goods received but simply as the same kind of sharing that exists between hunting companions or among members of the same extended family.

Shamanism[11] and Curing

A guardian spirit came to one through an accidental encounter or through being "pointed out" by a shaman, i.e. one who already "had been seeing it" for a long time. The preliminary mortification of the flesh—the fasting and self-torture—that are found over wide areas in North America where the vision is known was foreign to the Kaingáng. Nor did the Kaingáng prescribe any training for those who were to receive guardian spirits. The spectacular visions that are features of the guardian-spirit quest in North America were unknown. Kaingáng visions of spirits of the natural world were very simple: "One day Ketédn bent down to drink from a pool. When he looked up over his shoulder, he saw Toad, who said to him, '*Yúgn*, why do you come?' 'I am looking for tapir.' 'You will not see tapir, you will see *tateti*.'[12] Then Ketédn shot *tateti*." Many visions were of this simple character. Some were invitations, like Vomblé's vision of Bee, who invited him to come to his house. Occasionally someone lost consciousness through fear of the spirit and was told where to find animals while lying senseless, but there was rarely any visual or auditory elaboration of detail. The very appearance of the spirits remained vague, for they were described simply as looking like human beings or like the animals they represented. Encounters with the ghost-soul or dreams of supernatural

[9] See p. 43.

[10] See fn. p. 67.

[11] There are no Kaingáng shamans today; the few there were have died.

[12] An animal resembling a pig that lives in burrows on hillsides. It is about two feet long and somewhat less in height.

monsters at night have more definite content. This is consonant with the fact that the Kaingáng have devoted much more interest and imagination to the elaboration of the fearful aspects of their supernatural world than to the benign.

With Ketédn's simple vision of Toad compare the following horrible dream that Vomblé had of the *nggïyúdn* before Véye died: "I was the first one to see that the *nggïyúdn* ate Véye. I saw the *nggïyúdn* come with Véye. I saw that they were going to kill him, and I said to them, 'Why do you want to kill Véye?' But they said nothing. Then they said, 'He is a pig.' 'It is Véye [said Vomblé]; I used to go around with him.' They took hoes and led Véye off. I said, 'Leave him alone.' But they killed Véye with hoes. 'Why did you kill him?' 'It is a pig.' 'It is a human being, and it is taboo for you to eat it.' They seized his feet and tore him apart. I protected him. I thought I was dreaming. They put salt on him and ate him. When they ate him, it was taboo. I almost vomited. 'Come and eat [they said], it is like tapir's marrow.' But it was capavary.[13] Then I vomited and sat up. I ate dirt and almost vomited. Next day I told Véye, 'They roasted your ribs with salt,' but Véye said I was lying. Three days later he died."

Horror and the impulses to murder and cannibalism which the Kaingáng constantly and compulsively express are much more congenial to their imagination than the warm relationships with beneficent spirits of the natural world. It is true that guardian spirits are often mentioned in Kaingáng folklore, but most frequently simply as incidents in a murder tale. Stories whose central theme is a relationship with a guardian spirit are extremely rare. Being "shown" a spirit was as simple an experience as seeing it oneself. One day while an Indian was out with someone who had been seeing a spirit, the shaman would say to him casually, "Go over there and shoot those howler monkeys," and always after that the Indian would see supernatural Howler Monkey and find howler monkeys very easily. Such an experience might be accompanied by darkness and wind, but generally it was not.

"Yokégn was a shaman. He saw Fish and Wasp. He went hunting, and when he came back, he said to his wife: 'Let us go to the fish I saw. I'm going to get some for them [the children].' So his wife emptied a basket and carried it along with her. When they reached the spot, the water was shallow and there were some [fish] in it. Then he said to her, 'Come over here and have a look.' When she approached, she saw its men[14] in there. She stood there looking, and at last, he [her husband] asked, 'Did you see?' 'Yes,' she replied. 'Let us go now to the other fish that one eats all the time. They are good. Catch some of them.' So she took her basket and entered [the stream]. The shallow water came toward her in waves. She put her

---

[13] An amphibious rodent (*hydrochoerus capybara*) two feet long and twenty inches high.
[14] Fish in anthropomorphic form.

basket in the water for the fish, and they came along and plumped into it. He showed her so that he and she might both see it all the time." The essential features of this very mild incident are the simple nature of the instruction and the division of the fish species into supernatural untouchables and natural touchables. This was characteristic of every animal category—some of it was recognizable by the shaman as supernatural, and the rest was natural and might be killed and eaten. When we remember that the spirit a person sees constantly is his close friend and companion, we can readily understand this cautious examination of the scene by the shaman and his painstaking selection of the animals to be killed and those to be left alone. Some of them are children of his friend, and the rest are simply animals which the spirit gives to him for food.

Spirits control their species and keep them in inclosures from which they let them out from time to time. When they are angered, either because too many have been killed or because some have not been killed, they close them up again and animals become scarce. Failure to bring down an animal is an unfortunate occurrence which annoys the spirit, but refusal to take a tapir or deer or any other animal which the *nggïyúdn* offers is tantamount to refusing food from a human benefactor and can have but one outcome, death. Whoever turns away from quarry pointed out by a spirit is bound to fall ill and die.

The more we examine the ways in which the Kaingáng maintained the bonds that united them with supernatural benefactors, the more we discover that they duplicated in any number of details the complex of relationships and feelings through which security was maintained in their own society. One more point may be added. Over and over again, malevolent supernaturals are referred to by the sinister term of "different thing," but guardian spirits were never called by this term; for "different things" are dangerous things, and guardian spirits were friendly and helpful.

Like most primitive peoples, the Kaingáng obtain from spirits some powers to cure disease, but this side of Kaingáng supernaturalism was very slightly developed. In many cultures in which religious values rate high, the powers to cure and kill supernaturally bring great rewards. But the Kaingáng never killed supernaturally; the most they did in this direction was to throw people into a deep sleep so that they could murder them with lance or club. They did cure through the agency of the supernatural, but the shaman received no pay for his efforts, and his practice was generally limited to his own immediate family. The ministerings of the shaman were viewed as attentions naturally received from a close relative. No shaman ever extended the benefits of his practice outside his own extended family. Kaingáng culture did not define achievement in supernatural terms— shamanistic powers of any kind were not even something to boast about or to plume oneself on. The most that a very powerful shaman got from his fellows was a certain awe while he was alive and dread when he was dead. Almost anywhere in North America, the ethnologist may obtain for the asking stories of shamans with great powers to cure, even where he does not learn the esoteric lore accompanying them. Among the Kaingáng such stories do not exist at all. After diligent questioning, one does find out that Chu used to cure people, and that once Kemblén treated Klendó and he recovered; but supernatural healing was not a theme that the culture elaborated.

Kemblén was one of those rare individuals about whom supernatural influences seemed to cluster like lines of force about a magnet. He had lost an arm because of his refusal of power from Snake, who therefore bit him in anger. As he grew older he gradually accumulated the powers of Quatí, Monkey, Wind, and Fish, and in the end this was his undoing, for Quatí was out of sorts with him one day for some unknown reason, and he fell sick and died. Before he died, he showed two of his daughters, Anggló and Chantágn, his supernatural remedies. One day, after I had been among the Kaingáng for many months, Chantágn came to me, trembling with anxiety, and announced that for a price she would tell me about her father's medicine. There was no doubt about Chantágn's sincerity, and she was in real fear that her father might become aware of the fact that she was revealing his medicines and kill her. Although I ordinarily left windows open on the rare occasions when women were in my house, Chantágn's fear was so obvious and painful that I carefully closed all the doors and windows so that nggïyúdn could neither see nor hear what was going on, and prepared myself for a revelation.

At last, still trembling, Chantágn took out a little package wrapped in paper, unfolded it, and disclosed two plants, telling as she did so that one was to cure sickness in children and one was for sore eyes and that they should be pounded up and mixed with water. That was all—she asked her price and was prepared to leave. What a cold bath this experience was to me! For months I had been burrowing in search of just this kind of information with little success, and when at last Chantágn came to me straight from the source of power, I felt that surely now I should discover the real content of Kaingáng religion. I did, but it was little different from what I had known before. Naturally I questioned her. From her breathless replies in which one word stumbled on the heels of the next, I learned that Kemblén had received the medicines from Monkey when he was a ķëlŭ:[15] " 'Give it to your children,' said Monkey. 'Apply it to their sides. Let them lie on their backs on a robe.' He said to Howler Monkey: 'Give it to me. When I see that they are sick I shall get it for them.' Then Howler Monkey cleared the ground and showed it to him." To Chantágn the whole potency of the curing was in the herbs she sold me.

[15] Any male between the ages of thirty-five or forty is a ķëlŭ.

In all friendly relations a Kaingáng insists on superlatively developed emotional rapport and strong identification. A shaman's bond with the supernatural world was spun from the same emotional stuff as his tie with his fellow men, for he lived with the spirits, shared their food and his own, and adopted their children. Everything a shaman had from the supernatural he had by virtue of a strong and enduring emotional relationship with some supernatural being. After death he retained his connection with his guardian spirit, and even today the Kaingáng address their supplications directly to him, for he has real control over whatever forces the spirit directs. "Kukéye saw Howler Monkey. He died, and now whenever the others kill Howler Monkeys, they cry: 'Yúgn, Kukéye, it is I. Protect me!' "

When shamans performed acts which had been made possible by virtue of their connections with the supernatural, their associations with the spirit were made manifest. Since it was forbidden shamans to announce in so many words their actual relations with the spirit, they did it by means of stereotyped formulae which were direct enough but did not take the form of actual stories of their experiences. Instead of saying, "I have seen the spirit of Howler Monkey," the shaman asked a question which might best be translated, "Am I not probably the useful howler monkey?" And then he uttered its cry. This announcement was an affirmation or momentary actualization of his bond with the spirit. It was the shaman's deep emotional roots in the supernatural that made it possible for him to cure his patient, who was always a member of his own extended family and usually a very close relative. Thus, literally, deep spoke to deep, and through their intense and highly charged rapport, cure was effected.

Chu was once married to Thalú, but she "threw him away" and married another. One day her son Kukéye was bitten by a snake. He lost consciousness and sang in his delirium. "When his relatives heard this, they wept. Thalú blew on him. She rushed around him and sang:

> êng mbë thi tǫ́
> êng mbë thi tǫ́
> lô mbë ḳi nyang djô to nų
> êng ngglâ ya   tha   tôgn mê   nų ngglâ mu ve
> my dance place usual that about I dance
> êng ngglâ ḳų echǫ́ ḳôtëi ḳo ha wû êng nyatḳa
> my dance and I   fruit eat it   my mouth
> vëlë   ve[16]
> fall (plural)

[16] Elements not accompanied by interlinear translations are either meaningless syllables to carry the melody or untranslatable grammatical particles.

Then she went *hû hû hû hû*—she was imitating the macuca. She was saying in the song that the macuca was eating something. The food of the macuca is in its throat. That is what she meant by *nyatka vëlë*." A free translation of the little song is: "I dance in my customary dance place, and as I dance, the fruit tumbles into my mouth." The symbolism of the song and cry is transparent to the Kaingáng. "Probably," said my informant, "she is telling in her song about having seen macuca dancing. Probably she used to dance with them."

When Thalú had finished, she called to her former husband Chu: " 'Come and look him over.' He came over and looked at Kukéye, who was lying on a robe. He rubbed his hands over him and then blew on him. Then he uttered the cry of the howler monkey, *nggû nggû nggû nggû*. He spat all over Kukéye." He prophesied that the patient would live, saying, "I have seen that my offspring will eat pine pollen." Now was the time for Chu to announce his bond with the supernatural, and he cried, "Am I the voice of the useful *cipo* [vine]!" meaning by that that he "was" the howler monkey that sits upon the cipo. "He was saying that he was a supernatural being. Then he stopped and said to his relatives, 'Wash him with some other remedy.' So they washed him with *tutolo*. Kukéye went '*Ho*' and vomited blood. He opened his eyes. Chu had thrown all the poison out of him."

English is poor in words indicating existence. In English we may say, "It is a tapir," and to us this simple statement will seem clear and definitive. But to a Kaingáng Indian the statement, "It is a tapir," would seem extraordinarily vague. He would want to know whether the tapir was standing up or lying down, whether it was walking around or standing still. In the Kaingáng language there are words meaning "to be" that convey in addition some such concepts as these. There is still another that implies probability and blurs the edges of existential categories. All of these can have but one translation in English—"to be." When Chu says, "Am I the voice of the useful cipo?" he frames his utterance in the category last mentioned and in this way does nothing more than indicate his bond with the howler monkey.[17] The expression itself is really untranslatable; but its general feeling is one of indefinite assertion. It by no means implies that Chu is a howler monkey.

A striking example of the close bond between a shaman and the phenomenon from whose spirit he once obtained supernatural powers was provided me one winter's day during a storm. Kemblén, who numbered wind among his many guardian spirits, has been dead a number of years, but still his *kupléng*[18] is powerful and may influence the natural world to the injury

---

[17] Because the howler monkey holds on to the vine and makes a noise.

[18] Ghost-soul.

of men. One day Klendó, a man about sixty-five, and I were sitting together in my little house discussing the *kupléng*. Gradually clouds gathered
in the west. The wind began to mount, and at last with a rush the storm
swept up the valley. As the wind increased in violence the look of anxiety
intensified on Klendó's face. He gazed with frightened eyes through the
window before us, and his mind wandered as he watched in fascination the
rivulets of water trickling under the frame. At last the catch on the window
that faced the wind snapped, and with a burst of thunder and lightning
and a swirl of wind and rain, the window was flung open, drenching the
house in an instant and sending my papers flying. Klendó was seized with
acute terror, and jumping up with more animation than he had shown in
weeks, he dashed to the door, opened it a crack, and bellowed: "My
kôklá,[19] I am afraid of you; so stop! My *kôklá*, you are angry with me; so
you have made the storm!" Thus he shouted to his *kôklá*, his second father,
a man with whom he had had a most friendly relationship while he was
alive.

"Why was he angry with you?" I asked. "I don't know," he replied, with
that petulance that is so characteristic of the Kaingáng when they are
frightened. But in the afternoon he had an explanation, for he had stopped
to gossip and had learned that Kemblén's grandson had had a quarrel with
Yukwáya that very day. Kemblén, "therefore, became angry with her
[Yukwáya] and made it dark. Kemblén knew that Yukwáya was angry,
and therefore it became dark."

In characteristic Kaingáng fashion, people fall sick and die either because
they are attacked by some *nggïyúdn* who wishes them ill or because they are
seduced or "led off" by one who wants them for company. Thus the causes
of illness and death are oriented toward both extremes of the Kaingáng
world-view. In any event, the ultimate cause of death is complete soul-loss.
Seduction is accomplished either through invitations to visit a "good country," i.e. where the hunting is good and the honey plentiful, or through
sexual stimulation. When Vomblé's father tried to lure him away, it was
through promises of plenty, but Klendó almost died because a female
nggïyúdn wanted him for a sex companion.

The defenses against soul-loss are very simple. The victim may simply
say, "Let's go back," to those who wish to take him away, or he may re-
nounce his connection with the *nggïyúdn* if it happens to be an unconsum-
mated sexual one. If it is consummated he is lost and soon dies. First he
may go mad like Patklé, who copulated with a female *nggïyúdn,* or he
may rot inside, like Kulá. Whoever has intercourse with the supernatural
will not burn easily on the funeral pyre, and he is an evil omen to his relatives. "One night," said Vomblé, "Kulá called out to her brother: 'Waipó,

---

[19] Ceremonial father.

lift me up.' When he heard this, he woke up and took hold of her, lifted, and set her down. Then she said to him, 'It seems to me that you copulated with me,' but he replied: 'No! Probably *nggïyúdn* copulated with you.' She lay there awhile and at last died. When she was burnt, she exploded. She was *vai* [an evil omen] to them. She lay on her back with her feet in the air. She also said her husband [Véye] copulated with her; that is why she died. Probably the *nggïyúdn* looked like Véye. Her blood came out of her vagina."

Another way of bringing back the errant *kuplêng* is through calling it, but it does not always return. "I saw Nggemú's *kuplêng*," said Vomblé, "before the Brazilians killed her. I got up at night when the moon was high. Nggemú was sleeping a little to the side. Her *kuplêng* sat up. I thought it was she herself. It went out into the darkness. I thought she had gone to urinate, and I waited for her to return. I was awake, and I looked for her. I called out, 'Are you there?' 'Yes. When he [her infant] cried, I sat up.' 'I thought you went that way, and I waited for you.' 'I didn't go; I just sat up.' 'You went that way; I heard your noise.' Then Kuthúgn [her husband] rose and called Nggemú['s *kuplêng*]: 'Come here, Nggemú, come here! Come to the meat you put aside!' He was calling her *kuplêng*, but it probably did not come back, for nine days later the Brazilians killed her." It is interesting that mortals often use the same inducement to lure back the wandering *kuplêng* as the *nggïyúdn* do to draw it away; namely, food. Through the promise of plenty the *kuplêng* of a man is lured away by the supernaturals; through food the soul of a dead child is induced to return to its mother's womb, and it was through food that the *kuplêng* of Nggemú was tempted to return to Kuthúgn.

Behind the *kuplêng's* wish to snatch away its living relatives is its strong attachment for them, but in the case of the ghost-soul of a dead enemy the motivating force is revenge. When relatives lead off the unwilling *kuplêng* it is so that it may be cherished, but enemies seize the soul to punish the body. So, also, when supernatural beings other than ghost-souls take away *kuplêng*, it is for similar reasons. Thus the Kaingáng imagination follows out its pattern consistently both with *kuplêng* and with all other *nggïyúdn*.

Kuplêng may seduce, "lead off," or capture the souls of mortals, but devouring and shooting are the privilege of other *nggïyúdn*. For devouring there is no remedy—once a person is eaten, he is consumed and that is all, but for shooting there is a cure, and that is extraction of the missile, a reddish, wormlike object. Anyone may summon back a wandering soul or even cure sickness with an infusion of herbs or of bark scrapings, but only a shaman who has seen supernatural Pain can extract *thêyê*, the missiles which are shot into people by the monster Yunggí or by Pain.

"Tendó was a shaman. She took out men's *thêyê*. Her sister Kukú had a rash that was so red, it seemed as if she had been burnt. She wept all night. Next day Tendó went to Kukú's mother and said, 'Why did she cry all night?' 'She cried all night because of her *thêyê*.' Tendó looked at her feet. Then she fetched some water, put medicine in it, heated it, and washed Kukú's feet and rubbed them. She made her *thêyê* come out by kneading it. She looked and put her mouth to it and bit out the thing. Kukú's mother did not watch, for she was making a shirt. Tendó bit out the thing—she bit out many, and said: '*Nyọ*,[20] look here! This is what did it.' The *thêyê* were red and she put them in the water. The *thêyê* were red. Then she squeezed medicine over her and tied up the place."

In all *thêyê* extractions there was always the use of warm water, the universal panacea, with or without a medicine, the kneading to the surface of the *thêyê,* and finally extraction, not by sucking, but by seizing with the teeth and pulling—"biting," as the Kaingáng put it.

In our culture oral functions are often associated with ideas of destruction. Consider, for example, our vocabulary of oral destruction: "devour the enemy," "the jaws of death," "swallowed up in the sea," "biting humor," "eaten with rust," "gnawing hunger." Among the Kaingáng, however, oral destruction is relegated almost entirely to the realm of fantasy. The only beings that can actually destroy with the mouth are cannibalistic supernaturals and occasional masculine human characters in folklore. The situation in which oral functions are used for non-nutritional purposes on the human level is essentially a cherishing one—healing the sick. In curing, the Kaingáng spit, blow, and bite. A mother whose sick child refuses remedy or is too weak to nurse takes the medicine or food into her mouth and forces it between the child's lips. Women who esteem their husbands greatly chew their food for them. Although the cherishing motif predominates in oral behavior, there are two situations in which suggestions of oral annihilation appear. One is in the use of two curses[21] that are accompanied by spitting; the other is in the use of the term *nyat   ka   klédn ,*
                                                          mouth inside escape

to escape out of the mouth, which is employed at times to mean escape from a tiger or from a human enemy, i.e. from a "different thing." It is striking that the Kaingáng rarely use the curses—I do not know of a single instance in which they actually were used, and I regard them not as weapons actually employed, but as techniques known to exist.

The kneading that precedes the extraction of the *thêyê* is a special case

[20] Mother, or woman much older than the speaker.

[21] "So that they may go and die in one night they spit after them and say, 'When you go slip on this!' To lie there and die—that is a curse. They spit after him (and say), 'When you go may you do the same as *kôingglâdn* (a tree) and rot!' This *kôingglâdn* rots and falls at the slightest frost. They spit after him and he dies shortly."

of the Kaingáng faith in the efficacy of "the laying on of hands." We already know what the multiplication of caresses means to the Kaingáng in the way of security, and the gentle application of warm infusions of herbs or bark to all parts of the body of a sick person is not different in kind from the reciprocal stroking of two young men lying in affectionate embrace. Still another way of curing the sick is to heat one's hands near the fire and lay them gently on the body of the patient. This high valuation of cutaneous contact is one aspect of the Kaingáng special interest in sensation.

But the Kaingáng do not only cure from without, they also cure from within; and to that end they administer a variety of herb and bark infusions in warm water. These are rubbed all over the surface of the body, for the Kaingáng cannot conceive of treating the inside of the body without also treating the outside.[22] Anyone at all may perform this tender and solicitous task, and it is no rarity to see a Kaingáng step aside from the trail to cut a few plants for someone else or to see him come back from the hunt with a handful of herbs for medicine. A number of these herbs are used as panaceas—they are applied with equal faith to relieve a headache or a pain in the chest or to heal a cut.[23]

Of all the herbs and barks that the Kaingáng use to treat the sick, one alone is based on something more than this kind of selection. The use of áyólo nya tëi, "tapir's raw food," rests on a strong sense of its vital power. Tapir's raw food grows everywhere in the Kaingáng country. It is the favorite eating of the tapir and enjoys a wider use as a remedy among the Kaingáng than any other plant in their medicinal catalogue. But this herb is used not only to cure sickness but also to prevent evil. It is spread over the body of a dead tapir to please its kupléng so that it will not take all the rest of its brethren with it and leave mankind to starve, and in the same way it is placed all around the body of a dead infant to induce its kupléng to return to its mother. When a widow's hair and nails are cut, they are mixed with tapir's raw food before they are thrown into the water, so that they will not rot; and when she returns to camp after her isolation, tapir's raw food is strewn in her path to drive off the kupléng of her husband. So,

[22] Nowadays they do swallow the white man's remedies without rubbing them over their bodies.

[23] Their use is based not on exact knowledge of their efficacy in specific cases but on the simple faith that they are beneficial. The employment of herbs in this naive uncritical manner must lie at the roots of some of the great medicinal discoveries of primitive peoples, like quinine. Just as the Kaingáng scrape the bark of a number of trees and use them indiscriminately to relieve a variety of ills, the Indians of the interior of South America may have used the bark of the quina tree for a number of ailments until they observed that one disease in particular, malaria, yielded to it, whereas others did not. This marked the real discovery of quinine, one of the American Indian's great contributions to the relief of human suffering.

too, when a new-born child's ceremonial mother and father place its umbilical cord and placenta in the water, they wrap them in tapir's raw food.
Throughout life's crises, wherever the threat of death is great or where the
greatest stakes lie, tapir's raw food appears as a symbol to help the Kaingáng over difficult transitions.

When we review the techniques which the Kaingáng employ to cure
their sick, one in particular seems in perfect harmony with what we know
of the Kaingáng personality and world-view—that is the laying on of
hands which accompanies every curing, no matter what additional thera-
peusis is utilized. This is at once a way of reassuring the sick by reawaken-
ing in them deep-rooted intuitions of security and a device for bringing the
"physician" into rapport with his patient. Even herb infusions are not so
constantly resorted to as the laying on of hands. The ceremony used by
Thalú to cure her son is of a type well known throughout the primitive
world and particularly in the Americas. The most remarkable thing about
it, however, is that there should be only one such story from the Kaingáng
and that it is so well known and so outstanding that it is told almost like a
folktale. There has been nothing like it for a hundred years. *Thêyê* extractions also have been disappearing, for the last that the Kaingáng remember
occurred fifty years ago. The disappearance of curings by singing and by
extraction of *thêyê* are examples of the gradual simplification of the culture, which has been going on for centuries and of which we have abundant
evidence from social organization and folklore.

The techniques of biting, spitting, blowing, and singing were obtained
from the *nggïyúdn,* but the laying on of hands anyone could practice. The
application of warm infusions and warm hands has nothing to do with
the supernatural, except in so far as everything in the Kaingáng world is
supposed to have come from the supernatural. The history of Kaingáng
society has been one of long-continued disruption and of gradual reduction
in the circle of security. Thus, as the human world grew more and more
hostile, the supernatural, which was already alive with monsters and
charged with death, began to lose the modicum of beneficence that it had
had and the Kaingáng came to rely more on things they received directly
from those they had known since childhood. It is significant in this connection that the last *thêyê* extraction was done just about the time of the
last extermination of an extended family. The Kaingáng have not become
sceptical of the supernatural, but have come to rely little on its goodness.

Hunting Practices [24]

Since the Kaingáng have placed their faith largely in the efficacy of personal contact with the supernatural and the element of rapport is rarely

[24] All that is said here regarding tapir applies equally to deer.

missing in their dealings with it, the personal speech to the animal's *kupléng* is almost always a feature of hunting rites, whatever other acts may be included in them. When a tapir has been killed and eaten, its windpipe (called "the tapir's heart-tube") is wrapped in vine and tapir's raw food; and before it is burnt, a short speech is addressed to the tapir's *kupléng* in order that succeeding tapirs may stand still and allow themselves to be shot: "Look at your fine heart-bundle. I want to do the same to you—so stand looking at me!" The Kaingáng feel that when they are addressing one dead animal, they are addressing the species; for the *kupléng* of the tapir will influence its brethren if it has been properly treated. The whole effort of the Kaingáng is directed toward pleasing the wild animals so that they will come and be killed. This technique parallels, on the one hand, that by which dead babies are induced to return to their mothers' wombs and, on the other, the treachery through which vendetta enemies are lured to their death.

There is a striking parallelism between the way in which dead children are caused to return to their parents and the way in which tapirs are prevailed on to come to the hunters. When a tapir is killed, it is set up crouching on its legs, and tapir's raw food is pounded and squeezed over its body and head, while the hunter says to it: "Look here at the nice remedy I am giving you. When I see you, stand looking at me and when I go *hü* [i.e. utter the tapir's cry] for you, listen and repeat it." When a child under twelve dies, it is placed in a grave in a sitting position (knees tucked up under chin, like a tapir's forepaws), and the very leaves and vines that are used for the tapir's "heart-tube bundle" are placed around it and an infusion of them rubbed over the child's body. "The *kupléng* likes this and will come to the mother." In tempting the child's *kupléng,* an offer of food is made much the same as to the temporarily wandering soul of an adult and to the *kupléng* of dead howler monkeys. When a howler monkey has been killed, the hunter picks it up by the scruff of the neck and says in a conversational tone, directly into its face: "When the things I have planted, ripen, come and eat them. When the fruit is ripe on the trees, tell it to the howler monkeys and to the jacutingas and come with them to eat it. The fruit of the tree is good, and when you come I'll eat with you. Feel the warmth of my fire and defend me—defend me and my children." "I said this," Klendó told me, "so that it would protect me from the *nggïyúdn.* When it becomes warm in my fire, it will like it and protect me." The offer of food and the promise of sharing it are amicable demonstrations similar to those which lured the ill-fated Patklé and his family to their doom.

Dogs are treated in an animistic fashion to ensure success in hunting. An infusion is made of the plants that are used for the tapir's heart-tube bundle, and this is rubbed on the dog's legs and poured into its mouth. "I have treated you for the tapir," they say to the dog. "When you see one, pursue it until, when you have exhausted it, you bring it to bay. I'll follow your trail all over, and when I see that you have brought it to bay, I'll kill it." The poor dog is not offered part of the kill as a lure, for the Kaingáng rarely think of feeding dogs at all, certainly not with a piece of the precious tapir. All other animals are induced to yield to the Kaingáng through pleasant treatment or through the offer of food, but not dogs. The Kaingáng feel that dogs should run long distances through scratching, slashing, buffeting jungle day after day without reward.

Even in making an arrow "sick" the Kaingáng are animistic. Sometimes an iron arrow head is placed in the tapir's heart-tube bundle with the words: "My arrow, be sick. I am treating you so that you will be sick." An arrow thus treated will kill even though the wound be superficial. The technique of making something sick does not extend beyond this—the Kaingáng have never developed techniques of sorcery. They feel that arrows have *kuplêng;* not only do arrows weep and die if they are deserted or thrown away in the forest, but arrows can see when a man is threatened with death, and they will fall from their places in the house above him at night to warn him of his danger. "The arrows are with one all the time and can see what is going to happen."

One bit of hunting ritual has no reference to hunting efficiency. That is the ritualistic little meal the grown hunter eats with his closest relatives when he has at last reached the point where without fear of death from supernatural causes he may eat the tapir he has killed. Up to this point the *këlú* the fledgling male, must never eat of the tapir he has brought down himself, although he may share the kill of other men. When he becomes mature, "grown for a long time"—an extremely variable age—he eats a ritualistic dish of tapir meat, which someone who loves him has first thoroughly masticated and mixed with the charcoal of the tapir's heart-bundle. The preparation of this dish is essentially a service of love of one close blood relative to another. It comes at the time when the grown man is most likely to separate himself from the group with which he has spent years, and it marks the point at which he is no longer dependent on it for his food but may now launch out for himself. Previously, not being able to eat the meat of the tapir he had killed, he was dependent on others; no matter how great his prowess, he had to remain in the group or run the risk of starvation. This attitude is directed to the tapir alone; it does not apply even to the deer which is the next largest food animal. Other animals, particularly birds, are eaten in this ritualistic manner, but such meals come at any time at all and are repeated frequently throughout life. They are essentially techniques of imitative magic which are meant to increase the hunter's skill. A branch from a very thorny bush is burnt and the charcoal mixed with the meat of the animal and eaten "so the hunter's arrows will cut and tear like the thorn."

The bee, since it is a thing that lives and moves, is included in the animistic conceptualization of the world. When the Kaingáng chop out a hive, they say: "Bee, produce! I chopped you out to make beer of you! Yukúi's wife died, and I am making beer of you so that I can cut his hair." Or if they find that the larvae have eaten all the honey, they take the larvae and cry: "Bee, produce! It is I! I am alive! You ate up your honey and that is why you did not produce." And they throw a stick into the hive. After they have taken the honey they rub the sugar over the outside of the tree to show how high up the new hive should extend, and as they do so they exclaim, "Bee, make your honey go up along this way and leave off here" (at the limit of the sugar). The Yukúi mentioned in the formula is an imaginary person whom they use as an excuse for taking the honey. The implication is that since the post-mourning ceremony is extremely important, Bee certainly would not begrudge honey taken under pressure of such a necessity. When a Kaingáng cries, "It is I," he implies that the bee knows him, for such a statement can be intelligible only when the speaker is known.

Behind the requests, commands, and adjurations of the hunting and honey-seeking formulae of the Kaingáng lies not a faith in the magical power of words, but a deep conviction that people will do whatever they are asked and that any reason is sufficient in this society where reasons are unimportant and needs are everything. Whoever asks the Kaingáng to work for him must understand that they are motivated not only by hope of gain but particularly by their fear of refusing. Whoever stands his ground and asserts his rights can move mountains.[25]

Divining

There is scarcely a phenomenon in nature which has not at some time an immediate bearing on the small and insecure cosmos of the Kaingáng. But the feeling that things outside of a man's own body have direct reference to it is reduceable to a conception that most such things have a *destructive* reference. On the human level, the Kaingáng partially overcome this threat by extending their bodies through physical and emotional diffusion—the symbol of security is *ka lẽlẽ nyá,* to live in someone else. But everything outside of this social personality, that is to say, members of other extended families, is destructive. In the realm of the supernatural the

[25] This compulsive obedience is at the bottom of the feud victims' attendance at festas which they know are held solely to entrap them.

Kaingáng have attempted the same extension of their positive emotional relationships, but with little success. The supernatural, to them, is an embodiment of terrors; for it is burdened with portents of death, and no matter what benefits the Kaingáng derive from the supernatural, death always dominates their outlook. In *vayú,* divining by belching, the great preoccupation is escape from death; *ķumbëdn,* divining by insects in the ashes of the dead, is completely devoted to omens of death; *ķôplëgn,* divining with charcoal, is concerned with the location of animals that may be hunted and killed, or with the impending death of human beings, and the meteorological omens of rain, darkness, tempest, and flood are all portents of death.

The oral functions of biting, spitting, and blowing form part of supernatural curing techniques, but belching has been elevated to prophetic dignity. Through *vayú,* divining by belching, the Kaingáng obtain many important insights. Any adult who feels that he can divine by belching may take this function on himself, and he or she may be sought out and asked to drink an infusion of *matte* [26] so that his belches may give some information about the chances of death from the enemy, the hunting prospects in a given direction, or the whereabouts of a lost dog. The oracular belch always comes in answer to a request that is usually put to the practitioner in a form like this: "Belch to see whether, if I go to look for my wife and child, the enemy will see me." Then the practitioner drinks the infusion, and if he belches strongly it means "No"; and if weakly, "Yes."

Kumbëdn, divining by insects, is connected with the exogamous system which the Kaingáng say they possessed far back in ancient times. According to this tradition the Kaingáng were divided into five groups, with each of which was associated a set of personal names and a design with which its members used to paint their bodies. [27] The Kaingáng still use these designs, but their only functions for two hundred years or more have been to protect the wearers against *ķuplêng* and supposedly to provide a point of reference for this system of divining by insects. To each group belong certain insects, the presence of which in funeral ashes betokened the impending death of a member of the group. A certain fly and a little butterfly called *toto,* for example, indicated the future death of those who use the dot pattern; and other insects, among them all the different varieties of bees, a wasp, and insects that the Indians call *úpá* and *thathaķumbëdn* foretold the death of someone who bore the line pattern.

In spite of the precise way in which the Kaingáng formulate it, they

[26] This is the familiar *yerba maté* or *matte* that grows wild in southeastern South America, particularly in Brazil, Argentina, and Paraguay.

[27] See Appendix II for full explanation of this scheme.

were so incapable of adhering to any such formal scheme that in actual practise this system of *kumbëdn* was almost completely superseded by other interpretations. The insects that were named as having oracular significance for each group were rarely mentioned in practice, and interest was directed toward different insects and ones that had no personal reference. When a funeral pyre was extinguished the Kaingáng came to look at the ashes, and they could tell by the position and condition of an insect how, when, and where one of their number would die. "The *kumbëdn* of one who will die far away is on the edge of the ashes. The head points outward. A death near by is shown by the insect's head pointing inward from the periphery. . . . *Pónkôklá* points in the direction in which the man will be bitten by a snake. *It does not tell the name. Ndâdnwaichudndúdn*[28] is lying in the mouth of the *pónkôklá*. It showed the biting of Nyepá. 'A big snake will bite Nyepá,' said Konggó. Nyepá's *kumbëdn* was large. It was lying on the periphery of the place where Vádn was burnt. *They make vayú on these occasions, naming the people, until a big belch comes and tells who it will be.* If one is to be killed with a club by another group of our own people the *kumbëdn* will be intact. The *kumbëdn* of those who are to be killed by Brazilians will have shattered legs, or their heads will be cut off. . . . Another will have cut wings. If someone is to fall the *kônggó* [insect] will be crushed in little pieces. When Patá died the bee showed rumpled and with twisted wings. This shows that the person is going to die while entire [i.e. of sickness]."

Some of the associations in this abbreviated account of *kumbëdn* are clear; others are unknown to me. The significance of the shattered appearance of the *kumbëdn* of the victims of Brazilians and the intact condition of those killed by Indians was rooted in the belief that Brazilians always cut their victims into little pieces while the victims of the Kaingáng were always left whole. The origin of the belief that a crushed insect indicated a fall from a tree is self-evident, while the belief that *pónkôklá* foreshadows snake-bite was based on some association of this insect with the snake (*pón*, snake; *kôkla*, ceremonial father; hence, the snake's ceremonial father). The association of bees with the line-pattern group arises from a mythological connection between the line people and bees. Bees are the *mang*[29] of the line people, just as the tapir is the *mang* of the dot people.

Kumbëdn was sometimes used in association with *vavëgn*, a kind of war ritual intended to make the enemy sleep deeply. Before attacking, the Kaingáng "clean the ground and cut a stick. They take off the bark and scrape the stick. They sink the post and stamp their feet as they hold on

[28] An insect.
[29] Owned animals.

to it. Then the Brazilians sleep. This is done with the *poimbëngnggêlê* [tree]. As its fruit fall with the wind, so will men sleep. They sing thus when they make *vavëgn:*

> *mêng nê hoi ke nyang ve*
> tiger is
> *mêng nê klëgn mbëgn yô va tôgn mê   ê   ya   yukât*[30] *ku*
> tiger is animal large   trail   thereabouts its teeth
> *hui ke nyang vê*
> *mêng nê hui ke nyang vê mêng nê hui ke nyang vê*
> tiger is

[This song means that] the tiger waits for the tapir [large animal] on its trail and that they [the Indians] are going to do the same thing. *Yukât* means that the tiger seizes animals with its teeth."

There is another song:

> *nggaivá chu yïi chu ka eput kâi tôgn mê ke nyang mu va*
> a rat

which means that "*nggaivá*[31] is little, but it seizes birds, and therefore they want to do the same as it does. All the men go and make *vavëgn*. Then they walk a little way and come back and go to sleep. The next day early the shaman goes and sees the *kumbëdn* [and says], 'That one will be killed.' His *kumbëdn* is in his footprints.[32] *Kôlô*[33] or *patû*[33] lie dead in the footprint in imitation of death. It is his imitation."

Kôplëgn, divining with charcoal, is done in pitch darkness, and while anyone can do it, it requires rapport with the deer spirit. A pyramidal wick-like heap about a half inch high and six inches long is made of the charcoal of pine, cuqueiro, or canela wood, and as it is ignited they cry: "Deer, make *kôplëgn* with me!" In the darkness they watch the red starlike sparks appear and disappear as the glow travels along the wick very much as a cigarette burns, except that in *kôplëgn* there is no steady uniform glow but a constant twinkling as the burning proceeds. Then they can tell by the size of the spark and its location what animal will be killed and where it

[30] This is a word which I never came across elsewhere. In no Kaingáng song is the meaning clear from the context, because great liberties are taken with syntax. Very often when interpretations are given, the informants prefix their interpretations with "probably." Some of these are clearly fanciful.

[31] In this song we are faced with a problem similar to that in the first. There is much less evidence for the derivation of any meaning from the verse. The only words that mean anything are *nggaivá* and *tôgn mê*, which means thereabouts.

[32] On the trail.

[33] Insects.

will be encountered. Big sparks mean tapirs, smaller ones indicate deer, and so on down through monkeys and birds. If the sparks appear on the left side of the heap, the animals will be killed on the left side of the river; if they twinkle on the right side, the animal will fall on the right side of the river; and if the spark appears near the watcher, the animal will be killed near at hand. *Kóplëgn* never fails, because so many sparks appear that they cover every eventuality, and the Indians remember the details of the divination for a long time.

When an animal is killed weeks after the ethnologist hovered breathlessly over the beautiful little heap of glowing charcoal, he will hear an Indian say: "Ah! This is the jacutinga I saw in the *kóplëgn*." The impending death of human beings can be seen in the *kóplëgn* also, but no one can see his own death.

Totemism

In the religion of the Kaingáng, totemism, i.e. a close religious association between an individual (or a group) and some natural phenomenon, is simply a special emphasis in the general pattern of close associations between mankind and natural phenomena. The tiger and the tapir, the Kaingáng say, are Wanyekí's[34] *mang* because he made them in the very beginning when the first people emerged out of the shoreless sea in the east and over the "hard" mountains to the west. Some of these conceptions that link men with animals and plants appear in one of the confused origin myths of the Kaingáng, but it is impossible to establish clear connections between what is said in these obviously fossilized myths and what one hears from informants. The pine tree is believed to be the exclusive property of the circle people, but from the myth that refers to the origin of an (unnamed) animal from the bark of the young pine it is impossible to determine why the pine tree might not just as well be the property of the dot or disk people. The mark system has been confused for the past two hundred years. The association between Klendó (i.e. the line people) and the bee is explained as follows: "When Wanyekí came out first they found Klendó eating honey and therefore said it was Klendó's. A man saw Bee. Supernatural Bee has a name like man. Padnmbá [one of the line people] saw it and learnt the names. Then he said that the names were Klendó, Vomblé, Nyatkaé, Kanyahé, Waipó, Lugnmú, Vukthá, Pepó. *Nggïyúdn* said: 'Our names are thus. Let Klendó come with his offspring. His offspring are no more in the bad land.' When the bees heard this they migrated."

[34] Wanyekí is a male personal name and is used as a generic reference to all the dot people. Of course, in addition to Wanyekí there are many other names, both male and female, that belong to the dot people.

Far from permitting them control over species of plants and animals, the pessimistic totemism of the Kaingáng simply adds one more gloomy trait to the prevailingly somber character of their supernaturalism. Their totems are solely omens of death, for "When the Klendó are about to die there is no honey—there are only bees. When the Wanyekí are about to die the tapirs are very thin, because they are Wanyekí's *mang*. The pine tree belongs to Thethé [the circle people], and when they are about to die there are no pine cones. When they die they burn them in a dry pine tree. Before Chulí fell there were no pine cones—and then he fell. They burnt him in a dry pine tree. Before the Brazilians killed Kuikégn, the pines were the same way."

Like most peoples the world over, the Kaingáng reject certain things as foods while they accept others. But their preferences have little to do with their totemic ideas. There is a story in an origin myth of one of the line people who swam about in the water so much that he became a capavary, so that now the line people do not eat capavary; if they were to do so it would be like eating their own people. But almost no one at all eats capavary, nor do they eat armadillo or paca, that delicious fat little rodent that eludes the hunter like a streak of light. Some people abstain from tiger, but others eat its heart to make them valiant like the tiger, which roams and fights alone. None of these taboos are observed by everyone. Some animals from which the Kaingáng abstain were practically impossible for them to kill under the conditions of their old life, in which they had no traps or boats. The capavary is taken by trapping, the paca by trapping or by pursuit in a boat from which the hunter may kill it with a trident in the shallow water where it has hidden. The swift-flying and hypersensitive wild ducks are extremely hard to approach, and the meat of anteater and certain water birds has a very bad flavor. There seems to be less reason for abstaining from the toad, the armadillo, and the tiger. The Kaingáng say that they do not eat the tiger because its fat is white (not yellow like other animals') and that they abstain from armadillo because its bones break so easily that they are afraid their own will break.

All of these things that the Kaingáng do not eat are called *thangglïgn*, which is the term they use for anything dirty. People who eat things that are *thangglïgn* will lose their teeth, break their bones, or grow old prematurely.

Omens

The prevailing reason for the interest of the Kaingáng in omens is death. "I saw that before Padnmbá died it rained very heavily first," said Chukembégn. "Then the river rose after his death. The bees did not make honey—they just lived in the trees." All of this was because Padnmbá was one of the line people, and since the line people came out of the shoreless sea, rain and swollen rivers are auguries of death for them. But when dot people die the rivers dry up, because they came over the "hard" mountain. "Before Wanyekí died, the river dried up until you could hardly pass with a canoe. Then when he died it rose a great deal [fifty feet]. It flooded José's mill and carried off the corn."

If a man's arrows fall on him at night he says, "I am going to die, that is why my arrows fell on me." There is a way of seeking omens by shooting arrows into the night: "At night a man calls out, 'Come here!' The men come to him. Late at night they take their arrows and shoot out into the darkness and talk after their arrows—'Shall I grow old?' They will die if the arrow goes far and sticks in a tree. If it falls on the ground they will grow old. When my father's went only a short distance they joked: 'That one cannot see at night and lands in a tree.' His mother said he was about to die; therefore it happened. I myself did this when I was ķelú—I shot far and it fell in the earth."

Rain and drought are omens of death, but a particularly evil omen is the sun shower. Even when omens have some other significance than the fore-telling of death, the latter may be included in the portents. "They put their bows and arrows on top of posts and give them to the moon, saying: 'Moon, I give you my bow! Shoot an animal on my bow!' Next day when they come to them, cobwebs are all over them and fireflies are caught in them. This shows that they will kill tapir, for firefly is the tapir's ķumbëdn." But they can also tell by this technique when a man is about to die, because then there is no cobweb on his bow. Sometimes they would put their pots in a clear place and leave them there all night. Next day, "if there are cobwebs on them, the owner of the favored pot will kill a tapir and cook. If a person is about to die, it will rain on the pot."

There is, however, one way of taking omens that is not used to foretell deaths. It is by snatching meat from a pot. "Before they go hunting they cook a little deer, *tateti,* pig, tapir, monkey; the arm of a howler monkey, the wing of a jacutinga, or a hawk. They clear the ground and put these in pots. The men are all together, and they rush to them and thrust their hands into the pots. They can tell by what they take out what they will kill. One who will shoot nothing gets nothing." Sometimes, on the other hand, when they were about to attack the Brazilians, "they would cut up cloth into pieces and put them in a pot. They would then rush to the pot and snatch them out. They mixed earth and wax with the cloth. Getting earth showed that they would kill Brazilians; getting cloth showed that they would get Brazilian clothing. They would also put axes and knives in the pots and pieces of wood with which they indicated pots. One who would get nothing from the Brazilians would get nothing in the rush."

Control of the Elements

When the thunder rumbles distantly the Kaingáng growls back at it in annoyance. His face contracts in a scowl, and he looks up and expresses his anger by the same kind of growl with which he greets any animal that happens to disturb him. When the storm swells in intensity, when the thunder crashes, the wind roars, and the trees rock, he shouts in fear, "Storm, go away! I am afraid of you; so go away!" Or: "Storm, go away from me! You are killing me and my children!" Once a mild rain storm threatened to spoil the hunting for us, and as I lay by the campfire I called to one of the Indians, "Tell it that you have come hunting with your relative." So he obediently called out, "Storm, go away; I have come hunting with my relative!" Another cry is, "Storm, go where you were having intercourse with Chulúin," and at this reference to his traditional amour, Storm becomes ashamed and goes away. Thus, in the attempt to control the elements, the Kaingáng try to stimulate in them the emotions that are crucial in human society.

It is in weather control that the Kaingáng techniques of imitative magic are most highly developed, but even here the technique is rarely free from animism. Sometimes when there is a tempest they burn tapir's hair and throw the ashes up in the air with the cry: "Go away! Blow with my animal overhead!" "Probably," said Vomblé, "supernatural fire fights with Storm, and it goes elsewhere. Then the wind stops. The wind smells the ashes of the hair and goes away." When Kopaké heard the thunder, he would warm his hands in the fire and wave them, and as he blew he would say: "You! Drift away that way and do not notice me! Go somewhere else!" Vomblé describes this technique as peculiar to his brother. The blowing and the heating of the hands are reminiscent of Kaingáng curing practices. When the rivers rise the Indians may fill a basket with ashes and throw them into the water: "When the water smells it, it will disappear." One technique of weather control is free of animistic notions: when it rains incessantly and the rivers rise high above their beds, the Indians boil rain water until it all evaporates.

When the Kaingáng want rain they put their mouths to the water and blow. They take some in their hands and cry as they throw it upward, "Look here! Do like this!" "When the rain hears this, it comes down."

The sun and moon are also susceptible to purely emotional influences, for once when there was an eclipse of the moon the Kaingáng cried, " 'Moon, show me your big heart! Moon, do not die. I see you about to die; stop! Moon, be courageous!' and when the moon heard this, it appeared again." The sun also takes heart at this strong appeal to its courage, for once when there was an eclipse, they called to it: "My relative, show me your big heart! Be strong!" and when "the sun heard this, it appeared." If it has been raining a long time, the Kaingáng call to the sun: "Sun, appear; Sun appear; Sun appear; Sun appear."

Summary and Conclusions

As far back as they can remember, the Kaingáng have been a dying people. Hunted by foreign enemies and torn by conflict from within, they lived in the shadow of death, sleeping fitfully beside their campfires, awakening to peer with frightened eyes into the solid darkness around them. Nor did their imaginations conceive a happier life: their afterworld is a somber reproduction of this one. There the people still hunt vendetta enemies, there the honey tastes like water, and there there is no meat to eat but the grubs in rotten wood. Kaingáng folklore is a monotonous repetition of compulsive murder, revenge, and annihilation; they do not tell more than three or four humorous stories altogether—wherever one turns, there is the same gruesome emphasis. The Kaingáng even like the long tales of fights with the Kangdjá in which they were regularly worsted. In our survey of their religion we saw how preoccupied the Kaingáng are with death—not with the hereafter, but with the simple fact of death itself and its effects on the living. It is a striking fact that their most elaborate ritual complex has as its sole object the protection of the living against the dead.[35] It is true that a fair number of the Kaingáng secure guardian spirits, but the emphasis in their supernaturalism is not on the beneficence of the supernaturals but on their vindictiveness if thwarted and on the danger inherent in any contact with them. We have seen how threats from the supernatural stimulate the doubly toned emotion of anger-fear[36] and how this response finds expression in flights from the supernatural and in attacks on it. This flight-fight pattern is but a reflection of the behavior of the Kaingáng Indian in any similar situation on the human level. His reaction to a threat, even though the threat be nothing more than an outburst of violent language always takes the form of attack or flight.

Thus Kaingáng religion is not the expression of an "inner need" in the sense of an attempt of the organism to achieve stability. It is a naïve and pitiful projection of the Kaingáng social outlook and emotions on the supernatural, and it is far more a threat than a buttress to their security. What we see most clearly in Kaingáng supernaturalism is their feeling about their environment—the fundamental distinction between a person's own body (which becomes generalized into the extended family) and all other bodies, which are "different." One's own body provides one with

[35] See p. 181 and Appendix III.

[36] This argument is developed in detail in the author's "The Linguistic Expression of Emotion," *American Anthropologist*, NS, v. 38: 250-256.

security—it is one's only source. Whatever is outside is potentially destructive to one's body and must be brought close to it; nevertheless, since it is always outside, it remains forever an unknown quantity and a perpetual threat. The history of the reduction in number of the healing techniques among the Kaingáng as reflected in the disappearance of singing and *théyé* extraction has involved not only a gradual sloughing off of procedures that were dependent on some supernatural being for their effectiveness but also the dropping of treatments not directly applied to the body of the patient or not designed to stimulate his own resources.[37]

The peculiar psycho-physical orientation of the Kaingáng is his own creation, but the type of supernaturalism, animism, through which it finds expression is something which he shares with most of his Indian brethren scattered over the American continents. Everywhere in the New World the fundamental religious outlook is animistic, and the fact that the Kaingáng share this is an accident of their location on the South American continent. What the Kaingáng have done is to utilize this material to give form to their profoundest feelings.

[37] By a treatment not directly applied to the patient's body is meant singing; by treatments not designed to stimulate the patient's own resources are meant extraction of *théyé* and singing.

VII

The Processes of Internal Order

T HE EXTENDED FAMILY is the unit of security—outside all is uncertain and deadly. It is this dichotomy that underlies the movements of food and property and the handling of conflicts in Kaingáng society. In all these situations it is not so much that one individual acts over against another as that the entire group cooperates in an effort to keep intact the last shred of security that remains to them in a hostile universe.

Hunting and the Distribution of Food

The Kaingáng inhabit an enormous territory. Through this land they scatter in small groups in search of food, for there is not enough game concentrated in any one area to support a large population. The small hunting bands are made up of men who are related as brothers, as fathers and children, and as in-laws. This is the standard composition of the bands from the Kaingáng point of view. Sometimes men are associated who are first cousins or who have inherited hunting relationships from their fathers. The inheritance of paternal loyalties is very important in Kaingáng society. If two men have been close associates for years, their sons will be close companions by the pure accident of their fathers' association. To the Kaingáng such a relationship has a special warmth because it is a reminder of their parents.

Thus the hunting band, however ephemeral its composition, is made up of individuals who are closely related by consanguinal, affinal, and sentimental ties; and as long as the nightmare of vendetta has never raised barriers between them, the members of the group live without serious conflicts. Their life is not idyllic by any means—they have their quarrels, and sometimes they separate, but there is never any bloodshed. Stability is maintained by yielding to the aggressor, by grumbling under one's breath, and, at last, by going away—that is the end of all tension.

When a hunter kills an animal he rarely keeps it—even though he has no meat himself, he gives it away to a member of the band. He knows, of course, that he will get a piece of it, but if it is a bird and the recipient's family is large, it may be a very little piece. Under such a system of distribution it would be impossible for anyone to hoard meat even if the Kaingáng knew how to preserve it. It is also of little importance who the best hunter is, for all live by his prowess—his kills are the property of all. Not he, but the man to whom he gives his kill, receives the lion's share—the head of the tapir with its succulent neck. Whoever cuts the tapir takes as large a piece as he wishes, and no one murmurs—within his hearing.

One day, when I understood, at last, that the Kaingáng felt this way about butchering, I saw Vomblé, who had received a delicious young tapir from his brother-in-law, carry off half of it. I was somewhat puzzled because, since I was keeping a minute check on the distribution of pieces of the kill, I thought that Vomblé might divide it somewhere else and I might miss some information. As he stalked off down the river with the head and front legs of the animal on his shoulder, I asked him, "Who's going to get that?" "This is mine," said Vomblé. "All of it?" I asked in amazement. "Well," said he, slightly embarrassed, "I may give some to someone else." He did give a leg to his sister-in-law, but that was all.

Once the butcher has taken the head and whatever other choice morsels he may select, he will cut out large pieces for his in-laws, his brothers and sisters, and his hunting companions—and give the rest to whoever asks for it. Or he may simply let the women carry it back to camp, where it will be divided by someone else. Sometimes the butcher is influenced by the amount of meat he knows to be in the hands of other people. If they have plenty he may give them none at all even though they are close relatives.

Sometimes meat is even appropriated by people who had no hand in its killing, but it is impossible to call this thieving, for thieving can occur only where there are clearly conceived ideas of property rights which are buttressed by strongly felt sanctions. But in Kaingáng culture the whole concept of property is most closely tied up with this desire to keep peace among relatives. One day Waipó and I shot a tapir, but since it was growing late we took only a little of the meat in the expectation of getting the rest the following day; but when we arrived at the scene of the kill the following morning we found that other people had come from an encampment near us and had already got the meat cut up. They had taken it into their heads to divide the animal among themselves, and no one opposed them. Of course, they had not bothered about me any more than they had bothered about anyone else in my camp. I suggested that I should like to have a leg, and when I pointed to one the woman to whom it had been apportioned abandoned it without a murmur. If it had been Ndíli he might never have done so. When I got back to camp Chukembégn growled over what had happened to the meat: "We did all the work and they took the meat. The women are always that way. Kundídn probably took the penis and testicles —those who have no husbands always do that. Tomorrow we'll kill some animals just for ourselves." This was the last I heard of that tapir. There is really no great reason why the Kaingáng should quarrel over meat. Whoever gets none today will surely get some tomorrow, and in times of hunger the meat is divided among the whole group. Of course at these times the same emphasis prevails; close relatives are always thought of first, and the others get what is left over or nothing at all. When they are hungry, close relatives simply come and sit down where there is food, and he who has a quarter of tapir today may have none tomorrow, for his relatives may have eaten it all.

Students of primitive law frequently ask, "What happens if two men chase the same animal or if one man wounds it and another kills it?" Under certain conditions these are situations of potential conflict. For Kaingáng society the answer is that it depends on who the men are and even more on the native conception of the individual's role. Answers to questions of this kind can be given only in terms of the totality of native feeling and hunting technique. In Kaingáng society the individual is physically[1] part of a much larger group; he is trained to the suppression of counter-assertiveness, and his desire is to maintain peace almost at any price. He almost always hunts with a group of close kin, and the animal he kills is rarely his. If it is a tapir it is never his unless he lives alone. Thus, the interest in who killed the animal could be expressed only in terms of evaluation of the hunter. But skill in hunting is not stressed by the Kaingáng and plays no role in their judgments of individuals.

The basic tapir-hunting technique of the Kaingáng is stalking. One man tracks the animal without dogs and utters its cry until the deceived animal stops long enough to be shot. Under such conditions in the Brazilian jungle it is rare for two hunters to cross each other's trails during the day because they plan their hunts in different directions. I was able to find only one story of a dispute that arose over the crossed trails of two hunters. Characteristically enough, it goes back about a hundred and fifty years. One day Kongglúin wounded a tapir but lost its trail. Natkaé found it, however, and pursued the tapir until it fell into a stream, where he shot it again and killed it. When Kongglúin noticed his mistake he retraced his steps, and finding the tapir's track again, he followed it to where Natkaé had finally

[1] The strong sense of being one flesh and blood that the members of each extended family have justifies the use of this term. See Chapter IV, pp. 44-45.

killed the animal. "Come here," said Natkaé, "and cut it up." "Then
Kongglúin said, 'As I came along after the tapir your trail crossed its track.'
'No, it didn't. I shot it over that way and pursued it. Probably the one you
shot crossed this one's trail and went on.' Kongglúin's arrow was inside
the tapir, and he was about to take out the guts, but Natkaé anticipated
him, and feeling the arrow, he swept all the internal organs into the water.
But Kongglúin was watching and said, 'What was it that fell into the
water?' He came and pushed aside the insides and saw the arrow. As he
took it he said: 'Look here! Here is my arrowhead!' To which Natkaé
replied: 'Where then is the one [animal] I shot? Make a trail that way.
I'm going to look for the one I shot.' He lied, saying that the one he had
shot had gone in a different direction and that he had erred and followed
the one Kongglúin had shot. As Natkaé went away he said, 'It escaped!'
He broke his arrow and rubbed tapir dung and the blood from his own
scratches on it. When Kongglúin arrived in camp he said, 'Did you see the
trail of the one you shot?' 'Yes. I pursued it but it escaped.' 'Well, what
happened?' 'I followed it and it went downstream and my arrow fell out.
Here is the arrow I shot it with.' He had rubbed the arrow with the dung
a tapir leaves in its trail. Next day Natkaé went out again. The others had
gone to the tapir shot by Kongglúin. They heard Natkaé shouting [in the
distance], but he was lying. He reached them, carrying a broken arrow. 'I
shot another tapir,' but he had rubbed his blood over it. That is the way
he lied."

As an exposition of the point that to whoever shoots the animal first goes
the *credit* for having killed it this little story is excellent, but it stands alone.
Natkaé's interest in the tapir was not in the possession of it, for he had
already given it to Kongglúin before his deceit was discovered. What
Natkaé wished was to be acknowledged the killer. His shame arose not out
of his not having been the true killer but out of the discovery of his deceit.

The distribution of tapir may stand as a pattern for the distribution of
all game. In the pig-surround [2] no hunter eats the animal he has killed, for
he must distribute his catch to other people. Even if he has killed only one
pig he gives it away and gets back another one exactly like it. Once an
individual has received a piece of meat it is his with all the rights of possession we associate with *mine* and *thine*. No one but his spouse and relatives
by marriage may take it without his permission, and he may do with it
what he pleases. The meat a person has is his but his relatives may take it
whenever they wish; other relatives must be fed when they are hungry; he
must give to anyone who asks him, and he must always have regard to the
demands of hospitality and courtesy. While his meat is roasting slowly
over the coals anyone may nibble at it who wants to; whoever feels hungry

[2] See Appendix I.

in the middle of the night and finds himself without food may, if he is brazen enough, get up, and while the owner is asleep, eat the leg of his howler monkey or the rib of his tapir. He must keep his tongue between his teeth, for to refuse food is the most frightful sin the Kaingáng can imagine. *Ndegn,* to refuse, has such an aura of destructive affect about it that every time I heard it it chilled my blood. To hear *ndegn* applied to food is to expect murder around the corner. In times of plenty it does not matter how much meat a man has; in times of hunger food passes through his fingers like water. Still, with all this each of the Kaingáng likes to take the biggest piece even when game is scarce. For one or two days the bellies of his children will be full, but soon the meat is all gone.

This possessive feeling about food applies with somewhat greater intensity to pine nuts. These are often gathered by a man and his wife. He climbs the tree and jumps around on the boughs until he dislodges the great five-pound cones; and then he descends and helps his wife gather them up and break them open to extract the nuts. They fill their yard-deep baskets, and what they cannot use immediately they bury in stream beds to preserve them. The theft of a full unburied basket is rare—I know of only one case—but the theft of nuts from the preservation beds is quite common. The nonchalance of the Kaingáng about these thefts is perplexing to the ethnologist steeped in the traditions of western culture and trained to expect conflicts after theft. Nevertheless I never knew the theft of a basket of nuts to create more than a one-day grumble. Indians would protest to me about property people had stolen, and they would tell me in no uncertain language what they thought of such people, but they never did anything about it. It is not possible to formulate precisely the movements of food in Kaingáng society. When one has said that the primary emphasis is on giving to affinal relatives, to parents and siblings, to hunting companions, and to the friends whom one has inherited from one's father, everything has been said that can be about the structuralization of food distribution.

Kaingáng property arrangements are not a matter of checks and balances which ensure that for every piece of meat which A gives to B he may expect a piece in return. It is impossible to make them understand any theory of exchange other than that of outright purchase which they have learnt from the whites. I tried in vain to make them understand that when I lent them a scythe to clear their fields they should give me a little corn when it became green. Their understanding of reciprocity is in terms of lifelong symbiosis, not in terms of balanced exchanges. No accounts are kept, but in the back of his mind each man knows who has been systematically helpful to him and who not. Many of the conflicts within the extended families arise out of some failure to live up to the ideal of constant helpfulness and support, and it is at this point that one of the greatest weaknesses of Kaingáng social structure becomes evident.

All of a person's brothers and sisters, uncles and aunts, and first and second cousins are his *nungnyên,* and when a man marries, all of his wife's *nungnyên* become his in-laws. It is obvious that the number of any one person's in-laws will be enormous, especially when we consider the fact that he has in-laws not only through his wife but also through his own brothers and sisters and cousins and uncles and aunts. When we remember in addition how closely inbred Kaingáng extended families are it is at once evident that almost all the extended families may be in-laws to any one person. Since it is impossible to give attention to such an enormous number each man selects only a few. Owing to the fact that the lines of his selection are not defined for him, the group with which he throws in his lot is determined only by his own choice, and the character of the group of affinal relatives acknowledged by every individual is different. One man may associate principally with his wife's uncles and brothers, while another may ignore them almost entirely in favor of his sisters' husbands. There is no mechanism to fix and stabilize any kind of relationship. The consequent slighting or exclusion of some relatives and the general fluidity of the social scheme produce undercurrents of resentment that are ultimately drained off substitutively by the feuds.

Within the extended family feelings of rejection may be strong but they never break out into bloodshed. Although Vomblé did not see his brother-in-law Tokéle for a long time, all that passed between them when they met was words. "Tokéle used to shoot animals for me," said Vomblé, "but before he died he went away, so that I did not see him. [When I met him again I said to him,] 'I raided the Brazilians, but you went far away and I did not see you after that. I thought that when I went to attack the Brazilians you would follow me, but you did not. I was the companion of your [adoptive] father until he died; then I became angry with you. When your real father was killed[3] you were small, and he [the adoptive father] brought you up. At last you grew to manhood, but you went away and you did not see him die. Therefore I was angry with you. I thought to myself, if I were to see you I would be angry with you. *I am telling you this to no purpose.'* Then Tokéle said to me, 'I thought that you would be that way [angry]. When you went away I was going to follow you, but *yûgn*[4] asked me [to go with him], and so I went with him. That is why I did not see *yûgn* [his adoptive father] die. Are you going to be angry with me on that account?' 'Yes, I am. I went around with your *yûgn* and suffered hunger

[3] In a feud.

[4] His adoptive father's brother who was also his wife's mother's brother and hence a relative by marriage.

with him. That is why I am about to be angry with you—because you did not see him. He was always watching for you; that is why I who have seen you am talking to you. Now that I have done it I'm going to stop.' Tokéle also said: 'When I was your companion I shot animals for you. Then I went about with Kopaké[5] [Vomblé's brother] and shot animals for him. I went about with him; so I shot none for you, but you went around alone with *yúgn* [Tokéle's adoptive father], and so you are angry because I did not see him die.' "

Tokéle was caught in the confusion of his culture. His obligations to all of the individuals in question were real and pressing, but it was impossible to fulfill them all. His only excuse was that he was "asked" to go elsewhere by another relative by marriage, but it was not enough to soften Vomblé's anger. In spite of this resentment, however, Vomblé added that he was "telling . . . this to no purpose," for it is essential to do everything possible to remove the sting from an angry outburst within the family. In typical Kaingáng fashion Vomblé deflected the stream of interest from himself to his dead father-in-law by saying over and over again that he was angry because Tokéle "did not see him die." Failure to see a relative die is a theoretical offence which may be invoked to obscure the real causes of anger when it is felt necessary to do so. When Kanyahé brought about the murder of Patklé[6] the "reasons" he gave were (1) that he had been deserted and (2) that Patklé had not "seen his child [i.e. Kanyahé's wife] die." The true motive for the murder was that Patklé was "a different man" who had long had it coming to him. The real reason for Vomblé's anger appears in such remarks as "Tokéle used to shoot animals for me, but before he died he went away, so that I did not see him," and in similar statements in which Tokéle's desertion is emphasized.

The only way to avoid reproach was to wander constantly in search of other people and to live with them and give them food. But even this might fail. When the co-husband of Kapíli was killed in a feud massacre and Chukembégn, Kapíli's brother, was wounded, Kapíli needed another man to aid him in the food quest. But Yuvén, who had married his sister, was far away. "Yuvén and his children were his affinal relatives but never shot anything for him, and therefore he was angry and hungry." When Kapíli and the wounded Chukembégn at last met one of their relatives Chukembégn said to him. "Let Yuvén come and shoot some birds that I desire so much." Then the relative went away, and when he reached Yuvén he said to him: "Yuvén, Kapíli has called you. He said, 'Let Yuvén come to me and let him live with me.' Chukembégn and Kapíli called you to shoot birds for them." But Yuvén's coming did not solve the problem, for

[5] Tokéle's wife's first cousin—an affinal relative.
[6] See p. 58, Chapter V.

although he was willing to help Chukembégn, he felt quite differently about helping Chukembégn's brother, Kapíli. Kapíli had for a long time felt himself deserted by his wife's brother Waipó, and news of his anger had somehow reached Yuvén. But Waipó was Yuvén's co-husband, and Yuvén was angry, particularly because Waipó had died. "Yuvén came with many jacutingas. Wainlúin [his wife, the sister of Chukembégn and Kapíli] gave some to her brother Kapíli, but Yuvén ignored him. Kanyahé [Waipó's brother] did not speak to Kapíli." The situation between Kapíli and Waipó could be interpreted either as desertion on the part of Waipó or as desertion on the part of Kapíli. The close relatives of Waipó interpreted it, of course, in the latter way. This is the constant condition within the extended families: the streams of resentment are manifold, and the drying up of one does not mean the establishment of accord.

Property

In Kaingáng society there was only one reason for a man's accumulating property—in order to give it away to his affinal relatives when his little boy's lower lip was pierced for the insertion of the lip plug or when his little girl's thigh was pricked to make her "able to walk." In preparation for this festa of "blackening the children"[7] a number of men raided the Brazilians, stole their property, and came back and made beer for their affinal relatives. The people particularly singled out for recognition on this occasion were the child's *kôkla* and *mbë,* the male and female affinal relatives who buried the child's umbilical cord in the water and who on this day pierced its lip or thigh and symbolically "made" the child, thereby completing the process through which they become the child's ceremonial father and mother.[8] This was the child's ceremonial induction into the long series of activities through which in later life his bond with his father's relatives by marriage was maintained, with the vicissitudes to which all relationships were subjected in Kaingáng society. But it is not only the *kôkla,* the ceremonial father, and the *mbë,* the ceremonial mother, who received gifts on this day, but also other affinal relatives of the father, no matter whether he had come by them through his wife or through his sisters or cousins.

Accumulation of property is incomprehensible to the Kaingáng. Property is for use in the struggle for existence. It is not a means to prestige or power. Like most of the abstract values that our civilization has exploited, the concept of power over people is little developed among the Kaingáng. What property they gather above the immediate needs of existence is distributed throughout life to their close relatives. In days long ago, before the

---

[7] So called from the practice of smearing the children with charcoal. See Appendix III.
[8] See Appendix III.

Europeans invaded the land, there must have been much less emphasis on property than there is now. Two centuries ago the Kaingáng had only the things they made—weapons, clothing, and baskets—for they had no trade with other tribes. Once they began to steal from the Brazilian settlers, however, they acquired a large number of new things: iron for their arrowheads, knives, axes, iron pots, and the precious blankets. Frequently these are given away almost immediately to anyone who asks for them. To hold anything back is practically useless, because the article will be taken anyway—as happened, for example, with the deer skin I refused Ndíli. The following story indicates what may happen to desirable property.

"Kavá got an axe from the Brazilians. He took it out of a [Brazilian] house. Mumbégn went to another house, but it was closed, for the people inside would not open the door. Kavá came over, and Mumbégn said, 'Give me the axe.' He was going to break open the door. He broke open the door and entered. He looked for another axe but could not find one. '*Ai*,' said he, 'I'm going to take this one. It is fine.' So he took the axe and went to the forest. Kavá said to Mumbégn, 'Where is the axe I got?' 'I have taken it—ignore[9] it.' So Kavá ignored it and Mumbégn kept it." If he had protested, the same thing might have happened to him as happened to me or to Thegnmbégn. "Thegnmbégn went to the Brazilians and got a big knife. On the way back they [the Indians] shot a tapir and butchered it. The tapir was cut up with that knife, and then Wanengglό took it, for he wanted to steal it. Klakupú followed him and said: 'Give it to me, I want it. If he [Thegnmbégn] worries about it I'll say that I took it.' Thegnmbégn looked for his knife, and when he did not see it he followed them, and when he overtook them he said, 'Did you take my knife away?' But they answered, 'No.' Klakupú, who really had it, said: 'It is in that clear space where I was before. It is under the tapir dung.' Thegnmbégn returned to look for it, but at sundown he followed them again. Next day he said: 'My knife was a good one. Did you see it?' 'No.' Again he returned, and again he searched all about. The others waited for him and camped where they were. The following day he again searched and again returned to the others, but Klakupú had gone. Once more Thegnmbégn looked for his knife. He was searching with Kavá and said to him, 'Let's go; probably one of the folks took my knife.' By the time they returned the others had arrived in camp. 'Who saw my knife, folks?' said Thegnmbégn. 'I'm bent double with looking for it. If I had seen one of you take it I'd beat him up with my club and throw him out! That's what I was saying when I came along!' So Klakupú said: 'I took the knife! I took it to make arrows with. Now that you know it beat me with a club and throw me out!' But Thegnmbégn laughed and said, 'I meant that if someone *else* had taken it

[9] *Kakὁmὁ*, literally "ignore."

I would have done that to him.' "Probably," said my informant, "Klakupú
was Thegnmbégn's father's relative's child, and that is why nothing happened to him—or his mother's relative's child—therefore he took the
thing."

The ease with which Wanenggló relinquished the knife contrasts sharply
with Thegnmbégn's possessiveness. Thegnmbégn was also unusual in that
he decided to do something about the disappearance of his property. A
knife I once gave to an informant did not stay with him very long, but
with characteristic Kaingáng philosophy he did nothing to further its return. "Where is the knife I gave you?" I said to him one day after he had
repeatedly borrowed mine. "Ho! That disappeared long ago!" "Who took
it?" "The others." He had never even made the effort to discover who had
it—a simple matter in such a small community. Even when property is
borrowed it may never be returned unless the owner comes to claim it, for
the Kaingáng feel under absolutely no obligation to return what has been
lent to them.

In-laws are particularly likely to make free with one's property. Nowadays they are a nuisance to hunters who have laid aside stores of powder
and shot for hunting trips, only to discover, when they are ready to go, that
some son- or brother-in-law has come along in their absence, ferreted out
the hiding-place, and gone up the river, taking not only the ammunition
but also the dog and even the canoe. To cap it all, the in-law may lose the
dog in the forest and give only a small piece of the kill to his relative, while
he carries off a fat leg to his sweetheart.

Men and women own the things that they make themselves or which
have been given to them by their relatives. A woman has the right of dis-
posal of any of her possessions, and if she has an excess she may give away
what she sees fit. As for food, either the man or the woman may give it
away, and there is no feeling that it is "owned" by either one of them. As a
matter of fact the only time that the problem of ownership is important in
Kaingáng society is when a man has a number of desirable objects or when
a particularly desirable object makes its appearance. Excess objects are most
frequently the property of men, who have got them in a raid, and they are
given away to their close relatives. Women generally get desirable objects
such as scissors or knives or iron pots through inheritance or gift, but since
they usually have only one such article the problem of disposing of them
rarely arises. Like the distribution of food, the distribution of property
among the Kaingáng is conditioned not by a strong sense of reciprocity but
by the feeling of obligation to certain people, with the result that throughout life women may receive property from their in-laws without ever being
able to reciprocate. The emphasis in these cases is not on reciprocity, on the
evening-up of scores, but on relationship.

When a man dies, his most personal belongings, his bow and arrows and his lance and shirt and baskets, are destroyed. Theoretically everything else is, too, but actually the precious articles acquired from the Brazilians are kept—sometimes with apologies to the ghost. When Kakthí died during the epidemic of 1933 her son-in-law Yakwá could not endure to throw into her grave the beautiful steel knife she had inherited from her husband. So he kept it, and as she lay in her grave he spoke these words to her: *"Nyǫ, give me your knife—I am going to make it my own. Protect me from your husband—tell your husband that I took your knife. I have no knife; so I took it. Do not be angry with me. Do not leave me. If I fall ill I will ask you to protect me. I have given you all of your property and taken only the knife."*

Every death can be explained in terms of a ghost that has followed the owner of some bit of property that belonged to it while it dwelt in a living body and rapt him away to bear it company. Blankets and, in recent times, clothing are always thrown away, for they have been in close contact with the deceased. Dogs, in spite of their great value, are frequently killed, for "they always used to go around with him" and have become too closely associated with the dead person to make it wholesome for the living to keep them about. Dogs that habitually hunt with large groups of human beings have very diffuse loyalties and will obey almost anyone, so that the death of their owner still does not render them useless. The iron pots are generally abandoned, for to the Kaingáng pots are much more than simple cooking utensils—they are symbols of the living organism,[10] and when death comes much of its affect crystallizes around them. The *thúpǫya,* the widowed, must eat nothing from a pot until his isolation, his *waikómáng,* is terminated, nor could anyone who had killed a human being eat food cooked in a pot.[11] Thus, at death there is a general revulsion of feeling against those things that have been in close contact with the living, but the most valuable possessions are frequently kept in defiance of the *kupléng.*[12] Knives, scissors, axes, and nowadays guns are the things most frequently kept, and the "inheritance" of these objects is most frequently within the immediate family, with the husband or the wife taking the greater part.[13] When an object has been "taken," however, its fate is by no means settled. Although Yakwá took Kakthí's knife, a few days later he had handed it over to Vomblé, his mother's brother's son.

But probably the most striking aspect of Kaingáng inheritance is the way

[10] See p. 184. The ancient clay pots were broken.

[11] For the further discussion of ideas and practices associated with death see Appendix III.

[12] Ghost-soul.

[13] This has been inferred from a large number of specific instances collected by going through a hundred cases of inheritance.

in which the emphasis on obligations to relatives by marriage is followed through. Formerly if the dead man left any little children who had not yet had their lips pierced or their thighs pricked, a close relative, usually a brother, gathered the dead man's possessions together, prepared beer for the child's "blackening," and distributed the goods to the in-laws of the dead man. Perhaps the surviving relative also had children to blacken, and so on such an occasion his own property would also be distributed to his own in-laws.

Once property had been stolen from the Brazilians it flowed by gradual stages from the hands of the warrior into those of his relatives, and on his death it was either distributed to his in-laws or inherited by his wife and children. Societies like those of the Plains Indians of North America had made the distribution of property a device for the attainment of prestige, but when a Kaingáng gave away his booty he was doing simply what was expected of him as a relative. In many societies power tends to concentrate where property accumulates, but although the Kaingáng respect power they cannot tolerate any kind of intensification of it; for such intensification is felt by them to be disruptive. Through their insistence on the primary importance of the other person and their failure to reward achievement, the Kaingáng have suppressed processes that encourage the concentration of power in the hands of outstanding individuals.

The Meaning of the Feuds

One of the sources of aggression was the accumulation of resentments growing out of adultery and rejections by "deserting" relatives. Feuds and raids on the Brazilians provided substitute outlets for these resentments, and at the same time, by projecting the aggressions outside, operated to protect each extended family from internal disruption. A factor powerful in the perpetuation of the feuds is the Kaingáng feeling that once a force has been started it can never be stayed. Paralleling this on the human side is the belief that once a person has committed murder he will keep on.[14] With such a view of the natural world all that is necessary is that murder be committed once in order that there shall be perpetual distrust of the murderer. Given this attitude, the distinction in emotional ties within and between the extended families, and the peculiar social outlook of the Kaingáng, it is easy to see why things should have taken the turn they did: since murderousness is the attribute not only of individuals but also of groups, the groups suspect—and slay—one another forever.

---

[14] A parallel to this is not hard to find in our own society, for we believe that "a leopard cannot change its spots," and "once a criminal always a criminal." One of the fundamental bases of the theory of capital punishment is that a murderer must be got out of the way because he is likely to commit another murder under similar circumstances.

Social Forms and the Solution of Conflict

Students of social forms tend to interpret behavior in terms of the social mechanisms operative in a given culture, and when conflicts persist they explain such persistence as due to the absence of adequate social forms with which to handle them. Thus, in discussing societies in which feuds occur, they point out that vendettas are frequently stayed through some device such as the *lex talionis* or marriage between the warring groups and that where feuds continue it is because the society lacks a mechanism with which to stop them.

In discussing the solution of conflicts, however, we must understand what we mean by a solution and what personal factors are involved. A social mechanism is a device for handling a situation, and where the way of handling the situation accords with the kind of personality involved there is a perfect integration between the social form and the individual emotions. Often, however, this integration is not achieved. Let us consider a case in our own society. Before it was made illegal, a suit for breach of promise to marry was a device available to women seeking restitution for unfulfilled proposals. If a woman was successful in her suit one of the things for which the law compensated her was the "mental anguish" she endured. But such compensation was, at best, a solution for only certain types of personality. For many women the seeking of material compensation was repugnant and so irrelevant to their emotional needs that the idea never occurred to them. Thus, suits for breach of promise were adequate to the needs of only a certain type of personality, i.e. of the type whose status and whose emotions were measurable in terms of currency. The breach of promise suit would be a perfect mechanism only in cultures where the principal things involved in marital relations were the economic correlates of woman's status and where joy in the monetary gain from such a suit was so great that it allayed all mental anguish. In such a case of integration between personality and social mechanism there is a perfect structural and emotional balance between wrong suffered and compensation awarded. There is no residue of economic loss or personal suffering: it has all been washed out in a wave of economic satisfactions.[15]

Pepó, one of the personalities in a Kaingáng feud, was satisfied to live in peace after having killed the man who murdered his brother. A tit-for-tat solution of this kind is called the *lex talionis*. In other words, Pepó's nature

[15] But the man is in quite a different position, for the woman's gain is his loss, and depending upon the culture he will cherish resentment or accept his lot without complaint. Even in the case of the woman it is not certain that she will be satisfied. She may still hate the one who has wronged her and cherish the hope of getting even in some more direct way. If the culture produces resentful individuals who harbor grudges social forms may become mere stop-gaps, and the basic conflict must be resolved in some non-formal way.

was completely satisfied by the death of one man. If nothing more had come of the murder of Pepó's brother we could say that in this situation the conflict was solved through the operation of the *lex talionis*. But something else did happen, because Wainló, the foster son of Pepó's brother, could never forget the murder of his foster father. For years he nourished his hate until with the help of allies he exterminated the entire male line— sons, affinal relatives, and hunting companions—of the original murderer. Thus the *lex talionis* could not function because it was repugnant to the obsessive personality of Wainló. The *lex talionis* was no *lex* in Kaingáng society, not because the idea had never occurred to the Kaingáng, but because the people as a whole were incapable of accepting it. There are a number of instances of this kind in Kaingáng history. In the section of folklore I have given a long historical tale [16] in which it can be seen clearly how one man, Yokégn, tries twice to stay the forces of annihilation simply by refusing to take action, but in vain—his enemies literally force him to kill them. There are ample data even at the present time to show that such socially wholesome attitudes have appeared a number of times, but to no avail. As in our own society, individuals with insight are overcome and swept into the whirlpool by the obsessive behavior of others.

In Kaingáng society the men who have shown this special insight have never been the weaklings. They have, on the contrary, been among the most *waiķayú;* they have been the *waiķayú yônggï,* the very brave, the very vicious, the very dangerous. They were Thunder Storm, Pepó, and Yokégn. With the exception of Pepó they were physically powerful men, and they fought like tigers.[17] Pepó, who had been spared because he was thought incapable of harm, slew his brother's murderer single-handed and then walked into the enemy camp and cowed them all, so that Wanenggló, his chief enemy, lay awake night after night, slinking off in the day to sleep in hiding. Day after day he sent his wife to Pepó to beg him to spare him, until at last the exasperated Pepó exclaimed: "I've forgotten all about that. I killed the one who killed him [my brother]. Let him [Wanenggló] forget about me and sleep whenever he wants to."

Men like Thunder Storm, Pepó, and Yokégn were not "deviants."[18] On the contrary the Kaingáng looked on them as highly representative of their ideals. Indeed, Yokégn himself, although he twice tried unsuccessfully to avoid killing, deliberately plotted a holocaust[19] with the obsessive Wainló some time later. Thunder Storm too, although he was not inclined to

[16] Chapter IX, p. 134.

[17] *Waiķayú* men are frequently compared to tigers.

[18] The term "deviant" has been used in anthropology to describe the type of personality that is completely unable to adjust to the standard emphases of a particular culture.

[19] When he overheard a plot to kill him.

slaughter "different men," bathed his own lance in blood when social pressure forced him to it, and he loved to raid the Brazilians. No, we are not dealing with deviants here but with typical individuals who had developed the particular Kaingáng obsession with slaughter to a lesser degree, or whose fear of "other men" was not very great. These three were definitely of one type: they were as specifically peaceful with reference to "different men," as Kanyahé, Kundágn, and Nenggachá were dangerous.

VIII

Psychic Structure

ONE OF THE GREAT DIFFICULTIES that any society has to face is the necessity for building up attitudes that will preserve those within its limits but will destroy its enemies. Not only must such attitudes be created and fostered; they must be properly controlled and directed, for it is equally dangerous to cherish the enemy and to destroy the friend; one must help and trust friends but suspect and undo dangerous outsiders. But a society must develop within its very borders behavior trends that will at once cherish *and* destroy, according as the behavior is directed toward the in- or toward the inimical out-group. It is not enough to develop only cherishing behavior in the in-group and to tell its members that they must hate and kill everyone outside. People do not kill because they are told[1] to kill. Such destructive aggression must have an in-group behavior analogue, the expression of which must be salutary to the in-group. An example from our own culture is that of extremely destructive individuals who like to order their friends and families around. In this case the *control* of friends is the reciprocal of *destruction* of all non-friends, like servants (who are frequently discharged) and people not particularly liked (who are snubbed or insulted). Similarly, societies that are destructive to outsiders often exercise that impulse to destruction at home, but in some socialized way.

Such an impulse in Kaingáng society was expressed in the many-sided concept of *waiķayú,* self-love, which, when controlled, found its in-group expression in initiative, care for others, and staying awake all night to watch for vendetta enemies, and its out-group expression in attacks on Brazilians and on other extended families, but which when uncontrolled

---

[1] It seems unnecessary to argue that the men in the vast armies of modern times do not kill because they are told to but because they are driven.

found an outlet in attacks or designs on members of the same extended family.

The Development of Waikayú

When a male is ḳëlú he lies about caressing his hunting companions and spends his nights seeking young women. This is the period when he is childless, when he follows leaders, and when no specific judgments are made of him. But as he grows older, becomes chôi chí, grown old, he becomes waikayú. This gradual acquisition of the traditional stamp of approval is accompanied by two significant events. First, the growing man relinquishes his youthful caressing—men of forty or more rarely caress other men. Second, he acquires children of his own and need no longer satisfy himself through playing with the babies of others. After three children have been born to his wife the union is stabilized. By this time the man had taken active part in several raids on the Brazilians and might even have slaughtered some vendetta enemies. He was waikayú; he loved himself. Now he began to boast to his children of his capacity for beer and of his prowess in killing Brazilians.

The process of actually turning away from others physically may go quite far in some individuals. Klendó said to me, "Since I did not want to have intercourse I told my belly to my children."[2] It is significant that the introduction to a discussion of boasting should contain a statement regarding a reduction in sex interests.

Sexual relations, although enjoyable, are felt as obstacles to the achievement of waikayú, and any weakness or failure in social obligations may be ridiculed in terms of preoccupation with sex. In a story Vomblé kills Kuichó's relatives, but when Kuichó asks him where they are he replies, " 'They have forgotten all about you because they are too much taken up with copulating in the buttock-hole.'[3] They copulated so much that they forgot their father. Then Kuichó said, 'I thought so! They have been copulating so much in the buttock-hole . . . that they do not think of me.' " In similar terms Kundágn ridicules an enemy who manages to escape him: "You showed your manliness by setting women on their heads!"[4] The Kaingáng are the only primitive people known to me who made a special point of boasting to their own children, and this, too, is significant when seen against the general background of self-interest. One's children are extensions of oneself, one lives in them, and boasting to them is almost like boasting to oneself.

---

[2] This refers to his drinking beer.

[3] This is a Kaingáng vulgarism. The remark is readily understood as a reference to the customary Kaingáng manner of intercourse from behind.

[4] Another vulgarism. He is describing the position assumed by dogs.

When the fathers were mightily drunk they called their sons by their *nêklê*, the special boasting name that every male has, and repeated stereotyped phrases that referred to no specific deed but to their general prowess. "When my father wanted to kill someone," said Vomblé, "he was *waikayú* and he would boast to me, '*kakthú pi, kakthú pi chugn mbô pi chê ê pi.*[5] In order that my children may remember me when I am dead I say to them when they drink water, You will not die! The horses' children [the whites] throw their guns about the places where the children sleep and the children hide before them. Therefore I raid their dwellings, and they hide from me with their children.' " Thus the father boasted to his own children. He did not face a large audience and recount in detail the blows he had struck so that he might measure his prowess against that of another man and so that the people might check him if he lied. Boasting among the Kaingáng was not a means by which each man strove to take the measure of his neighbor and outstrip him if he could. Through boasting a man built up his own self-esteem, but boasting had a very limited scope and was peculiar in character.

The Constructive Aspect of Waikayú

Among primitives, individual attainments that make boasting possible are frequently stepping-stones to power; they may at times even permit a man to infringe on the liberties of the less fortunate members of his society. This is true to a certain extent among the Kaingáng also, but the principal function of *waikayú* is not to give unbounded sway to the whims of individuals, but to enforce good behavior; that is, such as is socially sanctioned. Thus, when Cha was bitten by wild pigs, Pandjumbúgn, who had to carry the stricken boy, decided that he was too much of a load and so deserted him. But as he went along through the forest the thought kept recurring to him constantly, "In spite of my boasting I threw him away. When the others hear about it they'll ridicule me." So at last, according to the tale, he went back, and, taking up Cha, carried him home. There are stories of men who have lost their lives because of their strong feeling of *waikayú*, for death itself was preferable to the ridicule that they would certainly draw on themselves if they failed to live up to the opinion which they had of themselves and which they tried to instill in others. When the Kangdjá descended on them one day in a great body, taking the whole camp unawares, their first impulse was to run away; but Tondúin shouted, " 'When you taste beer you boast and boast to the children, but now you are leaving them!' So they gathered up all their arrows. Thukúgn said, 'The women and the Kangdjá made fun of me very much and now the latter are coming!' Then they all remained and fought, and many were killed."

[5] Italicized words are Vomblé's *nêklê* names.

It was in times of great danger such as this that the two forces that are most dynamic in the integration of Kaingáng society, love of self[6] and love of others,[7] came into the foreground. The appeal to *waikayú* played its role side by side with the appeal through *ka lẽlẽ nyá*. The accusation "You are deserting me" would always bring back the fleeing Indian, even though to his own death. During the same battle in which Tondúin and Thukúgn lost their lives Kemblén was shot in the leg. When Kuklé made as if to go Kemblén called after him, " 'Affinal relative, you are deserting me!' So he [Kuklé] came back shooting, and the enemy went away. When Kuklé's arrows became exhausted, the enemy captured Kemblén. They tried to capture Kuklé but he ran away." Kuikégn lost his life under similar circumstances. He was about to leave after having slaughtered some of the enemy, but his wife, who had been taken captive, called to him, " 'You are leaving me!' So he came back and fought with them for her sake. He thrust her behind him and shot at them for her sake. Whenever he started to go she would say, 'You are deserting me!' and he would come back and shoot at them, until at last they killed him."

Like all nomads the Kaingáng were handicapped by those who were too old to move about easily. Yet they carried on their backs both men and women when they could no longer walk or walked too slowly. Kanyahé was so old that he tottered along on sticks and so nearly blind that he had to be led at the end of a bow. Yet he was not deserted. Even when they once seemed to have made up their minds to leave old Waimogué to her fate they took pity on her and returned and fetched her in carrying-bands like an infant. Few of the Kaingáng lived to a ripe old age under aboriginal conditions but when they did they were cherished to the last.

The typically *waikayú* individual was "dangerous" to outsiders. He was vicious, quarrelsome, and even, from our point of view, brave, for he would attack the Brazilians in the face of great danger and he was a great killer of tigers, the symbol of *waikayú* in the animal world. Aggressiveness finds mild expression within the extended families in the taking of the initiative, but initiative has a rather mild range. Movements of the hunting bands are determined almost entirely by the prevalence of game tracks in the region, and when anyone returns with the news that he has seen tracks somewhere the whole camp moves in the direction of the game. If the people are so far away from the pine forest that many days' journey would be necessary in order to reach it, some individual will suggest that they go there. His suggestion, however, has particular influence only over his own brothers and sisters and his close affinal relatives. Other people may choose to listen

[6] *Waikayú.*
[7] *Ka lẽlẽ nyá.*

to someone else. No Kaingáng has the right to take the initiative because of war exploits, hunting ability, or physical strength. Initiative springs from the same soil as *waiḳayú* and is its in-group expression. Many men who are murderous enough in their behavior toward "other men" and toward Brazilians, however, have never been known to take the initiative. When suggestions were made, they were the ones who just "listened and went along" with the others. It is also not without significance that the men who showed outstanding initiative were those who lived alone with their wives —who did not form part of a polyandrous or joint household.

Such a man was Kanyahé, who finally brought about the slaughter of Patklé and his male children. At one time Kanyahé had two wives, but after his early joint marriage experience with Yuvén and also with his own brother Waipó, he shared them with no one. He exercised considerable influence over his brothers, hunting companions, and in-laws. A description of the organization of an expedition against the Brazilians makes clear the extent of Kanyahé's influence in his own circle. "He said to his father, 'Father, I am going to command them to attack the Brazilians' camp site, for it is there that I am going to lie in wait for the Brazilians and kill them.' So when they [his relatives] returned from their hunting he said to them, 'Did you shoot any tapirs?' and they replied, 'Yes.' So he said: 'Shoot some more that your wives may stay by them and eat. In the meanwhile lie in wait for the Brazilians at their camp site where the roads cross, and when they stop on their way, slaughter them and take their goods. Then leave their things here and go where there are Brazilians' houses in the forest. There attack them and take their goods and we will make beer for our children['s blackening].' So Wanyekí[8] said, 'So you are saying that you are going to lie in wait for them?' 'Yes. I said I was going to lie in wait for them.' When Waipó[9] heard this he said, 'Well, then, lie in wait for them. I'll lie in wait for them with you.' Then Wanyekí said, 'Well, then, I'll lie in wait for them with him and you.'" In this way Kanyahé organized the arrangements and sentiment for the attack. The conclusion of the raid was characteristic enough—Kanyahé gave the knife he got to his half-brother Waipó, and Wanyekí received a knife from his co-husband.

But even those who "command" yield to the commands of others who happen to take the initiative, so that all aggressive personalities are at some time under the sway of others. It was remarkable to see how my informant, the blustering Vomblé, a man about fifty, yielded to the request of a crippled[10] boy of twenty-five who chanced to be interested in influencing

[8] The husband of Amendó. See p. 30. Amendó was sister to one of Kanyahé's wives.

[9] Kanyahé's half-brother. He was older than Kanyahé.

[10] He fell from a horse.

his behavior. One day the Kaingáng were planning a big hunting trip: they had got hold of a fine tapir dog and were all going up the river to try it out. "Are you going too?" I asked Vomblé. "If they command me to go I shall go," he replied. And when the cripple appeared at my window and said that they were all going up the river, Vomblé left me and went along.

The Disruptive Aspect of Waikayú

It is characteristic of the extremely *waikayú* individual that he directs his hostility toward his own group. He becomes quarrelsome and threatening and the hate against him grows to white heat. Vomblé sat for days with the picture of Nenggachá's family in his hands, gazing at it through half-shut eyes, while curious yelps grew and died in his throat. Nenggachá must have been long dead, but his offspring had been localized on a reservation in Palmas, and the agent, whom they later murdered, had sent their picture to the agent at Duque de Caxias. Although Vomblé was a baby when Nenggachá finally escaped, his memory was still vivid among the Kaingáng, for Nenggachá was *waikayú* to the extreme. He was "dangerous," he was "very *waikayú*," he was "no good," he was everything hateful. And as Vomblé regarded his picture he would say to it: "You were very *waikayú;* you wanted to kill me. No-good Nenggachá." The picture had an overwhelming fascination for him—it was the only thing he ever tried to help himself to in my house.

Nenggachá is famous in recent Kaingáng history—it is only of him that deeds of violence within the extended family are told, and the stories about him give considerable insight into his personality.

Nenggachá was one of Amendó's lovers, and like every lover he thought himself suspected by his mistress's husband. But to think a thing like this is, to the Kaingáng, the same as knowing it, and he projected into the mind of her husband Wanyekí the knowledge of his adultery and anger against himself. But anger against himself meant a threat to himself. Thus Nenggachá felt himself threatened, and he spoke angrily to the husband. Then the husband became angry with his mouth.[11] His co-husband was sitting next to him and he arose and danced. He jabbed Nenggachá with his club and he fell. Nenggachá's father Wanenggló came over and was about to strike the co-husband whose club was also raised when Wanenggló's brother-in-law seized the co-husband's club; so Wanenggló struck the co-husband and he fell. In this quarrel two families were pitted against each other, the family of Wanenggló and the family of Wanyekí, and at last Nenggachá ran off to his own camp, leaving his father beaten and bleeding on the field. When the two met again Wanenggló became angry with his

[11] He only spoke angrily—he did not strike a blow.

deserting son and said: "'That is your practice! Even when they do not drink beer they become jealous of you and beat you. Then something[12] spoke up for you and they beat him, and when you saw him beaten you ran away.' When Wanenggló and Nenggachá went away the others did not follow him, for Nenggachá was very *waikayú,* and he was very dangerous."

In spite of the fact that the Kaingáng agree that Nenggachá was extraordinarily dangerous, this story leaves us with the feeling that he was not nearly as formidable physically as the people around him, but that he was singled out, for some obscure and dreadful reason, to be the focus of the concentrated viciousness of the group in which he lived. Another story makes Nenggachá the center of violence, and here again it is difficult to discover why the fault lay entirely with him. During a festa everybody was drunk, and Yuvén and his co-husband Klendó were walking about. "Then Nenggachá said to Klendó, 'You are talking about me—I am angry.' 'I said nothing at all about you. What are you up to . . .?' Then Yuvén said to Klendó, 'Hit Nenggachá—I am angry at what he says.' Then Yuvén said [to Nenggachá], 'I am going to beat you,' and Nenggachá said: 'You deserted me. You said that you had been remembering me, and now you want to beat me.' Then Nenggachá became angry and sat up, struck Yuvén in the chest, jumped over the fire, and ran off, crying, 'In that way be angry with me!' Yuvén chased him and seized Nenggachá's lance and beat him over the head with the handle. Then Nenggachá ran off with Yuvén in pursuit." The affair ended in a brawl, with Nenggachá supported by his half-brothers and Yuvén by his brother-in-law. When some more of Yuvén's brothers-in-law returned from the hunt they wanted to go in pursuit of Nenggachá, but his mistress Amendó dissuaded them. "She was afraid that Thechá [another of her husbands] would fight with Nenggachá. He was going in pursuit of Nenggachá when Amendó lied. Nenggachá used to make love to Amendó, and therefore she lied. But Kopaké [Yuvén's brother-in-law] was angry with Nenggachá and [later] said this to him, 'Am I a child that you beat Yuvén and I let you all go without beating one of you?' But Nenggachá said nothing—he was probably afraid."

When the extended family of Kanyahé, of which Nenggachá was a member, later encountered that of Patklé, Nenggachá married two of Patklé's daughters and joined forces with him. When Patklé was killed by Kanyahé the only things that saved Nenggachá were his link with his old mistress Amendó and the fact that he had married a half-sister of Kanyahé. When she died he again feared for his life and fled, never to be heard of more.

[12] Meaning himself, Wanenggló.

In general, the Kaingáng feeling about *waikayú* individuals is that they are quarrelsome, vicious, and brave, but it does not appear from the preceding examples that Nenggachá possessed these qualities to a conspicuous degree. Indeed, what seems to be his most striking characteristic is his developed capacity for projection, which tends to get out of hand and find expression in threatening demeanor. In other words the cause of Nenggachá's antisocial behavior is an outlook in which the men around him are seen as living reproaches, perpetually storing up resentments against him. In this society, whose very vitals are torn by projected anxiety it is extremely difficult to prove that one individual has developed this characteristic more than any other individual. Nenggachá happened to be singled out as dangerous above all the others, and the beatings which he suffered were provoked by his anxiety rages. His extraordinary capacity for projection is what made him unbearable. Nenggachá is simply an exacerbated case of failure to project all resentment and guilt outside—against other extended families.

The feeling of being arrayed against the massed forces of destruction is hypostatized in *lu,* the concept of doom. "I shall go dancing to meet my *lu*" $\left\{ \begin{array}{l} \textit{êng lu} \quad \textit{kôtó ngglâ tâlé} \\ \text{my doom meet dance go} \end{array} \right\}$, is the striking phrase that appears in the origin myths. The Kaingáng say: "They are referring to death, and they say that something is killing them. That is what they call, 'I am going dancing to meet my *lu*.' When they first came out into the world they said in their strange language, 'I am going to meet my *lu* dancing.' They refer to their death as *lu*. My *lu* kills me and I die. When they are killed and they die they say, 'My *lu* killed me.' When a person goes to meet the approaching enemy—they are about to be killed. This is what they call my *lu*. 'Your *lu* is looking at you.'"

Thus the ultimate expression of the Kaingáng feeling of insecurity is *lu,* doom, the threatening world. The following diagram may make the Kaingáng psychic structure clearer:

MYSELF AND THE OTHER MEMBERS OF MY EXTENDED FAMILY [13]

What I think	*What I think they think*
1) My body is my fortress	
2) I live in them (*ka lêlê nya*)	3) We live in you
4) But I desert you and meddle with your wives	5) You have deserted us and have been meddling with our wives
6) so I feel guilt (*yôkthê*)	7) so we are angry with you
8) If you are angry with me I'll be angry with you too.	

[13] Read in numerical order. The language is my own.

Myself and the World Outside of Me (i.e. Other Extended Families and the Rest of the Natural World) [13]

My body	*Outside of My Body*
1) My body and those of my close relatives give security	2) Everything outside threatens. This is my *lú*, my doom
3) My body is in constant danger of destruction	4) and I must take action against the threat
5) Contemplating action I feel guilt	6) Feeling guilt I project: "The other person fears me because he knows what is in my mind."
	7) He fears me and therefore wishes to destroy me. This is my *lú*.

8) I must take action to prevent it.
9) I take action and feel guilt.

and I am so ridden by a sense of guilt that my very formulation of the customs of my tribe is expressed by *yôkthé*, guilt. When Klendó first came to me as an informant he wished to assure me that he would tell me everything faithfully, and so he said, "I shall tell you all about our *yôkthé*," meaning that he was going to tell me all about their customs. But *yôkthé* is used constantly to mean not only a person's habitual behavior but also his fault and guilt. A condition necessary to a healthy mind is that once it has embarked on a course it follow it through without remorse. It matters not how foul such a course may be, it is only necessary that the mind that has chosen it have no misgivings regarding its rectitude. Far from being content with the destruction they accomplished from time to time on members of enemy families, the Kaingáng were oppressed by a sense of guilt that often created conflicts within the ranks of the victorious extended families themselves. It was no abstract sense of inherent wrong in killing that gave rise to this feeling of guilt. The multitudinous cross-cuttings of relationship ties made almost any slaughter the source of guilt, for in all massacres some relatives had to be destroyed. The annihilation of Patklé and his offspring produced such strong feelings of guilt in Kanyahé and his offspring that a general quarrel ensued. The day after the slaughter Kanyahé's offspring went in pursuit of a man who had escaped. "Then Kanyahé became angry and said to Kuthúgn [14] and the other men, [14] 'Let him die alone. [15] You killed my in-laws; so stop your slaughter.' Then Kuthúgn [14] said, 'It was you yourself who ordered me to kill them, your in-laws, and I killed them; and now you're angry with me!' Then Kanyahé

---

[13] Read in numerical order. The language is my own.
[14] Kanyahé's offspring.
[15] The Kaingáng way of saying, "Don't kill him; let him die from other causes."

kept quiet. The men[14] were angry with Kanyahé." Soon after the fight Kuthúgn and Kanyahé quarreled over the pot of one of the dead men, and Kuthúgn burst out: "Those things[16] used to shoot animals for you, and then you told me to kill them, and when I did so you became angry. Let the pot be!"

Some of the men of Kanyahé's group had been loath to kill Yuplú, one of Patklé's sons, and this too was a source of ill feeling among the offspring of Kanyahé: "Kuthúgn went to invite them after Kanyahé ordered the slaughter. Now Kuthúgn [and several of the others] wanted to live with Patklé and his offspring, but Kanyahé ordered the slaughter, so that Kanyahé became angry with them and they became angry with Kanyahé. They were angry with Kanyahé because of the death of Yuplú. Kuthúgn said: 'Yuplú had seen me and came to look for me, and he talked nicely to me. He shot animals for me, and so I pitied him, but you told me to kill him; so because I thought that he would kill me if he knew about it, I did it to him. But you are angry with me!' Then Kanyahé became silent." Kanyahé's guilt-feeling found expression in anger against the members of his own extended family, and they relieved theirs by protesting that they had been asked to commit murder. There are a number of instances of this kind, all given in considerable conversational detail, but there is one that is so striking for its barrenness of such detail that it is worth describing. The entire situation was characterized by such extreme behavior and the men were killed in such cold blood and with so little provocation that it cannot but be significant that both my informants overlooked the murders in the description of the feuds and mentioned them only in passing. It was only through prying that I was able to obtain the descriptions that follow.

When the offspring of Vomblé[17] raided the camp of Kumbló and killed a number of women and children they also captured some boys. Long after, when these boys had grown to manhood and had hunted and raided with the grandchildren of Vomblé, one of Vomblé's grandsons was killed by a member of Kumbló's group who made good his escape. "Then the dead man's widow said to Kuthúgn[18]: 'Kill Kuvén and Wanyekí.[19] Their nyungnyên[20] [relative] killed him. When they see this they may go away. Kill them.' The murderer had no relatives, but Kuvén and Wanyekí had

14 Kanyahé's offspring.

16 The dead men.

17 This Vomblé was one of the male ancestors of the victorious extended family in the feud described in Chapter V.

18 A grandson of Vomblé.

19 Two of the captives, now grown to manhood.

20 For the exact meaning of this term see p. 177, Appendix II.

wandered around with him; so she called them his *nyungnyên*. So Kuthúgn and his brother-in-law Kiyitá went hunting with Kuvén. They went a long way but saw no tapir. Nightfall. Kuthúgn came along behind Kuvén and hit him with an axe and he fell. Then Kuthúgn said to his brother-in-law, 'Hit him!' So Kiyitá hit him." Wanyekí was killed in the same manner. Two other relatives of the widow went hunting with Wanyekí; one went in front of him and the other came along behind. One of them seized the victim and sat down on him, calling to the other, " 'Come here!' And he hit Wanyekí with an axe and killed him. Then they returned to camp."

Later the death of Monyá, another of the captives, was ordered, but "Kuthúgn heard and said: 'Don't! I killed one; so let him [Monyá] alone. He's alone; so let him be!' So they let him alone. 'I did not see the one who killed her husband; so I became angry and killed a substitute.[21] So let the other one [Monyá] alone and live with him. Let him shoot animals for you. Go with him to the Brazilians who killed your *nyǫ*[22] and let him kill some of them out of revenge for her.' That is what he said." And Monyá lived with them at the post until he died of influenza.

None of the murderers of Kuvén and Wanyekí would perform the act alone but insisted on collaboration. This insistence that someone else complete a murder is quite common in Kaingáng killings. In some cultures such an unwillingness to bear the full responsibility is associated with fear of punishment, but in Kaingáng society, where the entire group is always held responsible the aversion to committing the deed alone implies a feeling of guilt. The case in question is particularly significant in view of Kuthúgn's anxious protection of Monyá.

It is not enough that the Kaingáng should feel guilty about the people they have killed, but they must feel guilt because their own relatives have been killed by others. They sometimes feel that their relatives have died because they were not there to protect them. Kuthúgn and Koví went hunting together and separated, and when Kuthúgn returned he found Koví dead, for while Kuthúgn was away Koví was overwhelmed by vendetta enemies and killed. "Kuthúgn saw the place where Koví was killed and waited there all night for the enemy. Next day he met one of his relatives and asked him, 'Well, what happened?' 'The enemy killed him.' Then Kuthúgn became angry because of Koví [and said]: 'Now! I said to him, "Stay here," but he went just as I did and the things killed him.' " What had actually happened was that Kuthúgn had told Koví to cut out a beehive and had gone on, leaving Koví alone. The sense of guilt that op-

---

[21] The wording of the original has been slightly altered here for the sake of clarity.

[22] Any woman very much older than a person. See p. 177, Appendix II. In this instance, however, he is referring to a particular woman who had been killed recently by the Brazilians.

presses the Kaingáng is sometimes, as in the quarrel of Kanyahé and his offspring, absorbed into the extended families and digested in undercurrents of resentment, but in other cases, such as that of Kuthúgn, it finds expression in outbursts of anger which are rooted in a sense of personal guilt.

IX

Folklore

SOME COLLECTIONS OF FOLKTALES are not so much the tales that the folk tell as they are the tales that the investigator wished to hear. If he was interested in stories of celestial phenomena, he collected stories about the sun, moon, and stars; if he wished to trace the distribution of mythological plots over the world, he tried to unearth plots he already knew; if the student's interest was primarily religious his collection of myths included principally ritualistic tales. But the literature of any people is made up of *all* their tales, and no one can foresee in what part of the literature of a folk their fundamental motivations lie hidden. If a foreign student were to study only our religious tales, overlooking completely our novels, our humorous magazines, and the jokes and doggerel that pass from mouth to mouth among us, he would receive a false impression of our literature. Primitive folk also have different kinds of literature, and ethnologists should set themselves always to collect every tale they tell, without discrimination as to content. The Kaingáng are a striking example of a people who reveal all of the inner workings of their culture in one type of tale, while another type supplies little such insight. In plot content the latter is of the type one usually finds in collections of "mythology": the events move on the supernatural level or take place between animals that behave like human beings, or between human beings and animals with anthropomorphic characteristics. But the psychic structure of the Kaingáng is expressed constantly and clearly in an entirely different order of tale. It is in the story of feuds and murder that the Kaingáng reveal the dominating drives in their life. The feud tales, however, are always close to earth; feud happenings take place in the human world, not in the supernatural; and the actors in them are human. The occasional references to supernatural events in these tales are purely incidental to the development of the murder plot—they are never the main theme.

These bloody stories are never quoted in an effort to validate or explain any form of behavior. They may have served as a kind of depository of gruesome knowledge from which an aspiring murderer could gain many useful hints. They are full of descriptions of treachery and in general provide a background of detailed information relative to the execution of mass and individual murder. These bits of information are not sanctions, for feud tales are never quoted in order to validate particular murders; if these murder stories are sanctions then Machiavelli's *Prince* is a sanction. Kaingáng feud stories are direct expressions of the fear–wish-to-kill–guilt obsession that drives them constantly to acts of violence and panic. Events that occur in these tales are never cited as examples of behavior in the light of which other similar types of behavior may be explained or justified. It is quite different in the case of the Kaingáng origin myths, however. The origin myths are referred to to explain food taboos and observances associated with body paint designs. But the body paint scheme is of small importance in Kaingáng culture, and the food taboos are not dynamic. Thus the origin myths give sanction to institutions that are of small importance to the Kaingáng. The most important function of these myths is seen in the game of *wainyêklâdn*, in which two men sit opposite each other and shout the myths at each other, syllable by syllable, very rapidly, while they swing their bodies back and forth to the rhythm of their shouting. One man shouts a syllable, and the second man repeats it; then the first man says the second syllable, and the second man repeats it. If the origin myth begins, "When Wanyekí heard that many people were coming . . .", the men (A and B) playing *wainyêklâdn* shout as follows:

A shouts	and then	B shouts
When		When
Wa		Wa
nye		nye
kí		kí
heard		heard,

And so on to the end, the syllables separated minutely in a way that is a joy to a linguist pursuing the elusive structure of the Kaingáng syllable. The game of *wainyêklâdn* is played by two friends and serves no purpose other than that of drawing two people together. There are no stakes, and no goal is set. No one is downed, and no one triumphs.

Ruth Benedict has shown[1] how a people may express the drives that are dynamic in their own culture through the medium of widespread mytho-

[1] *Zuni Mythology*, Introduction. Columbia University Contributions to Anthropology, v. 21.

logical plots which they borrow and rework and reset to their own ends. The Kaingáng, however, have shown a striking reluctance to use outside material for the expression of their cultural interests. Those very stories that are widely distributed in the Americas show, in their Kaingáng versions, an almost complete freedom from the gloomy and blood-curdling attitudes that characterize the tales which the Kaingáng have developed themselves and which have not been recorded for other tribes. But these gloom-free stories do not even express consistently the lighter side of the Kaingáng character—its love of laughter and sex-play, its fondness for physical relationships and love of children. This does not mean, of course, that there is nothing of Kaingáng culture in them. But one may search in vain through all these myths for a consistent expression of motives that are dynamic in the Kaingáng culture. On the other hand, even a person completely ignorant of the culture could win from the feud tales a clear idea of what was driving it over the precipice.

It is impossible to tell how many of the tales of murder are purely imaginative creations and how many reflect actual happenings, though there can be no doubt that many of them do this; for stories of massacres in which great-grandparents of my informants are known to have been actors are told in the same way as tales of events which took place hundreds of years ago. In telling these massacre tales no attempt is made to connect them with later events. They exist of themselves, and the Kaingáng never try to unite them in historic sequence. No nexus of events is attempted further back than the fifth generation. As far as that point everything is joined in an orderly succession of well-understood happenings. But beyond that memory does not go, and it is this break between the fifth and sixth generations and even to some extent within the fifth generation itself that marks the limit of history and the beginning of folklore. Some of these murder tales may be fantasies, but the events that occur in them have such peculiarly specific quality and give one such a feeling of their necessity and uniqueness in the particular situation that it is hard to resist the conclusion that many of them are historical.

In Kaingáng folklore there is little of that building up of tales from separate plot elements that is so common elsewhere in primitive literature. Every murder tale and almost all of the stories containing plots that are widely distributed are told as fixed units. The differences that occur are between the well-told and the badly-told tale, not between the tale that is constructed out of one set of motifs and that which is formed out of another.

The Kaingáng have a clear idea of a period long ago when a number of events happened: their ancestors came out of the sea and over the mountains to the west then, and it was at that time that the animals had their war and tricks were played on the tiger. If at times they place Vomblé or Kanggúin or Mumbégn[2] back in that era it is not because they feel that these men were active in the happenings of those times but because they all existed so very long ago. Actually there is nothing mythological in their conception of these three men who played such an active part in their history[3]—they are never thought of as having given the world its present shape, nor did they ever war with supernatural monsters. They are real men from whom people of flesh and blood have descended. The named but shadowy men of the origin myths, on the contrary, have no existence outside of the stories in which they move. Descent is never traced to them, and their memory has little effect on the lives of the present-day Kaingáng.

The Murder Tales

1. THE QUARREL OF KUIKÉGN'S OFFSPRING

Kuikégn's children, Nduichó and Chukembégn, became angry with each other. Nduichó knocked his brother Chukembégn unconscious with his club. Then Nduichó said: "Am I useful *ndoyá*'s talking?[4] Now feel my weak arm!" Then Chukembégn fell. Probably Nduichó had seen the supernatural. Chukembégn recovered. He lay sick for a long time and at last healed completely. Then he came to Nduichó, and they fought. He knocked Nduichó unconscious. Chukembégn said: "I repeat what you said: 'Am I useful *ndoyá*'s talking? Let a strong man feel my weak arm!'" Then Kuikégn sat by his son, but Nduichó did not recover. Then he [Kuikégn] became angry. He took the double-barbed arrows of his dead ceremonial father,[5] rubbed them with something, and went in pursuit.

Now Payé was Kuikégn's affinal relative. Chukembégn had gone off with him [Payé], and Kuikégn went in pursuit. Probably the affinal relatives had been angry with Chukembégn. Kuikégn went after them to kill them. "I am angry because my child is dead," said he. He went to kill Chukembégn because he had killed his son. "My child died, and am I going to make my child suffer?" He was about to kill his own child. "I am going to kill Payé."[6]

It was night, and they were burning pine branches as they went along.

[2] These are the three ancestors of the extended family with which I lived.

[3] See p. 51, Chapter V.

[4] He is announcing his connection with the spirit of the *ndoyá* tree. The spirit of a thing is called its "talking." Spirits may be either benign or malevolent. When they are not malevolent (*kûlâk tµ*, not no good) they are benign or, as I have translated it, "useful." See p. 78, Chapter VI.

[5] His ceremonial father had died long before this story begins. Men sometimes carry the arrows of their dead relatives as mementoes.

[6] He decides to kill Payé, his relative by marriage, rather than his son.

Payé was about to walk around with his little daughter Ukó when Kuikégn shot him in the arm with his double-barbed arrow. He threw the child down and ran out into the night ducking, but Kuikégn shot him in the ribs and the arrow ascended into the neck region. Kuikégn took the child and returned to camp.

Payé's wife was Yokó. Kuikégn said, "Let Yokó take her child which they threw away and which I am carrying and pour some water into its mouth." So Yokó took her and went to look for Payé and Chukembégn. She did not see him and she came back enraged at Kuikégn. He said nothing. [Then Kuikégn said,] "Yokó is not here. She is looking for her husband all over. *nyungnyélé* is dead, so while her husband was unconscious he [the husband] was killed." Next day she saw him [her husband]. He was long dead, and his blood came out of his mouth. She brought him back. She became angry with her *yúgn*, Kuikégn. He said nothing. At last Payé and Nduichó came to.[7]

Nandjaví had cut Payé open to take out the arrow. He thrust in his hand. The arrow had come up along the heart. He lifted up his feet as he lay so the blood came out. He took out the clotted blood from the heart with his hand, and he recovered. They never died then, but nowadays they die.

The picture of disruption is frequently intensified in Kaingáng folklore through making the relationships within which the conflicts and murders take place much closer than they have been in reality. In the story that has just been told the initial quarrel is between blood brothers. It ends in the father's murdering his daughter's husband and the daughter's turning against her own father.

In the following tale the motive behind the initial violence is just as obscure as in the story of Kuikégn's offspring.

2. THECHÁ OF THE BURNING FIRE
Dramatis Personae

Thechá's Group	Kuichó's Group
Kundágn	
Thulí, *relative by marriage of Kundágn*	Ukó, *mother of Kuichó*
Kanyahé, *relative by marriage of Kundágn*	Mbliktó, *son of Kuichó*
Piké	Padnmbá
Thekplégn, *son of Thechá*	Laktógn
Tondúin	Koyivádn
	Kapíli

[7] In the first paragraph of this story the informant described Nduichó as dead, but here he has come to life. This is an inconsistency that may be understood better from the last sentence of this story.

Kuichó had seen *Véin*. Now when Thechá of the Burning Fire was old, Kuichó threw him to *Véin*,[8] and the latter ate him and he lay dying. Now when he lay dying he said to his children: "When I am dead kill Ukó's children. I took care of them, but they never give me anything of what they kill; and now that I am dying they will be alive." So Thechá's children and Kundágn and his in-law Thulí all went to Kuichó and his children.

The ones[9] who were living far away invited them to a festa. When they arrived Kuichó was walking around boasting to his son Mbliktó: "*Ko tei ko tei he pi*,[10] I sent Véin up my old father's rectum!"[11] Piké[12] was watching, and when he heard this he said to himself: "If it hadn't been for Thekplégn's father, Kuichó would not be here. He has killed old *yûgn!*" Then he went away weeping.

Piké told the children of Thechá, and Piké helped them because Kuichó had killed the man whom Piké called *yûgn*.

Now Kundágn and his in-law Kanyahé were on their way to kill them[13] when Kuichó's offspring went looking for honey. Kuichó was sitting beside the trail leading through the savannah when he saw Kundágn and Kanyahé coming along in the distance. He sat there watching them come along and then went back. When he reached his children he said to them, "Kundágn and Kanyahé arrived here and went away!" When they heard this they said, "They are coming to kill us!" So they constructed a platform above themselves within their house and remained beneath it.

Next day Kundágn came into their house and struck Padnmbá on the back through the floor, and he fell out in the darkness and went away on all fours. Then Kundágn shouted after him, "You are always becoming a man for men;[14] so I am going to kill you! You always set women on the tops of their heads[15] and become a man!" That is what he said to him. Then he killed Laktógn and went away. After he had killed him he said: "The deuce! I have killed Laktógn who never did the same[16] as the man,[17] and I am angry."

[8] A supernatural monster. See Chapter VI, p. 71.

[9] Kuichó's group.

[10] His nêklê. See Chapter VIII, p. 115.

[11] Like Yóin, Véin devours people's hearts. He thrusts his hand up the rectum and cuts out the heart. See Chapter VI, p. 70.

[12] This member of Thechá's group had been living with Kuichó.

[13] Kuichó's children.

[14] "You are always dangerous to us."

[15] Copulate from behind, the woman on all fours, her head toward the ground; hence, on her head.

[16] Was never *waikayú*.

[17] Padnmbá.

Then he went away. He reached camp. He kept worrying about it until he at last went to them and killed Koyivádn and Kapíli.

While Kuichó was lying awake Kundágn and his affinal relative, Kanyahé, went to watch them, [and as they crept along] their lance-heads struck together. [When Kuichó heard it he said:] "Death! If the folks[18] could kill me their hearts would come out!"[19] It was night, and Kuichó said to his offspring: "I heard the noise the folks made! They are near me!" So they all went out into the darkness.

Now Kundágn's old mother was lying on her back, with her knees drawn up at the entrance to a house near the fire; and when Kundágn dashed into the house he struck her. She became frightened and said: *"E! Kundágn, it is I!"* Then he said: "Mother, are the folks here?" "Yes," said she, for she had been asleep and had not noticed them go. Then Kundágn walked around there. Then they threw on the fire bundles of bamboo that the others had been drying for arrows. By its light Kundágn saw Kapíli standing in the doorway waving his club and called to his in-law Kanyahé, "In-law, the Kapíli we have been looking for is here!" Then he[20] leaped at him[21] and struck him and he[21] fell, and he struck him again. Then he[20] walked about the house singing. Koyivádn was kneeling against the wall of the house waving his club, and Kundágn called out, "In-law, the Koyi-vádn we came in here looking for is there!" Then he[20] leaped forward and was going to strike Koyivádn, but Koyivádn also tried to hit him and waved his club before him. Then he [Koyivádn] struck Kundágn with his club. He tried to strike Kundágn on the head, but he turned his head aside and the blow landed on Kundágn's neck. He staggered and fell on one knee. Koyivádn was going to hit him again. Kundágn's eyes were glazed, and he waved his hands in front of himself; and Koyivádn struck him repeatedly on the hands until he came to and stood up. Then Kundágn struck Koyivádn's club and knocked it out of his hands and struck him on the head. He struck him again and walked about singing. Then he said, "In-law, let's go!" Now Koyivádn's relatives were waiting for Kundágn at the entrance with drawn bows, and when he dashed out they shot at him, but he ducked and dashed away.

Next day he went on toward the fence.[22] He reached it, but his people had gone away during his absence. He remained there with his in-law Kanyahé and with Tondúin. Koyivádn and his people pursued him, and

[18] The term *nyêngôi* indicates relationship.
[19] They would be delighted.
[20] Kundágn.
[21] Kapíli.
[22] Anciently, the Kaingáng say, they lived in fenced communities.

when they reached the fence they shot at him. Kundágn's in-law would step outside to shoot at them, and Kundágn would say: "Stop! I can't move my hands, and if they kill you they'll kill me too!" But he paid no attention and kept on going outside to shoot until he himself was shot. Then Kundágn said to him: "The deuce! I said to him: 'Stop! If they shoot you they'll kill me with you!' But that one paid no attention and kept on going outside to them until now he is shot!" Then the others burnt the house down. They stayed inside until it was being consumed, and at last Kundágn said to his affinal relative, "Affinal relative, let's go out!" At last they went out and were killed.

In the meanwhile the house they had burnt in order to kill Tondúin fell on him, and he lay there silent, half dead. When he saw them go he went away. His back was all roasted.

Kundágn's hands had been beaten and crushed by Koyivádn. They were swollen, and he walked around with his arrow lying useless in the bow. Therefore he could not avenge himself.

A characteristic of this type of tale is its amoral, reportorial character: individuals commit murder, revenge is wreaked, and finally the avengers themselves are killed. The facts are told in perfect plot sequence without comment and without taking sides. An individual searching them for clues to proper behavior in given situations would almost always be confused, for although it is true in Kaingáng folklore that whenever a son kills his father or brother he too is killed, all murders whatsoever are avenged in folklore. In Kaingáng folklore suggestions regarding murders one must not commit are rare. Indeed, the stories describe murders that I have not been able to duplicate in the historical content of Kaingáng society. The actual Kaingáng at least draw the line at parents and full siblings, but the Kaingáng of folklore exploit these very relationships in murderous behavior. The only function I am able to see in the folk-tale murder of fathers and siblings is either the purely literary one of intensifying the affect or the more sinister one of giving expression to a deep-rooted desire to annihilate the closest relatives.

Like so many Kaingáng stories the tale of Thechá of the Burning Fire begins with an unexplained quarrel. "They were angry and they fought," or "they wanted to kill them and they invited them to a festa," is a characteristic opening. Whence springs this impulse to destruction? Why is everybody angry? The Kaingáng themselves do not search for reasons, for murder and rage are as much part of their lives as the tapirs they kill and the houses they build.

The second story reproduces some of the scenes of the ancient life of the

Kaingáng: their savannah dwelling-place and their large beehive-shaped houses with doorways. The device of building a false floor is known to me only in this context. The beehive-shaped house which the Kaingáng once built for me to illustrate their old life had no floor.

The repeated panicstricken flights of Kuichó's offspring in the face of two or three lone warriors is easily understood in terms of the character-istic Kaingáng flight in the face of an aggressive act. When the Kaingáng are attacked they run unless they are driven into a corner where they have to fight.

Kundágn's anger after he had dispatched Laktógn was not based on any feeling he had for him. Kundágn was angry because he was fright-ened. He had let someone escape who would certainly some day come to avenge the death of his relative, "So he kept worrying about it until he went and killed Koyivádn and Kapíli."

The first thing that Kundágn did when he returned to continue the annihilation of Thechá's murderers was to strike his own mother. This was an accident due to the darkness, and the character of the accident is significant for the understanding of the relationship between the two groups. Kundágn's mother was living with Kuichó's group, a sign that there was no profound break in social relationships between the two groups of people.

There are pointers in this story for future homicides. A good way to light up a house is to throw into the fire the dry bamboo arrow-shafts that are always stuck in the roof of every house. The thing to do during an attack is for a man to wait outside his own house while murderers are within and to shoot them when they come out; it is much safer than en-gaging in the hand-to-hand struggle that becomes inevitable in the interior. Kaingáng myth is indeed the repository of tribal lore—regarding how to slaughter kinsmen.

Kundágn's reaction to the wounding of his in-law was not sorrow but anger because his in-law's zeal had brought about his injury and left Kundágn crippled, with only one protector instead of two.

The story that follows treats of actual events that took place some five or six generations back. It is told precisely like a folktale, and though its principal character, Yokégn, is an historical figure well known to the present-day Kaingáng, the events in which he took part are not joined historically to preceding or succeeding events.

3. Yokégn Kills Pandjumbúgn and the Latter's Son-in-Law, Kuikégn

Dramatis Personae

Yokégn and	*Kuikégn and*
His *klą*	His *klą*
Ketédn, *son-in-law of Yokégn*	Kaklíli ⎱ *wives of Kuikégn; daughters of*
Waichúgn, *Ketédn's wife*	Anggló ⎰ *Pandjumbúgn*
Waimogué, *Ketédn's wife*	
Thanggié, *Yokégn's wife*	Yukúin, *son of Kuikégn*
and Waichúgn's mother	Yuplú, *son of Kuikégn*
Tombá, *Yokégn's wife*	
Thulí ⎫	
Thegnndádn ⎪	
Chuktídn ⎬ *affinal relatives of Ketédn*	
Tavádn ⎪	
Waivukté ⎪	
Yunggukthí ⎭	

Others

Pandjumbúgn
Kavá
Padnmbá
Padnmbá's wife
Chantágn, *Pandjumbúgn's wife*
Koikambégn, *Chantágn's infant son*

Ketédn went hunting and lost the trail. He slept. He wandered around lost. They went to look for him but did not find him. Ketédn's wives were Waichúgn and Waimogué. His wives thought he had died and went away in their widow's isolation. Then they cut their hair. Then Pandjumbúgn lived with Waichúgn and Waimogué.

Ketédn wandered around lost until he reached a different camp.

Ketédn fought with the Brazilians alone and killed four while he was lost. They were clearing a field. He took four axes. On his way back he met Kavá, who was with his offspring. Kavá went around with Padnmbá. When Kavá asked Ketédn for an axe he gave him one.

After a while Kavá became angry with him. Probably Ketédn copulated with Kavá's wife. It [the quarrel] happened at a festa. Ketédn went away taking Kavá's axe because the latter had become angry with him. Then Padnmbá said to his [own] wife, "Go after your relative and let him give you one of his axes." So she went. She shouted after him, "Wait for me!" He heard her cry and waited for her. When she caught up to him she said, "*Nyungnyên,*[23] I have come after you for one of your axes." He rested with her. Then they mourned because he was going alone. She pitied him,

---

[23] Relative. See kinship terms, Appendix II.

and said, "A tiger may kill you. When you go, and a tiger does not kill you, keep a look-out for me." She gave him her robe which she had brought along. It was new. Then he gave her an axe and she said, "*Nyungnyên,* take my robe and lie on it." He gave her an axe and went.

When he reached his relatives' camp his wives were living with Pandjumbúgn. Then Ketédn lived with them. He gave an axe to his wife's father, Yokégn. He said to his mother-in-law, "Thangglé, my *mbë,* get the bamboo I cut to make arrows with." She was Waichúgn's mother. He had two bamboo sticks.

He went to Yokégn with an axe, and Yokégn stood up and came to meet him, saying: "*Ai!* What is this? Gone for a long time and comes back carrying something? You threw away my children, and now you come back giving me something!" He was saying that he was going to be given something. "Ketédn, make beer for me with this axe!" He gave him all his axes. He kept his relative's robe and his own knife.

After a while Pandjumbúgn became angry because Ketédn lived with his wives. Pandjumbúgn left the two women when Ketédn arrived. Pandjumbúgn had no wives. Several days after Ketédn arrived Pandjumbúgn made a trough for Yokégn and made beer in it. Ketédn's in-laws, Thulí, Thegnndádn, Chuktídn, Tavádn, Waivukté, and Yunggukthí went on a somewhat long hunting trip, sleeping away from camp. Now Pandjumbúgn intended to kill them single-handed. He did not go with them. They shot tapirs and pigs and came back carrying the tapirs on large carrying-frames. When they arrived in the dance place they threw them down, and Thulí said to Pandjumbúgn, "Untie my frame." Then they held a festa. In the meanwhile he untied the frames. They took off the meat and gave it to the people. Pandjumbúgn gave meat to Thulí, Thegnndádn, and the others.

Yunggukthí came to the beer and drank some from a wax-lined basket. Waichúgn came behind him and took the basket from his hand. She took some beer, drank, and joked with him. When Pandjumbúgn saw this he came over and took the basket from her hand. Then Pandjumbúgn became angry with Ketédn and Yunggukthí and fought with them. He also became angry with Thulí, Thegnndádn, Tavádn, and Chuktídn. Yokégn was protecting them with his club so that Pandjumbúgn was unable to strike anyone. Then Yokégn became angry, and Pandjumbúgn stopped. Yokégn was going to talk to them. Pandjumbúgn looked at Yokégn and said: "I'll beat you! When men are angry with me I tear the clubs from their hands and beat them. I'll beat you." When Yokégn heard this he became angry and hit Pandjumbúgn and said, "*Now* beat me!" Pandjumbúgn fell. They danced around him, and when he did not sit up they hit him again and he died. Pandjumbúgn was the son of Nandjaví. When

they saw [that he had died] they stopped and Yokégn said to his offspring: "You don't have to be afraid of me, folks. Set the poor fellow out
in the burning-place." So they took him up and set him in the dance
ground, and he died there. They burnt him there. They stopped drinking
their beer.

Yokégn said to his offspring, "Pour out the poor fellow's beer for me."
He was going to dance. "I wonder whether he'll make some more for me."
He was saying that since he had been killed he would not make beer for
him [Yokégn] again. They poured out the beer for Yokégn alone. The
others did not dance. His offspring sat near him. Yokégn drank it all up
alone because Pandjumbúgn would never make beer for him again.

One day before Pandjumbúgn was killed Waimogué went for wood.
Pandjumbúgn came to her on his way hunting. When she saw him she
went away, and Pandjumbúgn became angry, [saying] "So that's the way
you treat me, eh?" But she went. Probably she told Ketédn. He [Pandjum-
búgn] was telling her that he was going to kill her husband and live with
her. She referred to what Pandjumbúgn had said to her.

Later Yokégn saw Pandjumbúgn's son-in-law Kuikégn. Kuikégn had
married Pandjumbúgn's daughters Kaklíli and Angglό. Yokégn went
along the old trail with his offspring, and Kuikégn was coming along in
the other direction. Yokégn went along the trail early in the morning, and
Kuikégn came to meet him. While they were resting there together Kuikégn's people came along and also Yokégn's offspring. Then Yokégn told
Kuikégn of how he almost died of hunger.[24] "I was hungry and went
hunting. I went on and was so nearly dead from hunger that I was retch-
ing. When I reached Thangglé [his wife] I said to her, 'Do not do anything for me.'[25] So she made palm-pith cakes and gave me fern shoots and
I ate them and vomited. I was sick. Then Tombá [another wife] cooked
some of the pine nuts she had kept in her odds-and-ends basket for her pet
parrot, and I drank the liquor and became well. If it hadn't been for that
I should have died. If I had died of hunger the others would have ridiculed me.

"The next day there was a big river. I swam it and on the other side
there was some fern [which I ate]. As I went further I saw some young
palms and I did the same thing.[26] As I was coming along I saw some
howler monkeys, and I put aside my wooden arrows and took my iron
ones. I shot a male. In the meanwhile it had started to pour; so I ran until
I reached the edge of the river, and it had risen a great deal. Then I stood

[24] I have introduced a long section from another version of the same story in order to give
a more complete view of the character of the detail that is incorporated into these stories
[25] This may mean "I brought nothing home; so there is nothing to do."
[26] Ate the palm shoots.

on the edge shouting, 'Throw me to the other side!' Then I tied up the monkeys and swam the river. Thangglé singed them and distributed the flesh. They ate it." [The informant adds: "When Pandjumbúgn heard his cry he cut a length of bamboo, and when Yokégn came along swimming he extended the bamboo toward him and dragged him out." The informant also adds the following: "Yokégn shot a deer and she [his wife] roasted it. Then she gave Pandjumbúgn a leg and put another leg and part of the back in a basket and hung it up. Then Pandjumbúgn's wife Chantágn took her son and stood on one leg so that she could hold the other in front of her vagina. She was standing without a robe, for she had put it over her husband with whom she had been lying; so she was standing without anything [on]. Now Thangglé was lying there looking at her [and said under her breath], 'What fool is eating the piece I set aside for them [my children] after having divided it up among the others?' Thangglé was talking because Chantágn had stolen her meat. Thus she would tear off a strip of meat and put it in her child's mouth. That is all. Yokégn shot a deer. When Pandjumbúgn was sick Yokégn treated him, and when he recovered he killed him."]

"In the meanwhile the river rose.[27] A line of bamboo had been stretched across, and that is why Pandjumbúgn's wife Chantágn's son Koikambégn, whom she was carrying, was almost killed there. The others would float holding on to the bamboo and letting their bodies stretch out downstream, but she floated upstream and was swung under it [the bamboo]. Therefore her husband said to Yokégn, "The one whose hair is gray at the temples is drowning!" So when she came to the surface Yokégn seized her. He was swimming toward her, and when he came alongside her she said, "My *kóklá*,[28] I am carrying him [her son]." "Well, then, hold on to him well. I'm going to carry you along." So he carried her and swam along until he reached the shore. [When they reached land] her child's belly was distended with the water it had swallowed. So he turned it upside down and shook it until the water poured out of its mouth and it came to.

So he went on telling these things to Kuikégn until the latter said, "Where is Pandjumbúgn?" He hadn't told him anything about Pandjumbúgn; so he asked about him.[29] Yokégn laughed[30] because he remembered that he had killed Pandjumbúgn. He asked again for Pandjumbúgn, and Yokégn said, "Yukúin's father,[31] Pandjumbúgn wandered around

[27] The informant has put himself in the place of Yokégn and is now telling the story as if he were Yokégn.

[28] Ceremonial father. Often used merely as a courtesy term.

[29] End of insert.

[30] He laughs to reassure himself. The Kaingáng laugh in difficult situations in an effort to regain their emotional balance.

[31] Addressing Kuikégn as "Father of So-and-so."

over there. When Ketédn was lost we thought he had died; so we ignored him. In the meanwhile Pandjumbúgn's relatives were killed by another group of his own people. They tried to kill him at night. He ran out at night, and they burnt torches in pursuit of him. He had gone without lance or bow. He became thin." Then he saw Yokégn, and Yokégn fed him.[32] Yokégn had killed an anteater for him, and he ate it. It was fat. Then he recovered. When he became well he lived with Ketédn's wives. "Pandjumbúgn was lost and arrived [in our camp]. I fed him, and he became well. He went around with me, and when Ketédn was lost he lived with his wives. Then Ketédn came back and lived with the women. When Pandjumbúgn saw this he wanted to kill me. When I saw this I became afraid, and I killed him. Now you have heard all about it." He stopped talking after a while. They camped there. At sunset Kuikégn mourned: "Now in vain have my spouse and I been bearing fine meat looking for the poor thing who we thought was still alive!" After a while he stopped. He became angry. At night he probably said to his wife, "I'm going to kill them at night." At night they slept, but Yokégn's wife lay awake and watched. Kuikégn sat up and took his lance, and Kuikégn's wife Kaklíli seized his lance. Yokégn's wife woke him and said, "My ḳôḳlá almost killed you." Yokégn got up and watched all night.

Kuikégn's son Yuplú was knocking down a tree for troughs. Yokégn said, "What fell?" Kuikégn answered, "Yuplú is knocking down trees for troughs." Before he made the troughs he said to Yokégn's offspring, "Make troughs for me, folks; I'm going to make beer in them for you." So Chuktídn, Thegnndádn, Thulí, Tavádn, and Ketédn went. Yuplú's trough was big. First one and then another helped and by midday it was finished. They cleared a space and made a place for it. Yuplú said, "Go out and get honey for me, folks." Tavádn, Chuktídn, Thulí, Thegnndádn, and Ketédn went; but Yokégn did not go. They brought back honey and mixed it in the troughs. The following day they went for more. Four days later they drank it.

Ketédn came with beer, and so did Yunggukthí. The others were dancing. As Ketédn came to drink beer Kuikégn was going to stab him, when Kuikégn's wife seized the lance. She did this because she was afraid that if he killed anyone they would kill him. Then Kaklíli followed Ketédn and said, "Kuikégn almost killed you." At last the beer became exhausted. It was not the baby-blackening. Kuikégn wanted to kill Ketédn. When there was no more beer they stopped [dancing].

Early next morning they all went away. They slept. Early next day they heard Yuplú knock down a tree for beer. "Who knocked down a tree?" Kuikégn replied, "Yuplú knocked down a tree to make a trough." Then

[32] The informant is no longer identifying himself with Yokégn.

Yuplú called them to help again. They finished making it and placed it in a cleared space. They carried it—they carry[33] troughs. Then he sent them for honey and they went out to look for it. Tavádn, Chuktídn, Thegnndádn, and Thulí were sent. They followed Ketédn. They saw a young coconut tree and sucked it.[34] Later Yokégn followed them and caught up with them while they were eating.

Kuikégn was going to shoot them. He wanted to shoot them, but his wife prevented him. He became angry with her and beat her with his bow, saying, "Seeing that they want to kill me I was going to kill some of them, but since you like being mounted by them you are trying to defend them!" Then he went around them [where they were camped] and went away. He had gone after them and was about to shoot them, but his wife prevented him. Kuikégn took her robe and went away.

The others went on also. They saw him in the distance with his naked wife, and they followed him, saying, "There's another enemy!" They were worried by him; so they called him "enemy." When they caught up to him they said,[35] "Ai, the old fellow frightened me!" Then Kuikégn went with them.

They saw some howler monkeys on the pines and shot them. When Kuikégn heard this he was going over, but his wife restrained him; so he took his bow and went away. He beat her. Then he pierced a beehive, took it out, and came back. Kuikégn arrived in camp before them.

Yuplú came to the beer three days later. He called Thegnndádn, "Thegnndádn, come make a festa!" He went and began. Then they all came.

In the afternoon Yuplú stopped and went to the house. Yukúin and Kuikégn also went. They were about to become angry. Yokégn and his offspring continued. Then Kaklíli came to Thegnndádn and said: "Stop drinking the beer I made for my nyungnyên [Yukúin]. It will become exhausted." Yukúin had sent her to tell him this. She gave them drink and then went back. They did not stop but drank it all up. Then, probably, Yuplú said to her: "Go over there and talk about it. Strike the one who talks back, and I'll come over." He probably said this. So she went to them and said to Thegnndádn, "Stop drinking the beer; it will become exhausted." "I will not! I made it! Beer is made so that it may be drunk up!" When she heard this she struck him on the cheek. Thegnndádn cried, "Hai!" and said, "If men want to kill me let them come over and exchange

---

[33] This remark was for my benefit. I had only seen the Kaingáng push troughs along the ground.

[34] They chopped it down and pounded out the fibrous interior of the trunk, which yields a cool and refreshing juice when sucked.

[35] Not within Kuikégn's hearing.

blows with me!" Then Yuplú came over behind her. Thegnndádn did not see him come because he was looking at the woman. Yuplú was about to strike him when Thegnndádn raised his lance. The blade fell off from the shock and hit Thegnndádn on the head and he fell. Kuikégn came behind Yuplú with his bow. He aimed an arrow, but his wife seized his bow and took it out of his hands. She also took Yukúin's. Waivukté and Yunggukthí seized Yukúin. They began to fight with Yuplú. Kuikégn took his bow and lance. He shouted to his wife: "Kaklíli, give me something! I'm going to pay back with it!" Yokégn protected him.[36] Yokégn took Kuikégn's bow and arrows from him, and Yokégn's offspring seized Kuikégn; but Kuikégn continued his shouting. Kaklíli took the blade from the lance and gave Kuikégn the handle. He hit Yokégn in the thigh and cut his leg with the corner of the handle. Yokégn fell on one knee and sent his wife for embira to bind up his leg. She bound it around over the wound. Yunggukthí, Tavádn, and Waivukté captured Yukúin. Yunggukthí said to Waivukté: "Hold on to him! I'm going to take a look at Thegnndádn." He went to Thegnndádn, seized his hair, and raised his head. But Thegnndádn was unconscious. Then Yunggukthí said: *"Ai! I'm going to kill him! He killed yúgn."* Thegnndádn was a child of Yunggukthí's father's [Yokégn's] relative. Then Kuikégn came over to Yunggukthí, still shouting, "Kaklíli, give me something to pay back with!" Yunggukthí hit Kuikégn on the head with his club. Thulí, Tavádn, Ketédn, and Chuktídn were fighting with Yuplú a little way off and they captured him. When Yunggukthí hit Kuikégn the former went to Yuplú. They were going to kill him.

Yokégn stood up and leaned on his lance. He wanted to go to Yuplú but could not. He called his offspring: "Let Yuplú alone, folks! He was *waikayú* only through his father's instructions!" So they let him alone when they heard this. Yuplú's lance shaft was all broken, and he threw it away. He grasped a trough gouge[37] that was lying in the place where he had been making a trough and took the handle and fought with them until it broke and he had only a little piece left. Nevertheless he continued to protect himself with it. When they heard their *yúgn* [Yokégn] they let Yuplú alone and came back with Yuplú. This is the Yuplú that [later] fought with Yokégn against Wanenggló. Yokégn said to Yuplú: "Yuplú, stop! I killed your father. If you become angry again I'll kill you! You were *waikayú* through your father's instructions. Nevertheless the one I killed is there! Stop! Fix him up and lay him out. I defended him but when he struck me I killed him. Stretch him out in the burning-place."

[36] The conciliatory attitude of Yokégn throughout all this is striking.

[37] A trough gouge is a small, sharp piece of metal with a slender handle about five feet long.

Thegnndádn recovered after a while, and Yuplú went around with them.

When Vomblé[38] was a young man he saw Kuikégn. Yokégn told this to Vomblé.

Then they burnt Kuikégn, and Yokégn said to Kuikégn's children, "Put the poor fellow in a clear space." He said to Kuikégn's children, "Don't be afraid of me. Put him in a clear space."

Then Yuplú went around with them. Yukúin had stopped when he was seized.

Later Wanenggló and his offspring saw them.

The general character of this tale, which is historical, is the same as that of the two preceding folklore examples; the theme, murder and revenge, is the same in all three. The third differs from the others principally in the amount of detail included by one informant.

The impulses that drive all these stories toward their bloody and disruptive ends are the emotional twins, anger and fear. In the third we learn that Kavá became angry with Ketédn because *"probably* Ketédn lay with Kavá's wife." This is a stock explanation, on a par with our own reasoning about stomach ache—"Probably he ate something." The real reason for the final break between Kavá and Ketédn was that Kavá's camp was a "different" camp and Ketédn was an outsider. Although Pandjumbúgn was inflamed because he had been deprived of his two wives by the return of their supposedly dead husband, it is also clear from the story that he was also an outsider in Yokégn's family. There is no safe haven for anyone in Kaingáng society outside the limits of his own extended family. The two basic groups in the drama are the offspring of Yokégn and those of Kuikégn. Ketédn got into trouble among the offspring of Kuikégn, and Pandjumbúgn met his doom among Yokégn's. Pandjumbúgn's fate is all the more arresting in view of the bond that existed between him and Yokégn. Yokégn had rescued Pandjumbúgn from starvation and then saved his child from drowning. When Pandjumbúgn, urged by impulses that he could no longer resist, tried single-handed to annihilate Yokégn and his entire family, Yokégn again stepped in to rescue this obsessed man from death. Yet Pandjumbúgn did not want the safety the pacific Yokégn offered him, and he was killed by the hand of his benefactor.

This story contains a number of the elements of demand and acquiescence that are so crucial in Kaingáng society. In spite of his anger Ketédn gave an axe to Padnmbá's wife when she asked him for it; Yokégn sprang into the swollen river to rescue Pandjumbúgn's wife and child when he

[38] The original male ancestor of one of the extended families. See Chapter VI, p. 51.

was asked, and Yokégn and his offspring attended the festa given to Kuikégn and his sons even though they knew that it was part of a plan to slaughter them. Another aspect of this state of mind is Thangglé's silent consent to Chantágn's theft of her meat. All she dared do was lie mumbling to herself and to call Chantágn a fool under her breath.

When the lost Ketédn at last wandered back to his father-in-law's camp he was greeted not by solicitous inquiries after his health or by curiosity about his adventures but by "You threw away my children!" Neither the dead nor the recently returned from the dead are beyond the reproach of desertion.

The constructive aspect of *waikayú* is seen in Yokégn's fear of starving because of the ridicule it would bring on him: he had boasted much but might at last die by starvation, a ridiculous death indeed for one who thought so much of himself! He must, therefore, make a great effort to save himself and to justify his great self-esteem. The disruptive aspect of *waikayú* appears in Yuplú's attack on Yokégn and his offspring. "You were *waikayú* because of your father's instruction," cries Yokégn. If we examine the behavior of the principal actors in this drama we can perceive two more characteristics of the *waikayú* individual: he perseveres in the face of great odds, and he continues in spite of the pacific demonstrations of other people. Pandjumbúgn, Kuikégn, and Yuplú, the most disruptive individuals, decidedly *overestimated* their own abilities. In Kuikégn we can see again the operation of the compulsive guilt-projection cycle: because he wished to kill Yokégn he believed that Yokégn desired to kill him. It was partly through the wakefulness of Yokégn's wife that he was not killed the first night he camped with Kuikégn. Sleeplessness is a great virtue among the Kaingáng.

Kaklíli, the only feminine figure of any importance in the story, is a confused and even pitiable person. All she receives for her efforts to keep her husband from committing murder is repeated beatings, and in spite of her eagerness to prevent trouble she is the one who eventually precipitates it and finally causes her husband's death by giving him a weapon to fight with. Had he been weaponless they might have seized him and dissuaded him as they did his two sons. Throughout all the feud stories, historical or fanciful, one cannot escape the conclusion that the Kaingáng women were driven helplessly on by the obsessive resentment-anger-guilt-fear behavior of their men.

The literary style of this story is excellent. In its apparently un-self-conscious way it has plot, heroes, and swift and exciting action. This is characteristic of most of the Kaingáng murder stories. In some primitive cultures the whole literary interest is apt to center around the personality of the story teller, for he combines the loose literary content of his culture into ever new patterns as he uses old material in any variety of combinations to suit his fancy. But among the Kaingáng every murder story is a complete unit that must not be tampered with. To put part of one tale into another would be like putting a chapter of *Alice in Wonderland* into *Pilgrim's Progress*.

Stories like the third above, even when they are much longer,[39] give the impression of being completely unplanned, but nevertheless there must be among the Kaingáng a definite feeling for drama that centers around some succession of events with an intelligible beginning and an esthetically satisfying end. It is this feeling that determines the selection of incidents in them.

The general type of motivation and incident—anger, revenge, the taking of other men's wives, festa murder—appear in all of the murder tales. But the particular context in which they come into play is different in each. Every tale is oriented about a different plot, and incidents other than those mentioned are various. The great value of the murder tales lies in the innumerable revealing insights they give into the operation of Kaingáng culture. For the Kaingáng themselves it is somewhat different. They derive obvious pleasure from the incidents of violence, enjoying the details of every blow and drop of blood. But they too like to follow out the varied plots, without which the stories would be monotonous. Unlike the ethnologist, they are little interested in the discovery of motivations and causes. The mere succession of incidents is enough for them, and they are swept along by the excitement of the events and eager anticipation of what is to come next.

Tales of Animals and Supernatural Beings

For the first tale of this type I have purposely chosen an extreme example—a story which, more than any other of its sort seems to reflect a little of the mood of the murder tales. But even in this legend of the war of the animals it will be seen that in spite of the fact that it opens with a festa which develops into a slaughter, the general tone is quite different from that of the murder story, and there is no elaboration of the various details of the Kaingáng psychic structure with which we are familiar. Thus, although at first blush my selection of this tale would seem to impair my general thesis of the lack of relationship of the animal and supernatural tales to the intimacies of Kaingáng life, actually it does not.

[39] I have a tale five times as long as that of Yokégn and Kuikégn which took days in the telling but which, in each version I received, begins with the same incident and marches steadfastly through the same plot and incidents.

4. The War of the Animals

The tiger was sitting next to the deer at the animals' festa. The ounce was sitting next to the tapir, the great hawk next to the porcupine, and the *hovo*[40] next to the armadillo.

Now when the deer began to sing Tiger said to him, "Look here, you're singing about me!" But the deer said: "I'm singing this way: 'Deer, your anus.' That's what I was singing." Then Tiger said to him: "You sang about me, and you sang: 'Tiger, *djô ve vê*,[41] Tiger, *djô ko tǫ wandô'*[41]— that's what you sang. Now then, [sing]: 'Deer, your anus. The place of defecating is the base of a tree. *Chǫ kla pi lô.'*"[41] That is what Tiger said to Deer.

Then as Deer danced around, Tiger seized him. At the same time Ounce seized Tapir and dragged him off, and as they struggled Tapir threw Ounce off and ran away. In the meanwhile Deer was lying in his camp site. Great Hawk seized Porcupine and killed him. Hóvo was going to seize Armadillo, but he entered the earth and escaped; he came out far away and ran off. Then Hóvo thrust his leg into [the hole] where Armadillo had entered, saying, *"Mbï tǫ yûi mbï tǫ yûi."*[42] But in the meanwhile he saw him come out far away from the place where he went in. Then he pursued him.

A woodpecker was piercing a hive [and Armadillo said to him]: "My *kôklá*, there's a fight on and I escaped. My *kôklá*, Hóvo is chasing me. When he comes here throw your axe into his mouth." That is what they[43] said to him. So Woodpecker put one of them at the base of the tree and covered him with earth and placed another in a basket which he stood on his thighs. Then he went on piercing the hive. In the meanwhile Hóvo came along their trail saying, *"Mbï tǫ yûi, mbï tǫ yûi,"* until he arrived beneath him. Then he said, "Have you seen my quarry?" To which he replied: *"Ívu*, it's been quiet around here. They may have gone over that way, because you can hear their noise." So Hóvo went to look for their trail. When [one] Armadillo saw this he said to Woodpecker, "My *kôklá*, throw your axe into his mouth." When he heard that he slopped up some honey with tree hair[44] and said to Hóvo, "Eat some of my honey." So he went for something to put the honey in. When Hóvo saw it he said, "Sit

[40] A kind of tiger.

[41] These are meaningless syllables that carry the tune.

[42] Hóvo's way of saying that Armadillo is no good.

[43] We learn here for the first time that there were two armadillos.

[44] A green, moss-like growth on the limbs and trunks of trees. It is used for mopping up honey as it flows out of the comb.

down[45] there for it. I am waiting open-mouthed down here with my people for the honey." Then he opened his mouth. Then the tree hair fell into his mouth and he swallowed it. Then Woodpecker wrapped the blade of his axe in some more tree hair and said to him, "Open your mouth." When he opened his mouth he threw it in, and it cut his windpipe. He fell in a heap. Then Armadillo said to Woodpecker, "Let me down." So he let him down. When they were all killed they [the armadillos] went away.

Chûlágn (a bird) tried to defend them. He went: *"Chûktú, chugn ve! Let them alone! Chûktú, chu ve!*[46] Let them alone!" At last Tekte[47] killed him.

Stories of battles among animals are common among the tribes of the New World. The general character of this tale could be duplicated in any number of groups. What is, perhaps, most typically Kaingáng in it is the festa settting and the peculiar seating arrangement—each animal next to the one he intends to murder. But here the specifically Kaingáng background fades. This tale would be at home in a large number of primitive communities, for it requires no unique cultural context. But the murder tales can be understood only in terms of Kaingáng culture and would be unintelligible outside its limits.

In spite of its resemblance to a feud tale—if men were put in place of the animals, the beginning would sound much like a feud brawl—the story of the war of the animals lacks the two motifs that give the murder tales their specific character: blood relationship and revenge. No animal tale contains them. In so far as this is, in part, a battle tale, the Kaingáng derive a certain pleasure from the fantastic struggle of the animals; but the murder theme is not developed. Porcupine's relatives never take revenge on Hawk, nor Hóvo on Woodpecker or Armadillo. It is a striking characteristic of the animal tales that only this one extends beyond three hundred [English] words. The reason for this is not hard to find. The Kaingáng have, in their murder tales, developed a literary form that is expressive of everything they feel deeply; and they have little need for other material.

As a second illustration of the animal and supernatural-being tales I have chosen a nightmare tale of Véin.[48] Kaingáng literary expression is

[45] We can see by the use of the plural form of "to sit" that several people are involved here. In this and the succeeding sentence we discover for the first time that several *hovo* are gathered together.

[46] Informants did not know what this means.

[47] A hawk.

[48] See p. 71.

devoted principally to the development of the death theme in various aspects. Among the tales treating of death are a number that deal with death caused by a tiger or by a supernatural monster. Where human beings are slain and devoured by supernatural beings or by tigers these creatures should be regarded as projections or hypostatizations of the great Kaingáng fear of death at the hands of vendetta enemies. In these tales the behavior of the attacking tigers or supernaturals parallels that of feud enemies, and the defence precautions taken are the same as those employed against enemy families. Like the warriors of "different" groups tigers and supernaturals strike and strike again; they pursue relentlessly and are satisfied only with total annihilation. And just as the Kaingáng run from their vendetta enemies or build protective fences around their encampments, so also they fly in terror from pursuing tigers and supernatural monsters or build fences to keep them off.

5. The Coming of Véin

The ancients saw Véin. Mumbégn's father's father saw him in the time when they still planted corn.

The women gathered it [corn] and were on their way back when they slept. They had no fire. Late at night Véin came for them. He came along flashing like a firefly,[49] and they spoke to him: "Let the one coming along with a torch of bamboo give some of it to me—I am lying here without fire." Then he came with his flame that was like burning bamboo. Then they made fire and stayed there and slept. Then he would lie down with a woman and copulate with his penis,[50] and her blood would come out. He copulated[51] with them all thus. He came to Chantágn at daybreak and copulated with her, and she almost died. She got up and ran off, and when she arrived [in camp] she said: "Some other thing that is like a man came with fire, and since we had none we asked for some, and he copulated with them all and they died. He copulated with me and I am dying." Then she fell and died. Then they all went off to some other men and told: "Some other nggïyúdn, the one that flashes, probably Véin, copulated with all the women." Then they made a fence. "He is coming behind you!" They finished the fence at night and waited for him. Next day they waited for him, and he pursued them. Late at night he was coming along after them. They were in a savannah. He reached the houses and circled them all with

[49] This refers to the way in which he gleamed, not to the size of the light.

[50] Since the verbs "to copulate with" and "to eat" are the same word, my informant found it necessary to make clear how the verb was to be understood in this context.

[51] The verb is, of course, the same as in the preceding sentence.

his arms. "Who asked for my upper arm?"[52] said he. He was probably carrying a fire. He ate them all. Some people in another house escaped and went to another group and arrived there. "The one that flashes killed all the men." Then they dug a trench around the house. Next night late he came along through the savannah. "Who wants my upper arm?" Then he came and killed them all again. The people from two houses escaped. There was nothing to be done. They looped a pine[53] and climbed up. They made a house in the pine by putting earth on strips of wood. They hoisted the earth up in baskets. There were three pine trees.

Amendó was mourning for her relatives. Her relative Kíyi[54] heard her and became angry. Probably he had seen nggïyúdn. [He said,] "When I hear her suffering I become angry." Then he waited for Véin. Late at night he saw Véin coming. He circled the houses again and said the same thing. When he saw that they were empty he stopped. He walked about and at last he saw their fire in the tree. When he climbed up Kíyi went "Kx," which is the cry of the owl, and he [Véin] exploded like a fire and fell down.

They put the women in the basket and lifted them up in it.

Then they all came down.

In this story Véin, the inexorable pursuing nightmare, is the counterpart of the relentlessly vindictive extended families. One village after another flies before him only to be annihilated. The terror-stricken people even build a fence against him as the Kaingáng did against other extended families even after they had abandoned their village life. Not only supernaturals like Véin are conceived of in this human fashion, but tigers too are looked on as bloodthirsty creatures which, having struck once, desire to strike again until they have eaten everyone.

The scene of this story is laid in the ancient villages in the savannah, and the women are pictured as returning from the gardens laden with corn. They are unaccompanied by their menfolk—an excellent opportunity for an enterprising male. There are a few other stories in Kaingáng folklore that reflect this fear on the part of the men of the community that while the women are away gathering wood or drawing water they may be persuaded, and all too easily, into a sex adventure. Nevertheless there is no instance on record of a man who was so aberrant as to attempt to accompany his wife on one of her customary errands.

[52] The meaning is not clear. It may indicate that Véin had fiery arms, but he is not generally so described.

[53] Made a climbing-loop.

[54] Kíyï, simplified to Kiyi, is the name of an owl.

An Origin Myth

The origins of things, people, and circumstances are explained in the series of myths that are used for *wainyêklâdn,* the myth-shouting game. The importance of these myths is primarily for this game, secondarily as a source of "explanations" whenever the Kaingáng feel moved to give any. For generations they have not been the bulwark of much that is vital in Kaingáng culture, but they contain echoes of things that may have been important at one time. The content of these myths is not very interesting either for us or for the Kaingáng. The incidents are confused and repetitious, and I have, therefore, abridged them where possible without impairing their value.

6. The Coming of the Groups[55]

Chuvái said to Chu,[56] whose other name is Chuvái, *"Yûgn,* since you are my *kôika hë,*[57] come in my road, which you like." Then I came in the road of *yûgn* Chuvái, which I liked, and came into his dance ground. Then we caressed one another and danced together. Now a *wangdjô*[58] whose name was Kíyi came down behind me and entered my dance ground. When I saw this I asked, "What man is this?" and the *wangdjô* whose name was Kíyi said, *"Ívu,*[59] I am *wangdjô,"* and I said: *"Hu ki mbô!*[59] Come in here and dance with me!" Whereupon the *wangdjô* whose name is Kíyi danced with me. I observed him and saw that he had no raiment, but nevertheless he danced with me. Then I approached him with my tied-up corn and suspended it from his upper arm, saying: *"Wangdjô* whose name is Kíyi, now then, swing your arms [in the dancing gesture] and dance with me. I am not *wangdjô.* You have no clothes, but dance with me." Then I danced with him.

In the meanwhile *wangdjô* whose name is Thekpopé came down after me and entered my dance ground. When I saw this I said, "What man is it?" and he replied, *"Ívu!* I am *wangdjô!"* Then I said, *"Hu ki mbô!* Come in and dance with me!" When I saw this I observed him and saw

[55] That is, the several divisions of people having different body-paint designs. See Appendix II.

[56] Mythological ancestors of the Kaingáng. In the origin myths it is often not clear just who is speaking.

[57] People having the same body-paint design as oneself.

[58] In the origin myths the Kaingáng are referred to as *wangdjô.* They, however, do not recognize it as a tribal designation. *Wangdjô* is also the word for the succulent top of the tapir's neck and for a supernatural monster. See p. 71. These meanings are all completely unconnected in Kaingáng thought.

[59] An exclamation.

that although he had no raiment he was dancing with me. Then I said:
"By means of *wangdjô* I make a road for men. I have white cloth." So I
approached him with some and put it on him. Then I said: *"Wangdjô*
whose name is Thekpopé and Patá, now girdle your *yôk̞të*[60] with my
cloth, my white cloth, and dance with me. I am not *wangdjô.* You have
no clothes, but dance with me." Then I danced with him.

In the meanwhile his *yôk̞të* were all married off. When I saw this we
caressed one another. Then I said: "Thus we are in-laws. Let us live in
one house together. When we have been married a long time we will have
one house only and divide our firewood into two fires close together."
Then I danced with him.

[The same procedure is gone through with two more men, Klendó and
Nuklágn. Then, abruptly.]

I danced along where Pathí cleared the earth before me. I entered my
other dancing ground. When I heard that many men were coming I
danced with fear.

In the meanwhile Pathí made a house over me of closely placed strips of
wood. I split wood. I had nothing to split for the house that Pathí made
over my head. Then I split young pine. Then after he built the house I
prepared *matté* for the divining by belching. After I prepared it I was
belching, when along came Pathí who was called Bad Mouth because of
his good teeth. His father had died. Now I was divining by belching because many men were coming, and he stood outside. Then I stuck my
head out of my big house and jerked him by the arm, saying: "Divine with
me! Since many men are coming I am going to divine by belching. Divine
with me!" Then I put the *matté* into his mouth and he vomited. When I
saw this I pushed him out. Then I said to him: "By this see! Because your
teeth are good you are called Bad Mouth, and your father died! Then you
vomited the *matté* I was going to drink because many men were coming."

Then I again divined by belching. After divining I stuck my head out
of my big house, and I saw that men had already passed along the road of
my *k̞óik̞a hë* Wanyekí. The Brazilian Thugnhé had passed along; no-good
Ndadnlé had passed along. Then I danced along after them and caught up
to no-good Ndadnlé. Then I said, "What man is this?" Then no-good
Ndadnlé remained silent. Therefore I thrust him to the side of the road of
my *k̞óik̞a hë* Wanyekí.

I was dancing along the road that Yognvái, whose other name is Pathí
had cleared for me to the land he had seen, when no-good Ndadnlé behind
me [said], "My name is Ndadnlé and Ndatúgn." But I paid no attention
and went dancing along the road that Yognvái whose name is Pathí had

[60] Women having the same body-paint design as a man; hence women having the same
design as Thekpopé.

cleared to the land he had seen, when there was the road of dangerous
Nevó crossing the road of my *kôika hë* Wanyekí. There the Brazilians in
passing had chopped down trees, blocking Nevó's road.

I went dancing along through the field to the base of Hawk Mountain
where live many men. I arrived there. In the meanwhile Black Water of
the good teeth came down after me and entered my dance ground. Then I
said, "Black Water of the good teeth, you may enter, but all our people are
married, including the young girls." Then Black Water became angry
because of the women and wanted to go away. When he went away he
said, "If you stay here and live together I'll come after you to cut you to
bits." When he said this he went away, but I remained dancing at the base
of Hawk Mountain among the many people.

[This is repeated with two other men, Chuvái and Kothá. Then the
story goes on:]

I remained at the base of Hawk Mountain waiting for my *kôika hë*,
Black Water. Then Black Water of the good teeth came along after me
and arrived at the base of Hawk Mountain. Then I said: "Black Water of
the good teeth, come here. I have been waiting for you to do battle." Black
Water had for a long time wanted to scatter the men at the base of Hawk
Mountain, and at last he put a *pepóbm* [bird] among them and scattered
the people.

I did not see which way Black Water went. Then I entered the forest
and was dancing when *yûgn* Chu, whose other name is Chuvái, came
down after me and entered my dance ground. Then I said to him: "Black
Water wanted to put a *pepóbm* among the people at the base of Hawk
Mountain, and he did so, scattering them. Then I entered the forest, and
here I am."

Then I looked and saw Kukuvá's gourd in the field across from me.
Then I went dancing toward it. I wanted to taste some [beer], but I was
afraid. Kukuvá was in the field, and I invited him and exchanged rattles
with him. I wanted to taste some of Kukuvá's beer, but I was afraid; so I
took some feathers of the tucan and put them on my rattle.

That is what they do, then they stop.

The fundamental confusion in which the Kaingáng have been living
for generations is shown in the contradictory behavior toward *kôika hë*
and *yôktë*. One's *kôika hë* are, according to the theoretical scheme, one's
closest relatives. One cannot marry one's *yôktë*, for that would be incest;
and all one's *kôika hë* are called by a kinship term indicating close relationship. These are theories which, although they may reflect historical fact,
have not been practised for at least two hundred years. In the origin myths
we not only find men committing "incest"—for Chuvái marries his own

yôktë in this myth—but actually fighting with their own *ķôiķa hë*: the nameless speaker in the myth fights with his *ķôiķa hë* Black Water. Kothá and Chuvái, two men the speaker calls by the kinship term *yúgn,* threaten to cut him to bits.

It is somewhat different in those instances in the myths where relationships through marriage have actually been achieved. The bridegrooms are pictured as sharing their property with the men of the other group and then caressing them and lying down beside the same fire. In a way this mythological behavior reflects the actual situation in Kaingáng society, but it is also in contradiction to the real state of affairs, for the relatives by marriage with whom one has one's strongest bond in contemporary Kaingáng society are members of the *same* group—a group which is closely knit together already by consanguineal and affective ties. Relatives by marriage on the other hand, no matter of what degree, are ruthlessly slaughtered if they are members of another extended family. In the myths marriage relationships are between *groups* of people, but what Kaingáng society is actually interested in is marriage ties between *individuals*. Thus the situation described so touchingly in the myth is either idyllic or antique; probably both—it is not real.

There is another important contradiction of everyday affairs in the mythological relationships. In the myth *ķôiķa hë* are pictured as fighting, as in the battle between the speaker and Black Water, while in-laws are described as living in sweet harmony. Now since, theoretically, *ķôiķa hë* are blood relatives, this means that blood relatives fight while in-laws love one another. But the more stable relationships in Kaingáng society are between blood relatives, not relatives by marriage.

Corn is a frequently recurring element in Kaingáng myths, and we meet it again in this myth in the reference to the ears of corn suspended from the arms of the dancers. The Kaingáng say that anciently they used to suspend ears of corn from their arms and dance holding their arms bent at the elbow and moving them up and down in time to the music. The Kaingáng women still dance that way, but without the corn.

Pathí is a character developed further in other origin myths. He was a young man with an enormous appetite, and his father fell from a tree which he had climbed in search of food for him; this was the origin of death. The possession of good teeth is a sign of aberrance and malevolence among these people who have such poor dentition. A mouthful of teeth is also an indication of insanity. Two of the evil characters in this myth, Pathí and Black Water, are spoken of as having good teeth.

The type of house referred to has not been built by the Kaingáng for two hundred years or more.

It is curious that the teller of the story should have asked Pathí to divine with him, for divining by belching, *vayú*, is a solitary affair nowadays; and it is even said that if anyone sees the diviner while he is seeking an augury he will not be able to perform.

No one was able to explain to me what the reference to the *pepóbm* meant.

Thus the small details as well as the general movement of the myth have little reference to the material, sociological, or psychological realities of contemporary Kaingáng life; nor is this story of the coming of the groups a collection of nostalgic memories of a golden age.

Appendix I

Material Culture

Hunting

STALKING, THE BASIC KAINGÁNG TECHNIQUE for tapir hunting, was described in Chapter II. I have called this the basic technique because all other techniques of tapir hunting are built on it. The core of the stalking technique is *following* the animal, and the Kaingáng do this whether they hunt with or without dogs. When they hunt the tapir with dogs one of two possibilities is open: either they can pursue the tapir by following the bark of the dog, or they can lie in wait for it beside one of its well-known runs and kill it as the dogs drive it. Now these two different kinds of hunting involve entirely different intellectual orientations. When the hunter follows the bark of his dog he acts directly; he swings into motion the moment his dog disappears into the brush with a yelp, and he follows persistently until he overtakes the dog where it has brought the tapir to bay or until it becomes too dark, in which case he tries to pick up the trail again the following day and continue the pursuit. But the technique of waiting is entirely different and so much at variance with the habits of the Kaingáng that they have never been able to carry it actually into effect.

Tapir run for generations in the same trails, *carreiras,* until they sometimes wear them down a yard in depth. Since, when a tapir is pursued it invariably seeks one of these *carreiras,* it is clear that anyone who knows the different *carreiras* in his neighborhood is well equipped for hunting. In the summer the hunted tapir frequently takes a *carreira* that leads to a stream, especially if the land is cut by many waterways and it is the habit of the white settlers to study the *carreiras* in the region carefully so that when they go hunting they can station men at all the spots where the *carreiras* debouche into the winding streams and can shoot the tapir when the dogs chase it into the water. This mode of hunting can, of course, be

153

employed on land also; but there it is much more difficult, because as the tapir comes charging along it is extremely hard to get a good shot. In the water, however, with the dogs snapping at it, its movements are very much hampered and it becomes an easy target. Hunting the tapir in this way calls for careful planning, long residence in one region, and the cooperation of a number of men. From the Kaingáng point of view it means changing the unplanned, solitary stalking technique to one of planned cooperation. How have they met this situation? Perhaps a description of my personal experiences will suggest an answer to the question.

Early in the morning we lead the dogs out, and as we move slowly along we search the damp earth underfoot for tapir tracks, pushing the brush aside where it obscures the ground, talking in whispers, stopping every half minute to disentangle the dogs from the brush or from a fallen log where the bark or bamboo leashes have become tangled. We have a definite objective: we are going to find a tapir track, and we must hold the dogs in leash until we have found it. We do not let the dogs scamper aimlessly about where they may bark at any little bird that flashes above them and so frighten all the game within a quarter of a mile or where they may dash off wildly after some lesser animal like a *tateti* or a deer.

At last the track is found, and the hunters begin to follow it methodically. They do not let the dogs go at once, for the tapir may have doubled several times in its rambling search for food, and it would be wasteful to let the dogs run over that unnecessary distance.[1] Perhaps the trail will show that the tapir has taken a route that would lead far off across a flat area where it might run and run indefinitely and never fall into a stream where it could be killed easily. The hunter who knows the land well seeks to control all these factors. At last when the hunters have become satisfied that it is well to let the dogs loose, they say to me, "Julio, you stay here. Here is a *carreira,* and if the tapir comes along you shoot it." Perhaps one of their number stays there with me also. Then the hunters go off, still leading the dogs, and disappear. After a while we hear the sudden excited barks of the dogs. When my companion hears them, his eyes flash, his body grows tense, and with a "Julio, you wait here; we'll come back for you," he is gone. All through the warm afternoon I sit beside the trail. The bark of the dogs has long since died in the distance. Somewhere beyond those ridges and trees that lie around me piled skyward one upon the other, brown figures are moving through the jungle, tense with excitement,

[1] Since, from the point of view of the dog, the track of an animal extends indefinitely in both directions—the direction from which it came as well as the direction in which it is going—it might be asked how the dog knows which way to go. The answer is that as it follows the track the scent grows stronger the closer it gets to its prey and vice versa.

listening with straining ears for the bark of the dogs which now seems lost, now appears close, now disappears in the distance as the driven tapir turns again in its path. Meanwhile I doze and slap mosquitoes. Never a sound but the calls of birds and the drone of insects.

At last as the sun begins to redden and slope steeply toward the west I hear the sound of breathless singing coming down the side of the hill before me. There in front is Kanggúin. From the distance I see that he is covered with blood and that something hangs from his back. Behind him, their faces beaming, their bodies blood-stained come the others. "Did you shoot a tapir?" I ask. "Yes. It was shot." "In the *carreira?*" "No. We followed the dogs and shot it." Now what has happened to all the elaborate planning? People are stationed in the *carreiras* but the tapir is not killed in any *carreira*. When this happens several times I decide on different tactics. Why keep my Winchester oiled and up to the minute? Why this endless fight against rust? Why lug two hundred rounds of ammunition along if all I am to do is sit sleepily beside the trail while others kill the tapir and I cannot even see what happens—who gives the tapir to whom and how they cut it up and divide it. Next time I insist on going along with the dogs and following the tapir.

When I make my revolutionary announcement the Indians are intrigued and somewhat disturbed. "Who will guard the *carreira,*" they ask, "if you follow the dogs?" "Somebody else," say I vaguely. "Well, then, give your revolver to Drunken."[2] Next morning we find a track almost immediately. In fact there seem to be two tracks. So Véye leads off the dogs along one track and Waipó and I go in the direction of the other, not knowing what will happen when the dogs are loosed. We descend a short slope, leap a tiny stream, and begin to wander along the other side. Suddenly a sharp yelp! Then short staccato barks splinter the forest quiet. "This way, this way, Julio!" Waipó calls in a hoarse whisper. We wheel about, leap the stream again, fight upward along the opposite bank, bend to the left, to the left. The high yelps of the dogs are almost in our ears. The tapir is not running! They have brought it to bay almost immediately. As we rush along through the thickets Waipó says, "Julio, Julio, a tiger, a tiger!" I shove a cartridge into the rifle chamber and keep going. "Certainly my Winchester is a match for any tiger," I think. "Do tigers eat .44 calibre bullets?" I ask myself excitedly. But we have come out on the edge of a little gully, and there, in a little place where it cannot turn around the gray bulk of the tapir struggles with the two little dogs that nip wildly at

[2] Ndjákemu, Drunken—So called because once when he wanted to sleep with Nandjá the young men hung around her door all night long so that he was ashamed to go in and next day was so fatigued from his vigil that he was like one drunk.

its thick hide. Waipó and I shoot, and the tapir is dead. The tiger was a joke to frighten the tenderfoot.

So! The very first day that I decide not to watch the *carreira* but to follow the chase I kill a tapir. What does it mean? It means that the Indians have not learnt to wait. On my first hunting trip with the Indians we killed eight tapirs, and not one of them was killed in a *carreira*. How could they be? As soon as the Indians hear the bark of the dog they are off in pursuit. All the tapirs are killed by pursuers, not by watchers. Day after day the Indians start with the same plan in mind, and day after day as soon as the dogs bark they abandon it. Thus the waiting technique regresses to the level of stalking,[3] i.e. to the pursuit of the quarry. In stalking, the hunter works in isolation, unaccompanied by man or dog. But in Kaingáng society, hunting with dogs is bound to be another matter if there is more than one man in the same hunting band, as there usually is. For if Kanyahé goes west, Chuvái east, and Waipó and Padnmbá in other directions, the moment they hear the dog bark they will start in pursuit. With the dog behind him the tapir may run far, and the farther he runs the more likely he is to meet with Kanyahé who went west or Waipó who went north. Thus, as soon as dogs are introduced the individual undertaking of the hunter becomes cooperative. What lies at the base of this cooperation is, in turn, the fundamentally non-individualistic orientation toward food. The tapir is eventually divided among close relatives anyway, and it makes little difference who kills it or whose dog brings it to bay.[4]

The small Brazilian deer is the animal next in size to the tapir. Nowadays deer are easily killed by turning dogs loose on their trail and waiting for the deer to fall into the river, where they are easily shot or clubbed.

---

[3] Leading dogs out on a leash is a thing the Indians do very unwillingly. They prefer to let the dog ramble about at will in the forest until it picks up a trail by itself and gives chase or, until the Indians having found a trail they call the dog and set it in pursuit. The only time they use the leash is in attempts to employ the waiting technique. Now since the waiting technique and leading the dogs on leash are both white methods *par excellence* and since the waiting technique is practically impossible for the Indians to follow out, it seems likely that the Indians learnt the entire procedure from the whites.

I believe that it is also significant in this connection that the magic formula to make the dog efficient makes no reference to the dog's driving the tapir along the *carreira* but only to the pursuit and the bringing to bay. See p. 85.

The Indians themselves say that they obtained their first dogs from the Brazilian settlers about two hundred years ago. It is striking how much the dog is treated like an outsider. See pp. 31 fn. and 86. There is no dog guardian spirit.

[4] Nowadays the pattern of division of the kill along relationship lines has been somewhat altered owing to certain practical considerations. Hunting parties may be organized on the basis of who has a canoe, who has dogs, and who has ammunition to lend. In this case the booty is divided in line with the contributions made to the organization of the party.

I have never seen a deer killed except in this way. It is child's play and was obviously learnt from the whites.[5] In the old days they were killed only by stalking or through a sudden encounter in the forest. They are rarely mentioned in folklore. After deer the pig-like *tateti* is the next largest game animal. I never heard of its being stalked, and the *tateti* that were taken during my stay among the Kaingáng were all killed cooperatively. Dogs drove them into their burrows, and a number of men combined to get them out. One day my dogs drove a *tateti* into a burrow on the side of a hill; while one man shoved into the burrow a bundle of flaming bamboo on the end of a long pole the others stood around with loaded guns, and when the beast emerged it was shot. Sometimes men wait above the entrance to the burrow and club the *tateti* when it emerges.

Peccary hunting I know only by hearsay. Although a couple of troops of peccary (called "pig of the forest" by the settlers) passed by while I was among the Kaingáng I took no part in their pursuit. The Indians, however, tell me that they surround and shoot them or stab them with knives on the ends of poles. Sometimes, however, they are pursued by one man alone. They are very dangerous animals when brought to bay, and it is well to keep one's distance. Formerly peccary were an important item of Kaingáng diet, but nowadays they have grown scarce in the vicinity of Duque de Caxias and are not found even far up the river. "*Nggïyúdn* has become angry with us," the Indians say, "and has closed up the pigs in his corral."

The Kaingáng have no bird snares, and all birds are shot individually with the bow and arrow where they are encountered.

Subsistence Figures

The following discussion is based on the data which I collected during a five weeks' hunting trip into the forests with the Indians. During that time it was possible for me to keep a fairly accurate check on the distribution of meat because the population was concentrated in one spot, and the entire organization of the camp was directed toward getting meat for everyone. Conditions at the post, however, are quite different. There the population is scattered along a half-mile trail and on both sides of the river, and it is therefore impossible to keep a day-to-day check even were such a check valuable—which I doubt, for in the region of the post game is ex-

---

[5] Waiting in a canoe for animals to fall into the river seems hardly removed from waiting at the termination of or along a *carreira*—a further suggestion that the entire technique was taken over from the settlers. The agent used to tell me: "When I first came into this region all you had to do was turn your dogs loose in the forest, and the animals would come tumbling into your canoe."

tremely scarce, and the Indians, instead of spending their time hunting, spend a great part of it tilling the soil.

The data that I offer present problems rather than solve them. They were collected at a particular time of the year: when the most important wild crop of the region, pine nuts, was ripe; when it was still warm and the tapirs ran slowly; when the females were heavy with young; when some wild fruits other than the pine nut were ripe and on the trees; when the bees were still making honey and their young had not yet begun to devour it. In other words, it was the most nearly perfect time of the year in the region where the Kaingáng would find it easiest to get food. Pine trees were abundant, which meant not only food for the Indians but also food for monkeys and all the four-footed animals that might live on the fallen nuts, particularly the peccary. Besides this the region was cut by many streams into which the dogs might drive the tapir so that the hunter could kill it easily. The difference that such a terrain makes in hunting tapir is amazing. Time after time dogs have been taken a little way up the river and turned loose on fresh tapir tracks only to run fruitlessly all day long because the lie of the land was such that the tapir need never drive toward a stream. The flat top of the ridge stretched for miles unintersected by any streams until it ended three hours journey to the northwest in the Deniker River. It was one of my grievances against the Indians that they would take my dogs to such a place against my will and let them run after a tapir until night overtook them, far out of reach of anyone, whereupon the Indians would return, leaving the dogs in the forest. Days later they would wander in, their snouts full of porcupine quills and their hides cut by the teeth of *quati*.

At the time of my study the Indians had hunted over the same area for almost twenty years. It is vast, and tapir are still to be found there; yet persistent hunting in one area must affect the number of animals, particularly when the favorite season for hunting tapir is the time of the pine nuts, i.e. when the females are heavy with young. Hunting by the settlers, although not very frequent, nevertheless occurs and may affect the quantity of game animals. On the other hand, during the five weeks' hunt the Indians had the use of my dogs—two well-trained tapir hunters—which I managed to keep fairly well fed. Under aboriginal conditions it would be rare for the Indians to have specially trained tapir-hunters, and they would never be well fed. This, of course, reduces the dog's efficiency.

Not all of the adult or adolescent males were armed during the trip, which, of course, reduced the efficiency of the group. Nowadays the young men never learn to shoot with bow and arrow, and if they are too poor to buy a gun they cannot hunt.

Figures for Five Weeks' Trip

Tapirs Killed: 7[6] $\times$ *Average Weight* 200 lbs. $=$ 1400 lbs.
Average population during 5 weeks   18 (not including infants)
Pounds of meat per person for 5 weeks   77
Pounds of meat per person per day   2$\frac{1}{5}$

The figures are self-explanatory as far as tapir are concerned. During this time about ten monkeys were killed and a number of birds of varying sizes of which I could not keep track. The weight of the monkeys as compared to the combined weights of the tapirs is so small that I shall not include them in the figures.

The figure of two and a fifth pounds of meat per day should be modified, as allowance must be made for the heavy hide, bones, and internal waste. Such an allowance would bring the weight per person down to less than two pounds. Not all of this meat remained in camp, for a considerable portion of it was taken away by Indians returning to the post. In addition to this meat the Indians were plentifully supplied with pine nuts most of the time and they sometimes had a fair supply of *tai,* a yellow fruit with a tasty pulp of very doubtful nutritive value. The quantities of other kinds of fruits consumed was negligible. The Indians also had along with them on this trip small quantities of corn and manioc meal and beans, and the new arrivals would bring food from the post. With all this, at no time could it be said that there was a surplus of anything but pine nuts. These were buried in a stream bottom to preserve them.

The Indians ate moderately; yet rarely did any kill seem to last us more than three days. This would mean about fourteen meatless days out of thirty-five. Fourteen meatless days would indicate that if the Kaingáng had eaten all the meat they killed they would have consumed not 2.2 pounds per person daily but 3.7 pounds. But probably as much or more than a third of the meat was taken back to the post. This would leave the original figure of about two pounds per person daily. To us two pounds of meat a day seems an extremely large quantity, but we do not view meat, as the Kaingáng do, as our principal food. To the Kaingáng, meat is the principal article of diet; everything else is garnish.[7]

Gathering Pine Nuts

An Indian selects several flawless bamboo stems,[8] cuts them down, splits them carefully from end to end into four strips about an inch wide, exam-

---

[6] An eighth tapir was killed the day before we returned to the post.

[7] This also makes quite a different picture from most of Melanesia, where vegetable foods are most important and meat is the garnish.

[8] Full-grown bamboo stems are about 15 feet in length.

ines them carefully for knots, and runs his knife along, chopping off the projecting nodes that divide the stem into short sections. This is done to make it all as smooth as possible. Now he throws one length of bamboo around the pine, inside out, and winds one end of the length around the other end, making a loop about four feet in diameter. While several feet of the first length are still unused he takes a second length of bamboo and slips it under the windings. Then he winds the first length around the second until he has exhausted the first length, whereupon he continues his winding with the second. Now he slips a third length under the second and continues the winding as before, and so with the fourth and last. He lets a short end dangle loose, flexes the loop about the tree to make it pliable, and gets inside of it. The loop is around him and the tree. He has an axe in one hand. He slides the loop up above his head, then throws his weight backward against it until it is taut. He places the soles of his feet against the rough bark of the pine and begins to walk up. Now his body is bent in an arc as his feet approach his hands which hold tight to the loop, and he shifts it upward again. Again he starts to walk, selecting spots on the bark where his feet will cling best. As he ascends he sinks the axe into the tree above his head so that he will not have to carry it. Each time he reaches the axe he again pulls it out and sinks it into the tree farther above his head. When he reaches the first little branch, twenty feet above the ground, he lops it off because he cannot stand on it and it impedes his progress. As he climbs he lops off one or two more such branches and at last reaches the first strong limb that projects horizontally. He climbs up on it and ties his loop to the branch by the loose end in such a way that he can step into it easily when he is ready to descend. Now he holds on to the trunk and cries, "Look out!" His wife moves a good thirty feet out of range of the cones that come hurtling down with skull-crushing force as her husband dances around on the branch thirty to fifty feet in the air above her and dislodges the cones with his weight. When the tree is emptied of its fruit he steps into his loop and descends rapidly in much the same way as he went up.

Now his wife and he begin the search for the cones among the brush. They gather them all together, break them open, and take out the nuts. A tree requires about half an hour. The amount of nuts obtained from a single tree is very variable. Then the couple go away, leaving the loop behind them, for it cannot be detached from the tree. A fresh loop must be made each time. Each person selects his trees as he wanders about. There are plenty of trees for all, and no quarrels arise. If a woman has no husband her brother or some other relative will knock down nuts for her. Sometimes two men help one another. Nuts are the property of the people who have gathered them. There is no pooling of the crop.

Distribution of Population

At the time of their pacification the Kaingáng were distributed on both sides of the Rio Plate within, at the most, three or four days' journey on foot from the pine forest. It is impossible to determine through questioning exactly what determined the movements of all of one extended family under conditions of minimum tension. It was not exclusively food. If it were we would expect all of the members of the family around the Rio Plate to have gone to the pine forest in the fall. But only certain groups would go. Within the extended families the movements were determined quite as much by the desire to attack or the necessity of fleeing from the Brazilians and the wish to look for one another as by the quest for food.

Fruit and Insect Foods

Other Fruit and Roots

While I was among the Kaingáng wild fruits were not important. They either gather fruit when it falls to the ground, climb up after it, or chop the tree down.

I never heard of the Kaingáng using any roots for food.

Wasps and Bees

We can see the wasps buzzing about the opening to their nest twenty feet above the ground in a huge tree that looks as if it were made of three trees grown together. The trunk forms a kind of cavern, and when we step inside we see that the part in which the wasps have built their nest is hollow all the way up. We collect wood and build a big fire at the base of the trunk, and the smoke rises as if up a chimney. We build another fire outside the trunk so that the wasps will not come down to annoy us. As the smoke pours out of the opening to the nest the wasps come with it, and soon there is a hum like a buzzsaw as thousands of wasps buzz about the entrance to their nest. When my two companions are convinced that the wasps have been completely evicted they take axes and go to work on the tree. When it at last crashes the nest has fallen through an arc of twenty-foot radius. No wasps are in sight now, but a fire is set on top of the tree near the nest to keep any chance wanderers away. Again the axes cut, and soon the structure of the nest has been laid bare: tier on tier of cells full of larvae and pupae. We take out the layers of the paperlike structure and in our hunger eat the contents raw. They are sweet, rich, and juicy. Now we build small fires and lay the cells against them to roast. Having eaten my fill, I receive no more. The two Indians divide the nest, the one who discovered it getting the larger share.

Honey is got out of a "dangerous" bees' hive in much the same way. Two or more men cooperate in the chopping and handling of the fire, and the honey is divided among them. Honey is a kind of free food, for when a hive is discovered anyone who happens along may share it. On the other hand, honey that has been collected is the property of whoever has found it, and sometimes it is hidden so that other folks will not take it. Wasps are not a very important food item for the Kaingáng, but honey is, although it is somewhat of a delicacy. No one thinks of making a meal of honey, but it is a godsend in the middle of the day.

When the Kaingáng were first pacified, says the agent, they climbed up to a hive if it was out of reach, but in these degenerate days they chop the tree down rather than climb it. Although the Kaingáng did not always climb up to a hive that was too far up on the trunk to be reached from a scaffold, they certainly did it frequently, and 1 per cent of the total number of deaths was due to falls from beehives. It was a hazardous occupation, for the climbing-loop might break or slip. Nowadays the most the Kaingáng do in this way is to build little scaffolds from which they chop out hives that may be six or seven feet above the ground. These scaffolds are made by lashing and cross-lashing posts to adjacent trees. Sometimes the scaffold consists only of a few steeply sloping posts that are tied together and leaned against a tree. The Indian stands on this uncertain perch and sinks his axe precisely around the edges of the hive so that it scarcely touches the delicate honey-laden cells. When the hive has been laid bare he places it entire in his wax-lined basket and sponges up with tree hair, a mosslike growth that clings to most of the trees in the forest, whatever honey has escaped.

Honey Beer

A man and his cousins or brothers decide to make beer for his in-laws. They cut down cedars, hollow them for troughs, and go to look for honey. After several days they have enough. Then they send their wives for water to fill the troughs. The honey is poured into the water, and the water is heated with hot stones. The stones are placed in special cylindrical baskets which are submerged in the water and suspended from rods placed across the mouth of the trough and moved from one end of it to the other. The woody stem of a fern called *nggign* is pounded and titrated and the red infusion mixed in the trough. This is to "make the beer red"; without *nggign*, say the Kaingáng, the beer would not ferment. This goes on for days, and then the mouth of the trough is covered with strips of bark and the beer is left standing several days longer. When it begins to bubble the Indians decide that it is *thô*, intoxicating or bitter, and ready to drink. The Indians say that instead of water the milk of a kind of palm is sometimes used and that this makes the beer particularly *thô*. Sometimes a little medicine is added for the sake of general good health. From time to time the beer is stirred with a long rod of bamboo, and the scum that rises is scooped off with the hands.

Preparation of Food

The women make pine-nut soup. A woman chews the raw pine nuts to a pulp, mixes them with water, and boils them. Sometimes they are pounded. The usual way of eating pine nuts is roasted in the shell in the coals.

Meats are sometimes boiled, and nowadays the broth is mixed with manioc meal and eaten. Most meat is roasted. This may be done in two ways. A scaffold of green branches is erected, a fire built under it, and the meat placed on it and roasted. Or a shallow pit is dug, a fire built in it, and green branches laid over it, the meat is then laid on the branches with leaves on top of it, and the whole covered with earth and left there for several hours. When the meat is taken off the branches it is juicy and delicious. The pit method is the best way to roast meat. In roasting meat in this way at least two people generally cooperate. One digs the hole while the other gets wood and leaves.

Small animals are spitted and broiled. Fish are broiled.

Palm shoots are boiled or eaten raw.

Këmê is made from the pith of the trunk of a certain palm. Leaves are laid on the ground and a cloth placed on top of them. The trunk is chopped vertically into strips; these are placed on a log and pounded with a stick. The mass is sifted in a basket, and the siftings are stuffed into a bamboo tube and roasted in the coals for five or ten minutes. The mass in the tube is then taken out, made into balls or cakes, and roasted in the coals. It tastes much like wet sawdust, and the Indians nowadays do not eat it even when they have the chance. Formerly it seems to have been fairly important in their diet. They mixed it with soup just as they do now with manioc meal. The Kaingáng say that in ancient times they used corn in the same way.

The Kaingáng used also to make a soup of the pollen of the pine tree. *Tai* fruit and wild *mamão* are roasted in the coals. Sometimes *tai* is pounded in a mortar and eaten.

Fire

When the Kaingáng move camp the woman takes an ember[9] from the last fire. Men carry no fire; so if they need it to roast nuts when they are hungry or to make fire to drive away wasps or "dangerous bees" they

[9] Any wood will do.

make it with a fire drill. They cut a piece of dry white canela about an inch thick, two inches wide, and two feet long and make a hole in it about half an inch deep, with a shallow groove on each side—Heaven knows what for[10]—extending over the edges of the stick. They also cut a smaller branch about a quarter of an inch in diameter and a foot and a half long; this is the drill. The Indian spits on his hands, places the drill in the hole, and begins to whirl the stick between his two palms, moving them up and down as he does so. After ten minutes he has no fire; so he calls another Indian and they alternate in whirling the drill. In five minutes more a wisp of smoke from the hole raises their hopes. They remove the drill and look—no spark. For five minutes more they drill, and then the spark comes. Sometimes the spark is on the end of the drill; sometimes it is on the side of the hole. Now the spark is placed on some dry palm leaves, and they blow on it until the leaves burst into flame.

I once saw two men attempt to make a fire with a three-foot base on which they could put their feet and a drill three feet long made of a long bamboo tube with a canela tip inserted at the bottom. They worked for twelve minutes without result. When a third man helped them they succeeded in obtaining a spark.

No sexual symbolism attaches to the fire-making apparatus.

HOUSES

Houses are built under pressure. It is theoretically woman's work, but in the excitement of sudden rain men and women cooperate. The woman goes for leaves for covering while the man cuts and sinks the heavy uprights and lighter boughs which are sharpened to a point at one end. He digs no hole for them but sinks them into the ground by raising them and throwing them repeatedly, with unerring eye, into the same hole, making it deeper with each throw. Sometimes two convenient trees are used as uprights. If the Indian should perchance decide to build the house long before the storm actually breaks and finds the ground is hard and dry he moistens the soil with whatever is at hand, even tapir soup.

When the uprights are in place the transverse is bound on about eight[11] feet above the ground. Now light boughs are sunk into the ground about nine feet in back of the uprights, *sloping away from them,* making an angle about 60° with the ground so that when they are bent over they will not break out. They are lifted and thrown into the ground just as the uprights were. The boughs are bent over and lashed to the transverse with

---

[10] What sparks were obtained were always in the hole itself or on the tip of the drill.

[11] Naturally if a house is built entirely by a woman it will be lower than if it is built by a man. Women may bind sloping posts against the uprights so that they can stand on them and reach high. The height of the house is much more variable than the width.

cipo or with palmito bark. The lashings are never knotted but twisted. When the arches have been formed—the number depends of course on the size of the house—transverse boughs are laid across them about nine inches apart and bound. The lashing is passed around both the transverse and the arched bough, and the two are approximated by pushing on the arch with one hand and pulling on the transverse with the lashing. For the lower transverses the foot and knee are used instead of the hand. All the lashing is done from the inside of the house, i.e. on the concave side of the arch. The arch is now covered from the inside with bunches of leaves by a simple weaving technique. The leaves are so placed that the tips hang over the lowest transverse (about a yard from the ground). The first transverse under which the stems are carried is about the fifth. Short separate sprays of leaves are also used, but because of their shortness they are carried under the third transverse. When there seems to be a chance that the bunches of leaves will slip they are tied, but generally they are not. In this way the entire arch is covered, each new bunch of leaves always overlapping that below. Now and then even in the pouring rain a woman will stop building to suckle her child. Every once in a while someone goes for leaves. *kunggluthâyâ* leaves are preferred for housebuilding because of their durability and the large coverage afforded by each bunch of leaves. The Brazilian settlers use them to thatch their houses, and they are called *palha* in Portuguese. If the Kaingáng have no *palha* they use palm fronds, or if they are in a grassy region they use grass. If there is no *palha,* palm, or grass they use bamboo leaves. Lacking all these, they sleep in the rain.

Since the arches in the house just described reach only to the main transverse that is supported on the two uprights and the ends of the house are not covered it is obvious that the house is completely open on three sides. There is another type of house, however, in which the arches make complete semicircles, with each leg of the arch imbedded in the ground. Such a house is really nothing but two of the simpler kind set facing each other, and that is the way such houses usually spring into existence. Sometimes, however, the entire thing is conceived and constructed as a unit, in which case the overlapping arches are bound to one another. Sometimes the Kaingáng make a simple lean-to by resting a bunch of palm fronds against the branch of a tree. Kaingáng houses are often built by more than one family in cooperation, but once the framework has been erected cooperative attitudes are dropped. Each family covers its own section of the house with leaves and remains completely indifferent to the fate of the other inhabitants.

Once, on their own initiative, the Kaingáng built for me a house of the type they say they inhabited when they dwelt in the savannahs and cultivated the soil. This house needed the cooperation of eight men, three of whom worked steadily. A heavy central pole nine feet high was sunk in the ground. Then a "ladder," i.e. a pole sloping from the ground to a point about four feet above the ground on the central pole, was tied to it so that the workers could reach the top of the central post. Six poles were sunk in a circle around the central post, about two yards from it, making the maximum diameter of the house approximately four yards.[12] Each pole was bent over toward the central post, caught by a man standing on the "ladder," and bound in place about a foot from the top. Five men worked to maneuver one pole so that it might be bent and bound: two held it in place, a third pushed it into an arc toward the center, and a fourth standing on the ladder pulled it down and in. The two arches first erected were separated widely to leave room for passage. When the arches were in place transverses were bound to them, the first one eight inches above the ground. The ends of the transverses were bound together. This frame was covered with *palha* and palm fronds all the way to the top.

Weapons

Bows

The Kaingáng told me that in order to make a bow a *kaktônggála*[13] tree is cut down and the trunk cut into sections and split with wedges. The desirable piece is then further reduced in cross section with an axe, and pointed at both ends with a knife. Then it is heated in the fire, rubbed with wax, and heated again. A short post with a fork at its upper end is sunk in the ground and braced with a second post. The bow is placed in the crotch, bent, and held in this position by another short post sunk in the ground. When the bow has been in the crotch for some time and thus permanently bent to its proper shape it is taken out and worked to the proper smoothness. This is all done by one person.

Nowadays Kaingáng bows have no howler-monkey tails on them, but at the time of the pacification the Kaingáng used to slip these tails over their bows to strengthen them. Whenever a howler monkey was killed they would cut off its tail, turn it inside out, and slip it over a stick of the same cross section as their bows. When they were dry they would turn them right side out and put them on their bows. One informant told me that the ancients used the tails of lizards. I never saw bows made.

---

12 Exactly 3.80 meters.

13 Known in Brazil as the *cablejuna*, a large tree yielding one of the finest and strongest hard woods of the Brazilian forests. The Kaingáng bow is from six to seven feet long and was often used as a club.

Arrows

Kaingáng arrows have one type of shaft and three types of heads, the iron head for tapir, deer, and howler monkeys, the barbed wooden head for smaller game, and the blunt head with nipple for birds.

The arrow shafts are made from bamboo which is cut while green, heated, and straightened and allowed to season. The longest shafts are used for the barbed wooden heads. These heads are whittled from a branch of *kôngûn*. They have a sharp point and have two edges, one of which is sharp while the other is provided with five barbs. The heads of these arrows (*lqlq*, thorn) are hardened in the fire. The origin of the use of the *kôngûn* for this type of arrow may be magical, for the tree from which they are taken is very thorny. When the heads are completed they are fitted into the shafts and bound in place with cipo, which is wound tight around the shaft at the junction of head and shaft. Then the whole is waxed and rubbed.

The next longest are the *ndó*, the bird arrows. These are whittled from pine knots. In shape the heads resemble inverted cones with nipples at the base.

The iron-headed arrows are the shortest, as is natural because of the great weight of the head, and the most difficult to make. These iron heads may be anywhere from three inches to almost a foot long and in average shape resemble very much the bill of the spoon-billed duck. Instead of being pointed at the tip they are perfectly rounded and are sharpened to razor keenness. They are also sharpened all along both edges. They have no barbs but end in blunt flanges. These arrows are used most generally at short range and make a terrific wound.

Iron arrows are made from metal stolen from the Brazilians, heated in the fire, hammered down with stones to the proper shape, and filed to an edge with a file obtained in the same way as the iron. The arrow head is finished with three flanges at the base, the central one fitted into a deep notch made for it in a short stick. This notch is filled with a strong black wax which gives the head additional support. Then the notch is tightly wound with cipó and the stick is fitted into the shaft which is wrapped with cipó and waxed.

Feathering for all but iron arrows is preferably done with the feathers of the jacutinga. The feathers are not split or wound around the shaft but bound on opposite sides of it. This is possible because only those feathers are used which have tendrils on but one edge. For iron arrows the feathers of the hawk are used. They are looked on as suited for the iron arrows because they come from such a powerful bird.

The making of arrows is done entirely by the owner.

Lances

The blade of this astonishing weapon is made from a single piece of iron that is worked by heating for days in the flames, pounding with stones, and then filing to razor sharpness.[14] The blade of the lance illustrated is 15⅛ inches from the tip to the bottom of the central flange, the actual usable length 12½ inches, 3½ inches at the widest point, sweeping gracefully in to a width of 2⅝ inches at the narrowest point. This was the only lance left among the Kaingáng when I came there; so it is impossible to make any general statements about the size of the blade; but I have been told that this is by no means one of the largest. Many, of course, must have been smaller, for the size of the blade depended on the size of the piece of iron obtained.

The peculiar shape of the blade might suggest that the Kaingáng lance was used principally for striking and not for stabbing. From stories it appears that the lance was used more often to strike than to stab, though stabbing was quite frequent. Nevertheless when we realize that the iron arrow heads were exactly the same shape as the lance heads it becomes clear that the shape of the lance blade was not determined by the fact that it was used more for striking than for stabbing. Obviously the drive of an arrow is always head on. The real reason that the lance was used more for striking than for stabbing was because the lance is a development of the club. The handle of the lance is exactly the same shape as a club,[15] except for the fact that the lance tapers toward the notch where the blade is inserted. The lance is grasped in the same way as the club. Kaingáng lance heads have had the same shape stages as the arrows.

Curiously enough, the lances were the weapons least used by the Kaingang. One would imagine that these lances would be ideal for slaughtering Brazilians, but the Kaingáng always left them at home when they went raiding. They preferred to cut clubs from hard woods just before attacking and to throw them away when they were finished. Sometimes they simply used their bows as clubs, but this involved danger of breakage. The Kaingáng say that they left the lances at home so that the women could use them to kill tapirs while they were gone.

The use of the lance *par excellence* was for murdering vendetta enemies. Most of the massacres were accomplished with lances. The Kaingáng beat time with their lances while they sang at the festas, so that they were fully prepared to turn upon their enemies suddenly and slaughter them.

In general the technique of making the blades is the same as for the iron arrow heads except that more than one man is needed. The heating and

---

[14] With a file stolen from the Brazilians.
[15] i.e. four-cornered; lozenge shaped in cross-section.

pounding is a long and tedious process, so that the men help one another. The blade is placed directly on the handle and not, as in the case of the arrow head, first on a wooden foreshaft which is fitted into the long bamboo aftershaft. The handle of the lance is ornamented near the upper end with an attractively woven glove of basketry.

Besides a large lance some men had in addition a little one, about one-third as big, which could be hung from the neck by a plaited band. It was useful for killing tapir.

Utensils

Beer Troughs

These are made from cedar trees. The Brazilian cedar is a mighty tree, dwarfing our North American variety to a weed. In order to make a trough a cedar is cut down and a section cut out. It may then be discovered that the log has a split in it, and in that case it becomes necessary to cut down another tree. This may go on for some time until at last a perfect log is secured. Then it must be moved back to camp, and since it is impossible for one man to do this several cooperate. If the log is on a hill the outer bark of the cedar which has been removed from the selected section is placed along the sides of the hill and used as skids. When level ground is reached the log is turned end over end through the "dirty" forest and rolled through the "clean."

When the log has been got into camp someone goes to work on it with an axe. He marks out the mouth, about eight inches wide, and hews away steadily until he can no longer strike accurately into the interior of the trough. Then he takes a gouge, a piece of sharpened iron bound on the end of a six-foot pole, and finishes the hollowing out. If he grows tired someone else takes his place. When the gouging has been completed the trough is stood on end and a fire made in it with dry bamboo to clean it. Then the charcoal is scraped out with an adze.

In order to guard against leakage wax is heated with a hot brand and rubbed over the ends of the trough. The ends themselves are also heated in order to make the wax run. When the trough is finished a shallow pit is dug to accommodate it.

If a trough starts to leak the festa may be hastened in order that the beer may be drunk up before it is all lost, or an attempt to mend it may be made by spreading wax over the outside of the leaking end and mixing it with ashes. When I saw this done once the effects were practically nil; I sent for some pails and pans and the beer was emptied into them. Melted wax was then poured on the inside of the trough and rubbed in with the fingers. This also failed to stop the leak, so the beer was consumed in a brief preliminary festa.

The size of the troughs varies from a yard to two yards in length. Their depth depends on the size of the tree, but they average about a foot and a half in external diameter.

Mortars and Pestles

Mortars are made when needed from fallen trees or from trees that are especially cut down for the purpose. Sometimes a mortar is no more than a hole in a fallen log. Mortars are always very small—never over a foot long, six inches or so wide, and three inches deep. Mortars are generally not transported but simply left behind in the deserted camp site. Small pestles are made for them from pieces of wood, but pestles of polished stone were also made until recently. These are about ten inches long. When such a pestle is found by accident it is called a "supernatural pestle."

Little bath tubs for the bathing of infants are also hollowed from logs. They are very shallow. The child is not placed in them, but the water poured in and then rubbed over the baby.

Baskets

From the point of view of use there are basically two kinds of Kaingáng baskets, those which are used for holding liquids and are lined with beeswax and those which are used for carrying burdens and are unlined. Both are constructed of bamboo splints. The former are much better in workmanship than the latter. They are made very carefully and, although unornamented, are fine examples of basketry. They are manufactured in one shape only but in a variety of sizes, from that of a small cup to a basket holding as much as a gallon and are used for carrying water and honey.

Each man makes his wax-lined baskets as he happens to need them, but the large burden baskets are sometimes woven by a group of men together just before they start out to collect pine nuts. Then they sit in a circle laughing and talking and holding up their handiwork for one another to look at. Since they are all made in exactly the same manner there is little for a man to see on anyone else's basket that he does not see on his own. They are all made with the outer green skin of the splint left on, and the interior and exterior show alternating bands of green (i.e. the outer side of the bamboo splint) and white (the inner side of the splint).

SPINNING

A certain kind of cord is made by twisting two fibers together against the side of the right leg with the palm of the right hand. It may be that the use of the leg instead of the thigh is due in the case of men to their wearing trousers and in the case of women to their unwillingness, since they have begun to wear dresses, to impair their newly acquired modesty by lifting them above their knees.

A KAINGÁNG BRIDGE

Two trees (A and B) are felled on opposite banks of the stream so that they will fall into it, and posts (C) are sunk on the downstream side to keep the trees from being carried away. A third log (D) is lashed to A and B just above the surface of the water. Then three sets of tall uprights (E) are sunk into the stream bed on either side of A and B and tied together at the top. At the bottom they are united by horizontal boughs (F) that pass across the top of D. A bough (G) is laid on either side of D and lashed to F. These structures, D and G, form the gangway. Now railings are made by tying long boughs (H) to E on both sides.

Ornaments

Lip Plugs

The Kaingáng no longer wear lip plugs. These were usually made from pine knots but some men preferred beef bone.[16] Still others liked to slip a fine deer bone over the pine-knot plug. There was a considerable amount of individual variation in the shape of the plugs, and the members of some extended families were distinguished by the shape of their lip plugs.

Dance Ornaments

These are made only for baby blackenings.

ķôndjáidn are, as the name implies, sticks about three feet long covered with feathers and stuck in the ground around the dance circle. Near the top they are provided with a tiny plaited square or disk and are usually surmounted by feathers. In making these ornaments the men do not try to surpass one another in originality, and all the ķôndjáidn are very much alike. The most striking innovation at the blackening that I witnessed was that of Chukembégn, who put the tail of a tesoureiro on top of his ķôndjáidn instead of the usual feather.

Lu are made of small basketlike objects set on the ends of poles about thirty feet long and set up on the dance ground. As the festivities mount they are lifted out of their holes and carried around on the shoulders of the men.

Smaller lu, about eight inches long, are held in the hand.

[16] Obtained from cattle killed in raids on the Brazilians.

Conclusions[17]

In spite of the incomplete character of the data some valid inferences can be made.

(1) Industries are overwhelmingly in the hands of the men, from the standpoint both of number and of importance. Before the raids on the settlers made pottery and clothing manufacture unnecessary the part played by women in the economy was somewhat more important than later when conditions made their techniques unimportant. The following table may make this clearer:

Industry	Male	Female
Hunting (CI)[18]	+	
Fruit gathering (I)	[+]*	+
Pine nuts (CI)	+	+
Honey gathering (CI)	+	[+]
Beer (C)	+	+
Cooking (I)		+
Fire making (CI)	+	
Houses (CI)	+	+
Bows (I)	+	
Arrows (I)	+	
Lances (CI)	+	
Clubs (I)	+	
Troughs (C)	+	
Mortars (I)	+	
Pestles (I)	+	[+]
Baskets (I)	+	
Spinning (I)	[+]	+
Robes (I)		+
Shirts (I)		+
Pots (I)		+
Carrying-bands (for infants) (I)		+
Dance ornaments (I)	+	
Lip plugs (I)	+	
Raiding Brazilians (C)	+	

The only important industry controlled by women was pottery, and when raiding the Brazilians loomed up as a new economic technique,

[17] My data on weaving and pottery are so scanty that I have not included them here.

[18] C=Industries that are organized cooperatively; I=industries that are individualistic; CI=industries that are sometimes cooperative and sometimes individualistic.

* Brackets represent participation in a minor way.

PLATE I

House

PLATE II

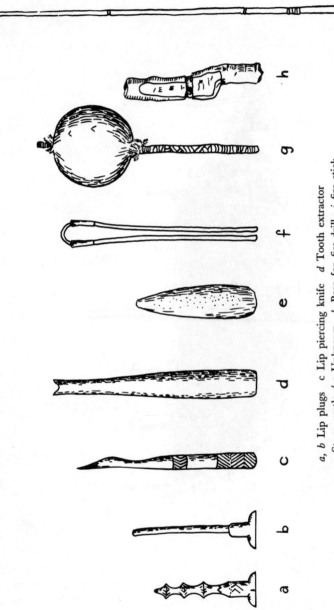

a, b Lip plugs *c* Lip piercing knife *d* Tooth extractor
e Stone pestle *f, g* Unknown *h* Base for fire-drill *i* fire stick

PLATE III

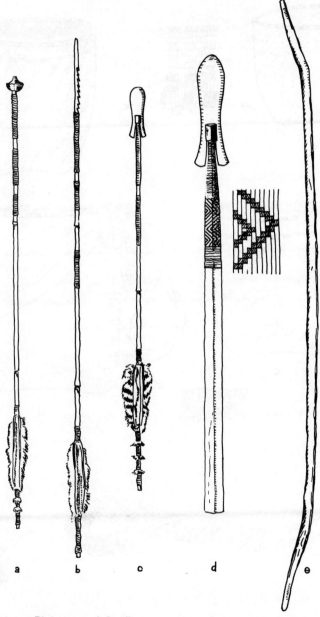

a Bird arrow   b Small-game arrow   c Large-game arrow
d Lance   e Bow

PLATE IV

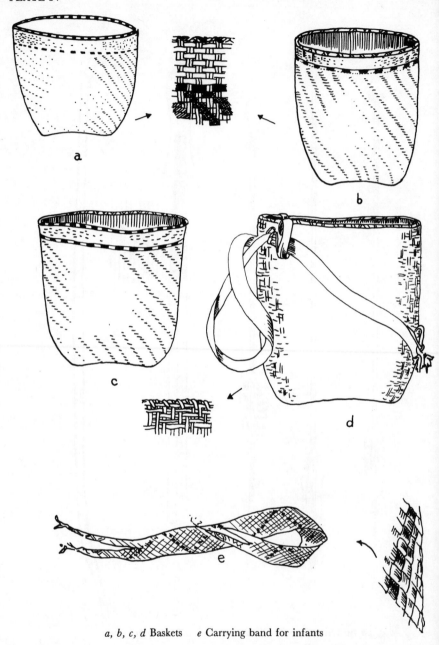

a, b, c, d Baskets   *e* Carrying band for infants

PLATE V

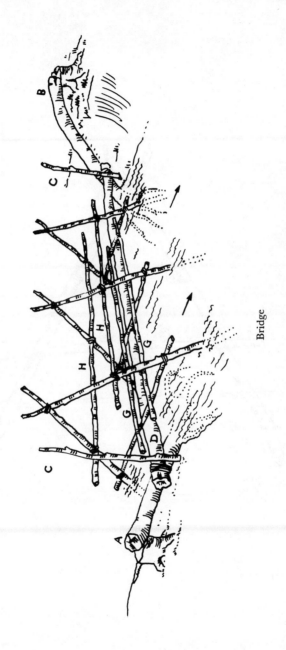

Bridge

PLATE VI

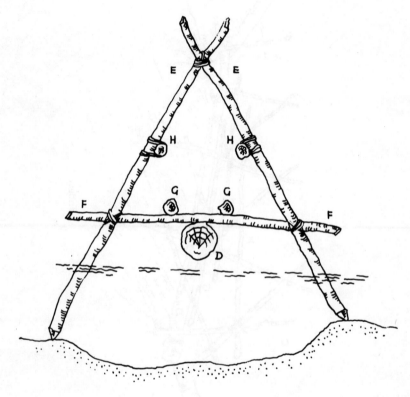

Bridge

PLATE VII

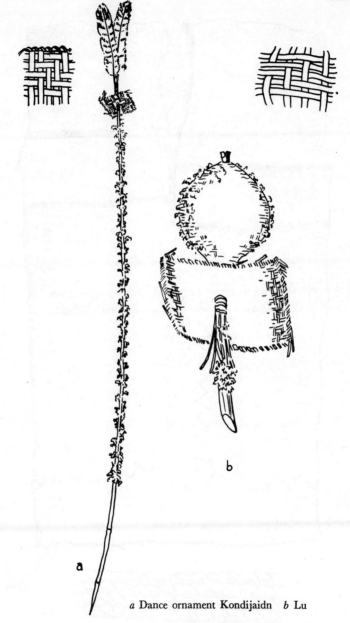

a Dance ornament Kondijaidn   *b* Lu

PLATE VIII

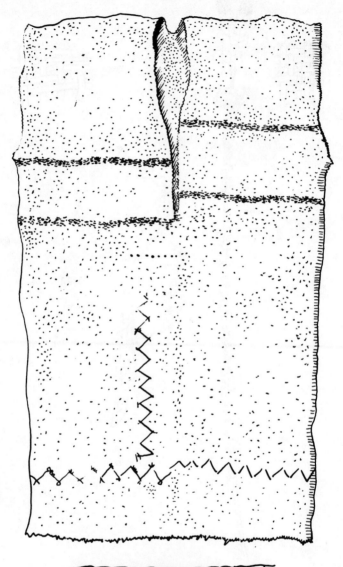

Shirt

women's role in Kaingáng economy became insignificant. They continued to make their contributions, it is true, but these were small compared to men's.

(2) Although most of the techniques seem better suited to an individual working alone, whenever circumstances become exigent several individuals cooperate, as, for example, in the making of lances and troughs and the hunting of tapir with dogs.

In general, the way in which each industry is practised is inherent in the natural conditions under which it is maintained. Tapir hunting is both cooperative and individualistic but fails to achieve the maximum cooperation because the Kaingáng are unable to put into effect the elaborate technique necessary for killing tapir in the *carreira,* the best way of hunting tapir. Peccary are usually surrounded, but they may also be pursued by a lone hunter although surrounding is unquestionably the best means of taking them. The only way the Kaingáng killed deer under aboriginal conditions was by uttering its cry until it approached or by coming upon a deer by accident. The best way to kill deer that I know of is to station men along the river bank and kill the deer when it is driven into the water by dogs. This seems possible even without canoes,[19] but I never saw or heard of its being done by the Kaingáng. Such a technique requires long residence in one place and a knowledge of the places where the deer will probably enter the water when it is driven by the dogs. Under aboriginal conditions deer were always killed by lone hunters. The only *tateti* hunts that I know of were cooperative, and this seems the best arrangement. Birds are not snared but are hunted individually.

Thus, for the most part, hunting techniques are fundamentally affected by the natural conditions of the forest. The hunting of tapir and deer by the waiting technique requires not only a thorough knowledge of the territory but a considerable number of men so that one may be stationed on every *carreira.* Neither of these conditions could well be fulfilled under aboriginal conditions. In other words, natural conditions in hunting prevented the systematic following out of the social ideal of cooperative effort.

In the table most of the industries appear as "I," but some of the most important, like hunting and housebuilding, are both C and I, and the very important industry of raiding is entirely C. If we throw this evidence together with the general emphasis in social life we will see that in spite of the preponderance of the "I" industries Kaingáng culture is really not individualistic but is cooperative under all of the most important conditions of life. Indeed, Kaingáng culture is oriented toward a degree of cooperation unusual in a tribe having so few social forms. It is unnecessary to sum-

[19] Richard Lydekker's *The Royal Natural History,* Vol. II, p. 462, describes a tapir hunt witnessed by Carl Schomburgk in which just this technique was used.

marize once more the attitudes and the procedures that express this cooperation, which reaches its highest expression in the prosecution of the
feuds. The search for food and the institutions of polyandry and joint marriage supply additional occasions for cooperation. Actually what we have
in Kaingáng society is a large number of individualistic techniques employed within a social framework that is essentially cooperative.

Appendix II

Body Paints and Kinship System[1]

THE THEORETICAL SOCIAL STRUCTURE, which has been largely so much cultural flotsam for at least two hundred years and probably much longer, divides the Kaingáng into five groups. To each group belongs a distinct body-paint design and a series of personal names. Throughout the six generations of the genealogies these names are repeated many times. All the people wearing the same design are *ķôiķa hë,*[2] good people, to one another. Each design has a name that describes its objective character, and all those who wear it are grouped together under one of the personal names belonging to the group. Two marks, however, the disc and the horizontal bar with vertical lines, are not distinguished by one particular name. The scheme may be tabulated as follows:

Group name	*Design*	*Name of design*	*Translation*
Wanyekí *ķôiķa hë*	•	*mêvídn*	scattered all over
Klendó *ķôiķa hë*	|	*ķalébm*	coming down
Kainlé *ķôiķa hë*	○	*ķuiķên*	in a ring
None	┬┬┬┬┬┬┬┬	*ķaķtêng ķų ķalébm*	horizontal and coming down
None	●	*ķanêm*	placed there

[1] This discussion is abstracted from a study of genealogies of more than 500 individuals. They include the ancestors of all the people on the reservation today back to the great grandparents.

[2] *Kôiķá,* relative; *hë,* whole, serviceable.

The names of the marks are simply descriptive. *Mevídn* refers to small dots scattered all over the body, *ḳalébm* to vertical lines drawn downward, etc.

All people having the same mark are *ḳôiḳa hë* to one another, but in addition a man calls all the women having the same mark as he *yôḳtë*,[3] and these women call him *ḳôiḳa hë*. He calls all men with a different mark from his own *wamǫ*,[4] and all women in a similar position he calls *plʉ*, sexual partner.[5] Women call all women with marks different from their own *wamǫ*, and all men in a similar position are called *mbâdn*, sexual partner.[5] Women with the same mark call each other *ḳôiḳa hë*. Men with the same mark call each other *ḳôiḳa hë*.

Even two hundred years ago a very large number of people had names from at least two groups, and a not inconsiderable number had names from three. Thus the groups are not separate. Within the obvious limits of historical investigation they have not formed the basis for any systematic organization. Marks do not descend systematically from parents or any other relatives to the younger generation, and there is no fixed system through which names are given to children. In general close relatives give the names of their own close relatives to newborn children. Individuals may have anywhere from one to eight names.

There was considerable disagreement among my informants as to the marks belonging to each person, and even though they might agree on his names they very often disagreed as to the marks proper to his names. Certain names, however, are associated by everyone with the same marks. Among the not inconsiderable number[6] of such names are the basic ones, Wanyekí, Klendó, and Kainlé.

The present-day Kaingáng say that people having the same marks cannot marry, but for two hundred years there has been absolutely no attempt to live up to the theory, and no feeling of shame is connected with marrying a person of the same mark. If the conversation happens to turn on the subject of the marks light jesting may arise in connection with some couple who both have the same marks. In general, however, the subject is sociosexually a dead issue.

Extensive checking shows that the marking scheme not only does not regulate marriage but also has nothing to do with the composition of hunting bands, the distribution of food and property, or the cremation of

---

[3] *yôḳ*, formal prefix; *të*, woman.

[4] *wa*, formal prefix; *mǫ*, dative. It implies the giving of something to someone and may actually have something to do with the belief that in the beginning some groups gave some of their personal names to other groups that did not have enough.

[5] See kinship terms p. 178.

[6] Exactly 49 out of 193, i.e. 25 percent.

the dead.[7] The only function of the marks is magical. When a person dies all the people around him paint themselves with their marks in order to frighten the *kupléng* away. "It sees them and becomes afraid and goes." A widowed person, a *thûpqya*, paints himself with marks other than his own on his return from his period of isolation in order that the *kupléng* may not recognize him. About five years before my arrival a number of people added the circle design to their other marks because when Kemblén died he told all the people to change their marks "so that the *kupléng* would see it and go away."

A number of kinship usages are explained on the basis of the marks. These will be discussed in the section on the kinship system. It is only necessary to say here that all such explanations are purely theoretical and do not support kinship usage.

THE KINSHIP SYSTEM

(1) *plu*, wife; women with whom a man has had sexual relations; women with marks different from a man, and with whom, therefore, such relationships are "permissible."

(2) *mbâdn*, husband; men with whom a woman has had sexual relations; men with marks different from a woman, and with whom, therefore, such relationships are "permissible."

(3) *yûgn*, father; grandfather; all males much older than Ego;[8] men who have had relations with Ego's mother.

(4) *nyô*, mother; grandmother; all females much older than Ego; women who have had relations with Ego's father.

(5) *nyungnyên*, all blood relatives excepting real parents and grand-parents and grandparents' siblings and own children. All members of the same extended family. It is often used specifically for Ego's own brothers, sisters, and first cousins, and for anyone about Ego's own age. In this case the term becomes reciprocal. It may be used also for anyone a little older than Ego. All individuals having the same mark as Ego.

(6) *yavï*, all people somewhat younger than Ego.

(7) *yi*, child; all people very much younger than Ego and the children of all the people with whom Ego has had sexual relations.

(8) *klq*, offspring. Tapirs and dogs have *klq*, but to speak of an animal's *yi* provokes laughter.

(9) *yômblâ*, (plural) *yëgnmblâ*, all the blood relatives of No. 2 and No. 1. In a more limited sense, all the No. 5 of No. 2 and No. 1 with the

---

[7] See fn. 1, p. 175.

[8] Ego=person speaking or spoken about.

exception of second cousins and their descendants and first cousins
once removed and their descendants.

(10) *lânglé,* co-spouse.

(11) *ḳaḳé,* relation. This term is not as strict in its application as No. 5, in
that its use may extend outside the extended family. It is used
regularly between cousins of all classes, rarely for aunt, never for
brother or sister. It is a courtesy term for people not related by
blood.

Although the major stress of this system is on relative age the culture
actually fails to take cognizance of it in any formal way. In the distribution
of food and property, for example, no one age class takes precedence over
another. Nor does the principle of relative age play an important role in
marriage. Marriage is on the whole between age-mates, although some
informants seem to feel that the man should be older than the woman.
Leadership is determined by personality factors, by *waiḳayú,* not by age.

The term *nyungnyên* expresses the attitudes within the extended families. Its use for blood relatives, combined with its extension to include a
much wider group, indicates precisely how the Kaingáng feel about members of the same extended family even when they are not related by blood.
Socially they are siblings to one another and the same blood flows in their
veins, no matter what the actual conditions are.[9]

I have frequently pointed out the wide difference in affect between the
relationships within the extended families and those that obtain between
them. Since, therefore, the terms *nyungnyên, yavï, yi,* and *ḳlą* are used
almost exclusively for members of the same extended family it follows that
they express a considerable amount of in-group affect. Since, also, the extended families are intensely inbred and the general sibling feeling is
strong, there is a correlation here with the fact that the kinship system
completely ignores questions of specific relationship. Since the kinship
terms at the most, therefore, express only generalized blood relationship
the most important correlations in the Kaingáng kinship system are with
age pure and simple, and with the affect associated with the in-group.

In Chapter VII I pointed out that the Kaingáng do not keep to the
theoretical formulation of their affinal relationships but that each man
selects particular individuals for attention. Hand in hand with this goes
the fact that although for all the Kaingáng the category of affinity[10] is the
same each person uses the term *yômblâ* in everyday life for a different

---

[9] An excellent example of this can be found on p. 122. Although Wanyekí and Kuvén
were not blood relatives of Kôi they were his *nyungnyên* because they came from the same
extended family.

[10] Relationship by marriage.

group of affinities. There is an additional variability in the use of this term due to the fact that some individuals prefer to use the age term series rather than *yômblâ*. Although some people are singled out as affinal relatives toward whom Ego has specific obligations he might never call them *yômblâ,* preferring instead to use the age terms.

The significance of terms 1, 2, and 8 has been discussed in Chapter III, and the further implications of 3 have also been discussed in that chapter.

Appendix III

Rituals

Death

WHEN DEATH COMES the emotional resources of the Kaingáng are mobilized to overcome the forces of destruction that have been set in motion. Death, the perpetual threat, has become momentarily actualized in the form of the *kupléng,* the ghost-soul of the deceased, and the most elaborate ritual forms the Kaingáng possess are directed toward the elimination of this threat. Of all the survivors at a death the one who stands in greatest peril from the *kupléng* is the spouse, the *thúpáya.* The Kaingáng feel that the spouses have had such intimate relations that there must be a complete wiping out of all the old contacts. The rites through which the *thúpáya* passes are intended, however, not only to safeguard his life, but also to protect the community. No one can be sure whom the *kupléng* will select for its companion, but since it clings most closely to the *thúpáya* he must free himself from the *kupléng* as soon as possible. The *thúpáya* is a threat to the members of his group—they are genuinely afraid of him—and the rites which he performs serve both to rid him of his personal fear of his dead spouse and to make him once more acceptable to his fellows. As Klendó put it, "They . . . make a festa when the husband or the wife comes back so that he [or she] can live with them."

Even before his spouse's bones are buried the *thúpáya* leaves camp for his widower's (or widow's) isolation, his *waikómáng.* "I did not want to see the bones," said Klendó; "so I left before she was burnt. I was afraid I would die; so I went to another place. I used to talk to her; therefore I was afraid to see her bones. I did not want to see her bones because I did not want to see her *kupléng* while I was asleep."[1] A man leaves camp alone, taking his bow and arrows, an axe and a blanket, but no pot, for *thúpáya*

---

[1] Up to this point all that has been said applies equally to men and women.

may not eat cooked food until they have completed the ritual series. If they did they would get hot inside and die. The *thûpáya* must refrain from all meat; all they are allowed to eat is honey and vegetable foods, and by the end of their *waikômáng* they may be very thin. If a widower encounters game he may shoot it, but he must not eat it. Instead he opens its belly and rubs the blood "all over himself to wash off[2] the hunting[3] that he used to do for his wife. This is called wiping[4] off and throwing away. He does the same with honey, bees' larvae, and bee sugar. He shoots tapir, pigs, deer, *tateti,* monkeys, jacutingas, howler monkeys, macucas, ururús [and a number of other birds]. He shoots several and does this wiping himself off."[5] By rubbing himself with the blood of game animals the husband removes one of the principal ties with his wife, for during her life he had shot game for her. Thus the whole ritual, including the fasting, is a transparent cleansing ceremony, in which the very terminology makes the psychological point clear. The Kaingáng do not feel that the dead are impure or that they contaminate, but that the *kupléng* follows the vestiges of its earthly life, to the peril of survivors.

The *thûpáya* does not remain so far away from camp that he is completely out of contact. Under aboriginal conditions that would have put him in actual peril of his life from human enemies,[6] but always remains close enough for some woman to prepare a sleeping-place for him every night. There he sleeps alone with two stems of the *nggign* fern[7] in his arms "just as he used to hold his wife.[8] The *kupléng* is afraid of these and goes away." Women remain nearer to camp than men, and if they have nursing infants they take them along. They do not always sleep alone, for often a woman who prepares the sleeping-place for the *thûpáya* and sprinkles it with protective herbs wraps her in her arms all night long in a protective embrace against her husband's *kupléng*. If there have been a number of deaths at one time, as from a raid by the *bugreiros* or by ven-

---

[2] *Waikupé,* to wash oneself.

[3] ê plu thi mô ê tô   pánúi yó
his wife her for he (instru- shoot place
                  mental
                  particle)
Literally, the place where he used to shoot for his wife.

[4] *Wainyekúi,* to wipe oneself. Without the reflexive it means "to wipe," as in cleansing the barrel of a gun.

[5] Women, since they have not the weapons with which to kill animals, simply rub themselves with honey.

[6] When the Brazilian Indian hunters, the *bugreiros,* were thought to be in the neighborhood, no one went on *waikômáng.*

[7] See p. 187 fn.

[8] Or husband.

detta enemies, the male and female *thûpáya* form separate groups and go off together.

The period of *waikômáng* is exceedingly variable. Until a few years ago the end of *waikômáng* was marked by *angdjüdn,* the festa of rattles. In preparation for this event, which marked the reacceptance of the *thûpáya* by his group, beer was prepared. But before the *thûpáya* returned he had to be completely cleansed of his spouse's "dirt,"[9] and to this end the people who went to fetch him cut his hair, "because when he slept with his wife their heads were together," and his finger nails. It is said of women that their nails were cut "because they used to get meat under their nails in preparing food for their husbands." The people sang during the entire rite of cutting the hair and nails in order to frighten off the *kupléng.* The songs that were sung during the death rituals are called *ëhëdn;*[10] some of them were sung only at certain points in the ritual series, while others are not ritual songs but are part of the general song repertoire of each man.[11] While the hair was being cut it was held with a bit of medicine to protect the cutter, and when the task was finished hair and nails were pounded up in a mortar with a number of herbs, including the ubiquitous tapir's raw food, and thrown into the water.[12]

"The hair is thrown into the water because they are afraid to let it rot on earth. The first-born [i.e. the ancients] came out along the water, and therefore they throw the hair into the water." Like tapir's raw food, water is a general life-symbol to the Kaingáng. In the same way the hair and nails of young children are thrown into the water "so that they will grow. Otherwise the children would dry up and die," and the umbilical cord is placed in the water for the same reason. The Kaingáng have great faith in bathing wounds with water, and all herbs are mixed with water before they are applied to the body as remedies.

The entire body of the *thûpáya* was now rubbed with tapir's raw food to cleanse him, and his head was covered with feathers or a feathered cloth, for the combination of the haircut and the feathers would prevent the *kupléng* from recognizing him. As he walked toward camp where the beer was waiting someone went before him scattering herbs in his path to frighten away the *kupléng,* and as they walked fearfully along they sang

[9] *Nyanggli,* dirt; taboo as applied to food.

[10] From the stem *hë,* whole, entire, sound. The purpose of these songs is to keep people well.

[11] See p. 192 this section.

[12] "They also cut the hair of her small child. Its father used to see its hair; so they cut it off." The hair at the nape of the neck was never cut off in this rite, for that would cause death.

whatever songs occurred to them. When those in camp heard the singing they too began and as the group entered the dance circle they were greeted by loud singing and the whirr of gourd rattles. "This is our song of fear. He[13] was afraid of her.[14] He was singing for her husband's *kuplêng* to be afraid and go away. He sang in front of her. When they saw him coming they began to dance with their rattles. The women came behind her, rattling. These rattles are for the *kuplêng* of the husband to fear and go away. Widows sit and the men dance around them. They dance about behind the woman. She is told to sit down. They are afraid of the woman. They think that if they stay there they might die; that is why they dance the woman. They are afraid of the woman because she used to live with her husband. That is why they have the *angdjidn*. When there is no more beer they go to the water and wash themselves and then wash their mouths with muddy water. They wash their mouths because they are afraid of the songs. It is because they sang with their mouths. They rub their bodies with sand and stones because they do not rot. I am going to be like stones that never die. I am going to grow old like stones."

Starting with the change of the body-paint symbols, as described in Appendix II, the normal activities of life were in part reversed, with the object of confusing the *kuplêng*. Instead of drinking his beer from a gourd or from a basket the *thûpáya* drank from a bamboo tube. A widow was *given* the drink because formerly she used to *give* it out to others, and she remained lying down in the morning when her children were already up because she used to get up to take care of her husband. "If she were to get up while her children slept they would die."

It is still dangerous to eat cooked food for a while, but after a few more days another rite overcomes the danger inherent in this act. "They kill a tapir and cook it, mixing *ndolǫ* or *kakleiklé* leaves in a clay pot with water. The water is brought to a boil with heated stones. They boil it and take it off and pour it into a plate. Then the people are called together and they drink the remedy and eat the meat."[15]

[13] A relative who was leading the group back to camp. Specific relationships are of no importance in these ceremonies.

[14] Although this is a description of a particular ceremony that took place when a relative of the informant died, leaving his widow, the description has equal validity for widowers.

[15] This has some striking parallels in the rites following the killing of men. "A man who killed a Brazilian did not eat from a pot. He roasted his food. They would pound the thorns of *chuin,* put it in a pot, and put water on top to boil it. Then they would drink it, and then they would eat from the pot. When they killed their own people they would do the same thing. They wanted to [be able to] kill men; so they pounded thorns and mixed it with water and drank it. When we are walking along thorns seize us and rip our skin; so they do this [pound thorns] so that they will be able to do the same thing. If one were to eat from a pot after killing the Brazilians one could not kill anyone after that. Some people would wash themselves after an attack on the Brazilians to protect themselves from [the scent of] dogs."

Now the *thúpáya,* after a period of approximately three to five weeks, could again take up his normal course of existence, except that he had still to abstain from sexual intercourse.

One of my informants gave me a number of ritualistic specializations in terms of the body-paint scheme. Although I consider them of very doubtful validity, I give them here for the sake of completeness.

(1) When a man comes back from *waikômáng* he is given his food by a woman of the opposite mark, because "they are different and therefore are not afraid."

(2) The period for which Wanyekí *kôiká hë* must abstain from cooked food is much longer than for Klendó.

(3) The former keep their body paints on for a much longer time.

(4) The Klendó *kôiká hë* use pine needles in the pot at the ritual of the first eating of cooked food.

The rituals of the *waikômáng* and the *angdjïdn* are limited to *thúpáya,* the widowed, for it is only the surviving spouse who must go through any procedure at all.[16]

Cremation and Burial

Vomblé's description of these ceremonies, which I never had the opportunity to see, since the Kaingáng no longer burn their dead, is so clear and vivid that it needs practically no elucidation or paraphrasing; and I therefore give it word for word.

"They place him on a blanket. Arrows are placed beside him. Feathers are placed on him.[17] His arrows are broken. The bowstring is cut and the arrows tied with it; also the wrapping for future arrows. The bow is chopped in half and tied together with the arrows. His head is laid to the west and his feet to the east because the *kupléng* dwell in the west. He will see the road and go that way. If they were to put him on the other way he would err. The wood [of the pyre] is waist-high. They place him on it and pile wood on top of him until it is as high as a man. They sink posts on the side all around so that the wood will not fall down. They put wax[18] and meat in his hands and say: 'There! Take it and go and leave me! You go to the many.' They pound him on the chest [and say]: 'Leave your animals[19] to me and go! When I am suffering [hunger] I'll shoot and eat them. Leave your people and go! Leave the honey for me! You went to

---

[16] All inherited property, however, should be wiped off with tapir's raw food.

[17] I do not know why.

[18] Symbolic of honey.

[19] All game animals. The *kupléng* is asked not to take the souls of the animals with it.

the many!' When a person has many children [they say]: 'Leave your children and things to me and go. When they are hungry they will kill and eat them. Now the [things] I have given you to be your own are there [in your hands]. Take them and go. But leave the rest of the things that are here for me and go!' This is also said to women. Then they talk again. They call his name and say: 'Speak well of me. I suffered much with you. Do not be *vai*[20] to me! Speak well of me. I suffered a great deal with you, and so I am putting you in a prepared place.' Then they set fire to the pile with flaming bamboo. When they set fire they sing." There is no special song for igniting the pyre.[21]

"When they burn a man they go off and sleep. Much later they come back to his bones. They go around toward his head and say to him: 'I come to see you. Do not be *vai* to me. I suffered a great deal with you—do not be *vai* to me.' Then they come to the pile. The bones are whole if the pile burnt slowly. If the corpse is *vai* it did not burn completely but fell off the pyre beyond the stays. *Vai* means a threat of death—he has seen someone die without walking about. Patá fell in the direction of the place in which his people would die. Children are never *vai*,[22] but men and women are *vai*. Kutá exploded and fell off the pyre—she was *vai*. She was foretelling the death of Pepó [her husband]. Next day they went there, and only her arms were burnt. The fire burnt out alone. Then they made another fire for her.

"The people who burn them treat themselves with *tutólo* and with *mbë* leaves. *Ndâyâ waikôktô* is also used. These are pounded. They smell like orange[23] leaves. They are rubbed over the hands and body for five days.[24] When they walked around burning them [i.e. the corpses] the smoke enveloped them and stuck to them—so it is this that they wash off.

"When the fire is out they throw the ashes off the bones and gather them together in bark. When they gather up the bones they make a big basket for them and put fern in the basket with *kungglú* and *tai* leaves.

[20] To be *vai* means to be supernaturally dangerous. Specifically it involves a prediction of death. The capacity to be *vai* is limited to dead bodies—which show that they are *vai* by not burning on the first pyre. The informant's explanation of the command "Speak well of me" is that "he should not be *vai* to them." This does not seem very illuminating.

[21] See p. 192.

[22] Children are also never burnt; nevertheless this absence of threat in dead children is correlated rather with the attitude toward children than with ceremonial procedure. Children are universally loved.

[23] Since they have been on the reservation the Kaingáng have become familiar with oranges.

[24] A very doubtful period both from the standpoint of fixity and from the standpoints of the informant's notions of time and number, which are extremely vague.

They carry the basket with the bones and go to another place to bury them. They carry a long stick, leaning on it, [and they sing:]

1) *nde te   tę ve*
   what carry

2) *nde te   tę ve*
   what carry

3) *vâ ma la nyakthô te   tę ve*
   look you sun faeces   carry

4) *vâ ma la yudn   yô klam tę ve*
   look you sun come out place under

Since the words are in perfect syntactic order the obvious translation is:

Line (1) What is being carried?
  (2) What is being carried?
  (3) Look, you. Sun's faeces are being carried.
  (4) Look, you. Under the place where the sun emerges.

I have no explanation of the significance of this song. Klendó said that they sing the song "that it should be light [in weight] and that the people should not slip.

"They sing this song because they are afraid they will die. They are afraid they will slip—a person who is about to die will fall, but one who will live to old age does not fall. If there are many of them they do not sing this song, but if there are few they sing. After carrying the bones they wash themselves with clay and rub themselves with stones. They all do this, not only the one who carries the bones. [They say,] 'I am going to be like the old stone—I am never going to die.' They do not bury the bones in the place the person died—it is not good."

As they walk along they cut *nggign* (fern) repeatedly and throw it away. "They carry it [*nggign*] so that the carrying of our bones should be no more.[25] It is to rub out the sweat caused by carrying the basket. . . . At last they pound the *nggign* and wash themselves [with the titrated sap]."

When they reach the spot where they intend to bury the bones the ground is cleared, and hole dug and lined with fern, the bones and the basket placed in the hole, and a little house erected over the grave by the women.

[25] It is clear from the phraseology and from the general ideology of death ceremonies that this is a way of severing contact with the dead. The precise symbolism, however, eludes me. *Nggign* is a fern with a short (about four feet), woody, extremely thorny trunk that grows exclusively on heavily wooded hillsides. Besides its function in death ceremonies it is used to ferment beer. When titrated it produces a deep red juice.

"When they burn a man or woman they throw away their firebrands after the burning and make a new fire with a fire drill, for if they remained beside the old fires they would die—it was the fire by which the dead used to sleep."

Keening

The Kaingáng mourn in a rhythmic chant heavily interspersed with sobbing and snuffling. When a number of people come together at a death they all keen, but most of the keening throughout the year is done by individuals who start to think about their dead relatives and burst into tears. Keening is most commonly heard in the very early morning or evening, when the Kaingáng have nothing to do and it is not yet time for a meal. Nevertheless people may start to keen at any time at all and wherever they may be. Although the Kaingáng feel that it is respectful toward the dead to weep and are scornful of those who do not, they do not particularly select large crowds to weep in. The lusty voices of the Kaingáng carry wonderfully in the cool air before dawn or after sunset, and I have heard them as much as a quarter of a mile away. In a small camp it would be unnecessary for them to raise their voices so in order to be heard, but nowadays when the settlement stretches for half a mile on both sides of the river a powerful voice has its advantages. To me this mourning was always unintelligible, but anyone who has ever tried to understand a sobbing person in our own society will understand that my difficulties were not simply linguistic. The only way I could obtain texts was through informants. The chants thus obtained are a good sample of the general drift of the occasional keening, but since they were not uttered under the influence of emotion and were not taken down while the individuals were actually mourning they lack somewhat the variety of the "natural" product and are greatly reduced in length. Nevertheless they are faithful.

During the very early part of my stay I heard Angglό keening at a festa, and with the help of my interpreter, who gave me snatches of what she said with the interpretation, I managed to record a great deal.

Angglό's Chant

I am weeping. I forgot my daughter's[26] name and now I am remembering. I loved[27] her much, and now I can love her no more. I desire very much to see her again. She used to call me mother. Before my daughter died she wept much. I desire to see my daughter today. My father[28] always provided food for me, but now I am hungry; that is why I am weeping.

[26] Angglό had one child who died.

[27] Ka lêlê nya.

[28] Now she begins to mourn for her father.

I am always bewailing my father. Before he died he suffered much. I thought that my father was alive, but he is dead. I always forget my father, but now I am remembering him. My father had many relatives, but I alone am weeping for him. I feel like weeping all day long for my father. He used always to get food for me. I wish to see him. I weep all day long for my daughter. When my father was alive I used to call him "father," but now I cannot. He always gave me food. I pity him. My father loved me much, but he left me and went away. I am forgetting my father a great deal. He suffered much. I desire to see my daughter who called me "mother." Before she died she called me "mother." My father used always to bring food for me, and now I wish to see him. My father died and never remembered me. My father died, and now I pity him. I am suffering because of my daughter. I cannot sleep because I am always thinking of my daughter. Whenever I eat I do not forget my daughter. She is there now [where she died, at the Post].

Kulá's Chant[29]

I am remembering my mother.[30] I want to call her mother. I am remembering my mother. I am the one who called her mother, but now it is all over. I am remembering my mother. When my mother would look at me she would remember that my father had seen me and she would weep—now that is all over. I am remembering my mother. I and my children used to call my mother mother—that is all over. I am remembering my mother. I want to see my mother. When my father would return after leaving me he would think of how I suffered, and he would weep. Grandmother, whose name I bear, would think of my sickness and suffering.

Kundídn's Chant

One of my nyǫ[31] would see my brother and me suffering, and she would come to us to weep. I suffered with him. My brother and I had no father; so he and I wept for my children. He and I suffered. I want to see my father.

Kundídn has lost all her nearest relatives—husband, parents, brothers, sisters, and four of her five children—and it is probable that if she had continued longer she would have mentioned her mother.

[29] This and the succeeding chants were obtained from informants. Kulá is Angglós's sister, but this chant was recorded eight or nine months after Angglós's, when their mother had died of the grippe. Kulá lost one baby many years ago—apparently she had stopped mourning for it.

[30] Literally, "I am remembering what mother looked like."

[31] See Appendix II.

Kuthúgn's Chants
I. For His Mother

Mother saw me and mourned every night. I was suffering. I forget what she looked like. I was hungry. I forget what she looked like. I forget what she looked like. I suffered. I forget what she looked like. I suffered. I am always weeping but I never see her. I forget her.

II. For men

Nyungnyên shot things for me. I suffered. I forget what he looked like. I used to wander about with *nyungnyên,* and he loved me. I used to go about with him, and I forget what he looked like. I forget what he looked like. *Nyungnyêlê*[32] and I suffered a great deal and I forget him. I forget what he looked like. [Then he sings:] *e ko yo ho nei mo ko ma ve yo na ta ko ma chudn ve yo ne ta ko ma chudn ve.*[33] I suffered with *nyungnyên* a great deal and I forget what they looked like. I attacked other men with *nyungnyên.* I used to shoot things with them. I forget what they looked like.

Klendó's Chants[34]
I. For His Wife

I do not see my wife. Will I see her? I go with my wife. I do not see her.

II. For His Mother

I do not see my mother. Will I not see my mother? I forgot my mother.

III. For Véye (Who Died a Few Weeks Ago)

I do not see *nyungnyêlê.* I do not hear *nyungnyêlê* call me *yûgn.*

IV. For a Father's Brother

I do not see *yûgn.* I forget what *yûgn* looked like. *Yûgn* lived in me.

V. For a First Cousin Once Removed

I do not see *nyungnyên.* Will I see another who looks like her? I do not see her.

Vomblé's Chants
I. For His Relatives

My relatives shot things for me, and now I and my children are suffering.

---

[32] The term *nyungnyêlê* is a form of *nyungnyên* that occurs only in mourning chants.
[33] This song has no meaning.
[34] These and the chants of Vomblé were recorded while they were my informants.

II. For His Father

My father used to set food before me, and my children and I ate it; and now my children and I are suffering. My father would weep when he saw me because of my mother's having seen me.[35] Now when I am suffering I think of my father's face.[36]

III. For His Mother

I and mother had no *yûgn*,[37] and I got nothing for her for a long time.[38] Since she left me I have no mother.

IV. For Véye (Who Died a Few Weeks Ago)

My *klạ*[39] came to where he had seen me, and I had forgotten him. My *klạ* and my many relatives shot things for me. My *klạ* and I have no father. I am remembering his face and his leaving me.

To the Kaingáng these are all tender chants of remembering, forgetting, and regret, and they are striking for the complete absence of any elements of fear. So, too, there is only one resentful expression—in Angglo's chant where she says, "My father died and never remembered me." It is curious that the Kaingáng, who desire less than anything on earth to see their dead relatives, should express in their mourning chants a desire to see them. The chants of Klendó and Kuthúgn, with their monotonous reiteration of "I forget what he looked like" and "I do not see him" may be pure and simple expressions of their horror of seeing the dead again rather than elliptical statements which might be completed: "I forget what he looked like, he has been so long dead; and how sorry I am."

The chants of the three women are of the occasional type, i.e. of the type chanted whenever the mood comes on one, whereas those of the three men are of the type uttered at funerals.

While I was among the Kaingáng the women did much more keening than the men. The Indians, however, could not be made aware of the fact that there was any difference between the amount of keening done by the women and that done by the men.

Death Songs (Ëhëdn)

The following songs may be sung as the funeral pyre is being ignited:

[35] His mother was dead.
[36] Literally, "his appearance."
[37] She had no father, and therefore he had no grandfather.
[38] Vomblé's explanation: "I would go to look for meat and not find it."
[39] See Appendix II.

I

a to na a wa lê hê nų yô nê ķê ya ma mbû vô yô
ta to na ha vâi ķëgn yâ nggâ ķô yêyê ķo yïgn mbâ
ha yê ķô yïgn mbâ.

Vomblé said, "They do this so that the *kuplêng* will go. If they did not do this it would take the living away."

II

ķi yë ų tô ķô pando mê lêlê nya
ķûi ķi yë ha lêlê nya ķų
ķûi ķi yë ų tô ķô pando mêêlêlê nya ķų
ķûi ķi yë lêlê nya

Vomblé explained: "They say to them that when they were alive they climbed trees.[40] Then they say *'ha ha.'* When the *kuplêng* hears this it goes off. If they did not sing this all the souls would come and live with the living, and then the living would go with them."

III

la ķônang yuķê[41] *pïtpïli vadnvala*
la ķôna yuķê pïtpïli vadn vala

"This song is sung so that the pyre may burn," said Klendó.

IV

1) *hëi   tê*[42] *vê hëi   tê vê*
   intact   intact
   sound
2) *vâ ma la yudn*[43] *yô ķlą të*
3) *hëi tê vê hëi tê vê*
4) *vâ ma la lâdn yô   ķlą tëi të*
   look you sun down place
5) *tô vai tê vê*

[40] The interpretation is clearly one of accommodation to what Vomblé feels to be the ethnologist's taste for interpretations. The song is made up of syllables some of which, though identical with meaningful elements in the Kaingáng language, have no conceivable meaning in the present context.

[41] The first five syllables have a general resemblance to what might be translated as "sun's eyebrows"; the two succeeding words might be translated as "ururú" (a bird) and "fever" respectively. Since, however, no explanation was vouchsafed by the informant and the reference is not clear, it seems best to reserve judgment.

[42] A predicating element.

[43] See p. 193.

Vomblé said that they sing this song "so that the *kupléng* will not be *vai* to them. [When they say sing] *hëi tệ vê* they are saying that when it is burnt the bones will be intact." But he immediately added: "They never sing this song. They sing their real song," i.e. their personal songs. Klendó said that this song made the corpse *vai*. "Kangdádn sang this song, and that is why Patá did not burn. It has [a syllable]*vai*[44] in it—that is why." But then, on the other hand, he says, "When Patá's *kupléng* heard this it probably became afraid and went away." Another interpretation of this song by the same informant is that "he is singing in order that there should be no *kumbëdn* on the edge of the burning place where the sun comes up."

Klendó, who is usually silent when asked for interpretations of songs, thought that in line 4 the "place where the sun comes down" referred to the sun's being alive and red and that *tệ vai tệ vê* meant that the edge of the ashes [toward the west] is evil-omened.

Although Vomblé and Klendó give different interpretations of this song there is a general agreement between them. Both informants feel that the effect of the song will be to make things *hë,* sound, well, but Klendó feels that it also involves certain dangers because of the presence of the syllable *vai.*

The following are hair-cutting songs:

V

kaichâ yûpï tê kô
wa kậ na yô anggû kâi mô a nê
yangvê yukï kunê anê vavû ho
anê vavâ kaichâ yûpï tê kô
kaichâ yûpï tê kô
wa kậ na yô anggû kâi mbô anê
nang vê yûkï ku nê anê va vû ho
a nê vâ hâ

This song has no meaning whatsoever.

VI

ų nų yômên ho lâ wa
kï kë lâ kalê hê
ų nų yômên hô lâ wa
kuyo kaichô
ų nų yômê hô lâ wa
kï kë kalê hê [and then repeat from the beginning]

[44] See line 5.

This song has no meaning whatsoever. Said Vomblé: "This is our song of fear. He is afraid of her [the *thûpáya*]. He is singing for her husband's *kuplêng* to be afraid and go away."

CEREMONIES FOR THE KÔKLÁ [CEREMONIAL FATHER,] AND MBË [CEREMONIAL MOTHER][45]

The Placenta and Umbilical Cord

When the child is born the placenta and the piece of the umbilical cord that was attached to the child are wrapped in medicinal herbs, placed in a little basket, and sunk in a stream, and a sharpened stick is forced through the basket to keep it from floating away. This is called by the term *pâyú,* which means to steal or to conceal. *pâyú* is done most usually by a brother of the mother and his wife. Through the series of rites that begin with the *pâyú* of his umbilical cord the child is bound to his father's affinal relatives.

The Baby's Meal of Cooked Food (Yôgndêyê)

Soon after the child is born its ankles are wrapped loosely with about twenty turns of cord, its *patthêyê*,[46] foot cords, and these are kept on for two weeks or so. Then the father decides to make a *yôgndêyê* for his child, and he goes out hunting, with perhaps a brother-in-law to help him, and hunts intensively for a number of days to get together enough meat for a big feast. When the meat has been collected the *mbë* and *kôklá* as well as all the close relatives of the child's parents who happen to be around, together with friends, are invited to a feast, and while their guests dine the parents look on without eating. Were they to eat, the father would never be able to shoot game again.

These ceremonies are almost always conducted in high spirits unless the hosts are stingy, and then everyone is rather gloomy and there are secret grumblings afterward. Everyone sits down wherever he wants to, the more distant relatives keeping discreetly in the background and joining but mildly in the conversation, the in-laws acting as if they "belonged," pushing the pots around and dishing out the food. When everyone has eaten as much as he can, or as much as there is, the men start to sing and the baby's mother hastens to remove the *patthêyê,* and when they are all unwound the party wanders off, carrying with it the remains of the feast. Depending on the quantity of meat, the party may last from a half hour to an hour.

[45] The explanation of all these ceremonies for the child is that if they were not performed the child would die, that it would not grow up, or that it would dry up and die.

[46] "The *patthêyê* are put on so they may be taken off at the *yôgndêyê*."

After the feast the *patthêyê* and the piece of the umbilical cord that was attached to the mother are wrapped with herbs and thrown into the water. Some time after this the child is given a name, but there is no ceremony of name-giving.

The Baby Blackening (Waichëdn)

This was the most joyful ceremony of the Kaingáng. Every few years, whenever there were enough children to warrant a baby-blackening, a large number of the people of one extended family used to come together in a big camp. While the men with children to blacken went out with their brothers and first cousins to get honey for beer, the others made dance ornaments[47] and hunted. The Kaingáng[48] cannot restrain themselves as the day of the festa draws near, and night after night as the beer ferments the men walk back and forth across the camp circle carrying their babies on their backs and singing. When at last the beer is *thô* the women paint their husbands with a black mixture made of charcoal and the sticky sap of a tree and stick feathers in it, and the men put little square hats of embira bark on their heads and wide bark belts around their waists, with bark tassels hanging down. Some of the belts are painted with black paint or animals' blood in crude designs that represent nothing at all. Now some men and women pass around the beer while the men stand or sit and sing, beating time by pounding on the ground with their clubs and lances. When the men have been singing awhile their wives come and stand or sit behind them, moving their arms slowly up and down in time to the music. Everyone sings as he chooses and as loud as he can, while clusters of young men stand around the older ones to try to learn the songs. There is no attempt to achieve harmony—everyone sings a different song, self-centered, musically oblivious to his surroundings. As they stand shaking their rattles or pounding their weapons on the ground—dancing, the Kaingáng call it—they stop from time to time to drink the beer. All day long and until late at night they drink while the women now stand, now sit, beside them, drinking beer, nursing babies, cooking food, eating, mourning, singing, quarreling. Every once in a while a group of men and women break out of the circle, grasp the *kôndjáidn* and the *lu,* and walk across and around the dance circle in a confused singing knot, drunk, intense, and unsteady. This staggering around the circle is called dancing

---

[47] See Appendix I, p. 171.

[48] Since the Kaingáng abandoned their lip plugs a number of years ago *waichëdn* has been given up. What follows is based on observations made at a *waichëdn* that was arranged for me. The actual piercing of the lip was done against my wishes and over my protest.

but bears not the slightest resemblance to the rhythmic artistic form usually called dancing. The Kaingáng make no effort to execute a formalized dance step. All they do is walk; yet their word for it is dancing, and they use the same term for the Brazilian polkas. What the word really means is something like "motion on foot while singing." Little children of five or more are not excluded from the festa but drink their beer, try to sing, and march around with the others. Sometimes two or three little boys will take a gourd of beer and go off by themselves and drink it, shaking rattles and singing.

At some time during this festa the children's lips are pierced. I saw only one child pierced—a boy about two. While Chantágn, its mother, held it on her lap, its grandmother forced beer into its mouth by pressing her lips against the child's and squirting while it wriggled and bawled to high heaven. This was to make the child sleep. Now while the child's mother, aunt, and some other women wept, the child was bathed in beer, wrapped in a blanket, screaming all the while, and laid down on a small heap of blankets. While the child was lying down it was coaxed to nurse to quiet it, even as its kôklá sat by swinging the little piercing knife in time to his own song. "They sing," say the Kaingáng, "so that the child will become frightened and go to sleep." While we may credit the Kaingáng with deep knowledge of infantile behavior under stress, it was clear that in this case the infant was completely unaware of just what was to happen to him; for in spite of the beer and the nursing he was wide awake when his lower lip was marked with three parallel black lines and his upper with one. These were centering lines made so that the piercing would be precisely in the middle of the child's lower lip just under the red part.

Now as the completely terrorized infant is held down by a number of people, while its mother and other women around it weep and the loud singing goes on, the kôklá thrusts his fingers into the child's mouth, distends the lip, and thrusts home with the knife. The child wriggles and screams, seizes the knife, and tries to pull it out as its mouth fills with blood and saliva. Now that the knife is extracted they try to insert the tiny lip plug, pushing and twisting and turning while the baby howls and the blood streams from its lip until at last the plug breaks in an ugly splintery end. Evidently the hole is not properly made. Again the kôklá distends the little lip and thrusts again with the knife. This time must be the last, so he twists and twists the knife until he is sure at last that the hole is big enough. When the plug is successfully inserted it is bound around on the outside with a bit of fiber to prevent its slipping back. Then one of the men takes water in his mouth and squirts it over the wound.

The piercing over, the kôklá picks up the baby, slings it in a blanket on his back, and begins to walk back and forth across the circle singing. Then he and the rest of the men stop and shout, "This is your [the infant's] making," followed by:

> *hili* about twelve times; and then *lililihilihilihililiholo changa changai yetyetyethohoho.*[49]

Vomblé said that the cries were in imitation of the cry of Water's Talking, a water-dwelling supernatural monster. Since, however, the water monster has no part in the extremely scanty ideology of this ceremony, I regard this explanation as very dubious.

Following the baby's "making" they play the game of *kavígn*, with soft bags[50] made of the inner bark of the embira tree and stuffed with tree hair. The bags are supposed to be thrown back and forth between the parents and the children's *kôklá* and *mbë*, but everyone joins in the fun of tossing the bags high in the air across the dance ground and catching them when they are thrown back. Meanwhile the people shout: "Come here! Catch my animal";[51] and *kaví kaví kaví* or *të të të*[52] or *tektektek*.[53]

When the beer is gone the camp breaks up.

Although the Kaingáng do not say so, it is clear that the ceremonies of *pâyú* and *waichëdn* have the purpose of giving the child a ceremonial father and mother. The *kôklá* or the *mbë* are usually brothers or sisters of the mother. They perform the first formal act after the child is born by putting the umbilical cord, the symbol of its birth, in the water; and at last they "make the child" at the ceremony of baby-blackening. On this occasion they receive presents along with the other affinal relatives of the parents, but they are especially rewarded for their services in the lip-piercing.

[49] Instead of these syllables they might also shout the following: *chui* (about 12 times); *yo* (about 4 times); *chui yoyoyoyo o halalala halalala holo* (about 6 times); *tivi* (about 12 times), followed by *vivivi tivivivivi net* (about 5 times); *ho* (about 4 times); *tivi* (about a dozen times); *vivivi tivivivi ho* (4 times).

[50] These are plaited especially for the occasion and then thrown away.

[51] "Probably the first ones to come up [in the very beginning of things] referred to these as owned animals [*mang*]. The long bags are men and the short ones women. They are called his wives."

[52] Vomblé said that this was the cry of the dot people, who were imitating the small hawk called *tëtë*.

[53] The same informant said that this was the cry of the circle people.

Appendix IV
Songs[1]

WITH THE EXCEPTION of the rare curing songs and the funeral song recorded in Appendix II, all Kaingáng songs are completely made up of meaningless syllables. But their meaninglessness is of a peculiar character, for often the syllables themselves have meaning in an absolute sense; that is to say, they exist in the Kaingáng language as meaningful elements, though in the songs their arrangement and sequence is such that no meaning is derivable from them. It is as if we were to make a song in English of the syllables *to, sigh, fly, me,* and so on. There are words in our language which have the same phonetic structure as these syllables, but if I make up a song of these words alone, in the sequence given, it is obvious that they have meaning only if we insist on a very arbitrary definition of the word "meaning." My informant Vomblé, however, was not beyond arguing that the songs he sang did "mean" something. Perhaps it was his desire to make the Kaingáng songs seem like the Brazilians' songs; perhaps it was his imaginative mind that prompted him. His interpretations are given in complete indifference to the syntactic and even the phonetic structure of his language, but they are always prefixed by the expression *tógnnyangló,* "probably," which indicates that he is speculating as to their meaning. The proper thing to do, of course, would have been to ask him to interpret the same song a month or so after recording in order to see whether his interpretation varied. I feel sure that the results would have shown considerable variation. Unfortunately time did not permit this.

Each Kaingáng song has from twenty to thirty stanzas. There is very

[1] The song given here was one of four recorded from one informant only. Everything in this section is based on information obtained from Vomblé unless otherwise stated. Since I had no recording device it was impossible to make a musical analysis of Kaingáng songs.

little melodic variety, and quite a number of songs are sung on one note. They gain their variety from the difference in the syllables and from the rhythmic patterning.

Men and women know the songs equally well, but men make more of a show. They sing to impress their sweethearts or prospective sweethearts; they sing at festas; they sing while they work; they sing in the quiet hour before dawn when they are lying awake under their coverings; they sing in the evening as they lie beside the fire squinting along an arrow to see if it is straight. They never sing in unison unless a group of young men are learning from an older man at a festa. Generally when the Kaingáng learn a song they listen attentively while it is being sung and then go off and practice alone. I never suspected that the Kaingáng youngsters who heard my Apache Indian songs knew them until I asked them to sing for me. Then they sang them without a mistake. It was the same with North American myths that I told. They would ask me to repeat the same myth until at last they corrected *me* when I left something out. But before that they had never given a sign that they already knew them.

The name of some man who is supposed to have made it up in the very beginning is attached by tradition to each song. Anyone may learn from anyone at all. From Vomblé I got the impression that there were a limited number of songs and that very few were composed anew, but I had no opportunity to confirm my impression.

I give below an analysis of the lyrics of the first ten stanzas of one song.

Padnmbû's Song[2]

I

(1) *nê yô vudn vudnê ḳa la ye nya yugn lë yô mba tôgn mê*[3] ⎫
(2) *nê yô vûn vû nê ḳa la ye nya yugn lë yô mba tôgn mê* ⎬ a
(3) *nê yô vûn vu ne ḳa la yem*   a—
(4) *a tô êng mu lo ne a teng dje to va ḳa ḳle to to me*   b
(5) *nê yô vûn vudne ḳa la yem*   a—
(6) *a tô êng mo lo ne a teng dje to va ḳa*   b—
(7) *nggôyo cho me*   c
(8) *neyô vûn vu ne ḳa la yem*   a—

Interpretation: "Probably: when the ancients came out [there was] the smoke of their fires." This interpretation is derived from the first five syllables of line 1, which are frequently repeated in somewhat modified form throughout the song. *Nêyô vudn vulu,* in Kaingáng, means "smoke."

---

[2] I.e. song of the mythical Padnmbû as sung by Vomblé.

[3] The division is merely to assist in comparison of lines. For meaning of symbols see p. 204.

II

(1) *a yugn nê kẽgn yë to un vẹ*   a(x)
(2) *a yugn nê kẽgn yë*   a
(3) *na tobm nat kûlû wanyêkô*   b
(4) *te to vâi mê pô*   c
(5) *ta tộ yëbm*   d
(6) *nyêki klạ nê ya*   e
(7) *të to vâi mê pô*   c
(8) *pi tộ yïm lok tộ yë a tû kê*   f
(9) *ta tộ yë*   d

III

(1) *a vẹ tû va*   a(x)
(2) *a ve tu ve*   a(y)
(3) *a kï nya*   b
(4) *a vẹ kû a yô ve na vẹ tụ kû yô yâ a kïm*   c
(5) *a kô nyang ve*   d
(6) *a kô nyang ve*   d
(7) *a vẹ kû a yo ve na wẹ tụ kû yô yâ kïm*   c
(8) *a kô nyang ve*   d
(9) *a kô nyang ve*   d
(10) *a kï nyam*   b

IV

(1) *a tộ lugn ve yâ mu nya*   a(u)
(2) *a tộ lugn ve yâ mụ*   a(v)
(3) *ye tộ lugn ve yâ mụ kû*   a(w)(x)
(4) *yûgn ndô ye tộ a ve na vẹ tụ nê tẹk tạ*   b(y)
(5) *lugn vẹ kô yô hëm kû*   a—(z)
(6) *yûgn ndô*   b
(7) *yi nê ang djâ kaichâ ku pan hëm ôgn ve lô kû* c
(8) *yûgn ndô*   b
(9) *yi nê ang djâ kaichâ kupan hëm*   c
(10) *yûgn ndô*   b
(11) *yi nê ang djâ kaichâ ku pan hëm*   c

Interpretation: "Probably they made their bird arrows [*ndô*, lines 4, 6, 8, and 10] of pine knots [*kaichâ*, lines 7, 9, and 11], and they are telling about it."

V

(1) *vêle vê*	a
(2) *amblïgn nê tệ wa*	b
(3) *vêlê vedn vêlê*	a
(4) *naichû nyêkï⁴ klą nê ya ti yô kle ko tự to*	c
(5) *amblïgn nê tệ wa*	b
(6) *vêlê vedn vêlê*	a
(7) *naichự môklâ⁴ klą nê ya ti yô kle ko tự to*	c
(8) *amblïgn nê tệ wa*	b
(9) *vêlê vedn*	a

Interpretation: "Probably something was shot [*yôklé*, somebody's hunting prize, lines 4 and 7] and they did not eat, [*ko tự*, lines 4 and 7]. They left it. Probably Nyekï [line 4] is joking with him and telling him about his camp [*nêyá*, lines 4 and 7]."

VI

(1) *êng wai nyê të la ha nự kâ*	a
(2) *nyêkï⁵ klą nê ya ti yô kle kû lâgn*	b
(3) *wai ve lo tộ nê*	c
(4) *êng wai nyê tëbm*	a—
(5) *êng wai nyê tëbm la ha nự kâ*	a
(6) *kanggûï⁵ klą nê ya ti yô kle kûlâgn*	b₁
(7) *wai ve lok tộ nê*	c
(8) *êng wai nyê tëbm la ha nự kâ*	a
(9) *kïyïtá⁵ klą nê ya ti yô kle kû lâgn*	b₂
(10) *wai ve lok tộ nê*	c
(11) *êng wai nyê tëbm*	a—
(12) *êng mự hự yë*	d
(13) *êng wai nyê tëbm*	a—

Interpretation: "Probably when they joke with him they say, 'The animal you shot [*a*, your; *yokle*, hunting prize, lines 2, 6 and 9] is no good [*kulagn*, lines 2, 6 and 9]. When I eat it I get diarrhea and my insides become dry.'" References to diarrhea (*chukchúyu*) and dry internal organs (*ndju kanggá*) do not appear in this song.

VII

(1) *lugn mô kë yô kô yô kë*	a
(2) *lugn mô kë yô kô yô kë*	a

---
⁴ Male personal names.
⁵ Male personal names.

(3) *lugn mô kë yô kô yô kô*   a
(4) *lugn mô këm*   a—
(5) *a tô nê hu vâ wa hu va ve hû vâ wa*   b
(6) *lugn mô këm*   a—
(7) *a tô a tô nê hų nyang mbâ ve ve hû vâ wa*   b₁
(8) *lugn mô kë yô kô yô kô*   a
(9) *lugn mô këi yô kô yô kë*   a
(10) *lugn mô kë ko këbm*   a—

Interpretation: "Probably: they came along and camped." The only reference to camping I can discern is the syllable *nê*, which really means, "One person camps" [lines 5 and 7].

VIII

(1) *yô nya a tô të ye tô a ko kô yâ mô*   a
(2) *wai ve yâ mô*   b
(3) *a yugn ndë yûgn mô*   c
(4) *wai ve yâ mų*   b
(5) *kô kų mbâ hâi kô kų mbâ hâi kô ko mbâ hâm*   d
(6) *yô nya a tô të ye tô a kô ko yâ mų*   a
(7) *wai ve yâ mų*   b

IX

(1) *ang dju lê lê kôinggëgn hë pe wai ndjë na yâ*   a
(2) *ang djû ma ak tê nô a yon wai ndjë tadn vâ*   b₁
(3) *ang dju lê lê kôinggëgn hë pe wai ndjë na yâ*   a
(4) *ang djû ma ak tê nô a yo wai ndjë tadn vâ kâ wa*   b
(5) *wai ndjë tadn ve kâ wa*   b—

Interpretation: "I don't know. Probably they were watching for him [*ti*, him; *yâ*, for; *lêlê*, look or watch]; watching for him to come along. Probably they mean *kôinggëgn mbëgn waindji wa* [the big man laughs]. Prob-
                    man   large   laugh
ably he joked." (See line 1, *kôinggëgn* etc.)

X

(1) *ndo ko kë*   a
(2) *ang ndo kô kë mbô*   b
(3) *êng nya mô*   c
(4) *ang ndo ko këm*   b
(5) *yô vâ*   c

(6) *nê yâ mbô na e ye lo tobm*   d
(7) *yô vâ nêng mǫ ve yô vâ ma yô vâ vebm*   e
(8) *ndo ko kë*   a
(9) *ndo ko këi*   a
(10) *ang ndo ko kë mbô*   b
(11) *êng nya mǫ*   c
(12) *nat kû lûi[6] wanyêkô[6] te to*   f
(13) *yô vâ nêng mǫ ve yo vâ vem*   e—

Interpretation: "Probably he became ill from something and they carried him." The whole interpretation is derived from the syllable *te* which appears for the first time in line 12. *te* is the participial form of the verb meaning "to carry on the back."

Little can be done with song analysis without phonographic recording; nevertheless I have analyzed the lyrics of the ten stanzas given, with the object of discovering whether the syllables follow a specific form. Each song has at least two definite syllabic patterns which are repeated over and over again, but the arrangement of the patterns does not follow any order except a general kind of alternation with other patterns. In the analysis below, each syllabic pattern has been marked with one of the first seven letters of the alphabet. When the pattern is repeated with something left out a minus sign is placed after the letter: b—, when the pattern is repeated with some modification it is marked with an inferior number: a_1. Occasional syllables which occur at the beginning or end of well-defined patterns but which are not repeated when the pattern is repeated have been indicated by one of the last six letters of the alphabet placed in parentheses: a(v).

The following schema shows the arrangement of syllabic patterns in the ten stanzas:

(1) aaa—ba—b—ca—
(2) a(x)abcdecfd
(3) a(y)bcddcddb
(4) a(u)a(v)a(w)(x)b(y)a—(z)bcbcbcbc
(5) abacbacba
(6) abca—ab_1cab_2ca—a—
(7) aaaa—ba—$b_1$aaa—
(8) abcbdab
(9) ababb—
(10) abcbcdefaabcfe

___
[6] Male personal names.

Appendix V

The Kaingáng Language and Ethnological Investigation

Ethnological investigation has most always had to cope with two great difficulties: lack of funds and the physical and psychic hardships of field work. These difficulties have necessarily limited the length of field trips. At the same time it has become increasingly evident to ethnologists that a speaking knowledge of native languages is such a tremendous aid to investigation that some attempt has to be made to learn to talk them even in the limited time available. The difficulties seem, at first glance, insurmountable, particularly when we recall our difficulties in mastering languages of our own Indo-European group, which at least have the same grammatical categories as English and many similar words, even though pronunciation may be radically different. The grammatical categories of primitive languages, however, are frequently quite different from those of the Indo-European family; and their phonetic structures are often utterly foreign to our own linguistic habits.

The thoughtful student of language and culture is sometimes inclined, therefore, to doubt the possibility of learning to talk an exotic language in less than two years of hard and steady work. If he knows any primitive language at all through having studied its grammar and vocabulary he is aware of its phonetic subtlety, its strange way of formularizing the natural world, the richness of its vocabulary, the illusiveness of its idioms. Now although all of these observations are correct, they are not always *all* true of any one language. Languages that have completely strange phonetic systems may have grammatical structures that are not so very different from the Indo-European; languages with difficult morphology may have simple syntax and phonology.[1] When doubts arise, therefore, about the

---

[1] It is not always necessary, as we well know, to speak a foreign language grammatically in order to be understood and to understand. We must be careful, however, not to under-

possibility of gaining a working knowledge of a language in a short time, it is not really possible to satisfy these doubts unless something is known about the general structure of the language (phonetic, morphological, and syntactic) and its categories. It is also necessary to know what we mean when we speak of "easy" and "difficult." The morphology of a language may present overwhelming difficulties of analysis, but some of these difficulties may be quite irrelevant in learning to talk it. It may be almost impossible to get at the meaning of some troublesome elements, yet the elements themselves may be used in such a formal way that it is unnecessary to know their meaning. All one needs to do is to know where they occur and then to use them mechanically.

When all these factors are taken into consideration, however, the fact still remains that the language *is* utterly strange and that the possibility of mastering so much strangeness in time to use it as a tool in field work seems slight. I shall, therefore, give here an account of the precise nature of the conditions encountered in an attempt to learn to talk the Kaingáng language so that the reader may be able to form a just idea of the problem.

I outlined the general pattern of the Káingáng language in a recent paper [2] and shall not, therefore, go into detail here. Of the eighteen consonants there is really only one that does not occur in English, a labiodental *m*.[3] Of the vowels there are four that do not occur in English, but of these, two are familiar in French and German, and a third in Russian.[4] The fourth occurs nowhere else that I know of, but it is so much like the sound of the diphthong in English *sure* and *gourd* that it would be easy to produce an equivalent of it that would satisfy the natives. Most of these vowels can also be nasalized, but these nasalizations are familiar to students of French and Portuguese. There are no consonantic clusters[5] in Kain-

---

estimate the importance of speaking grammatically, for some natives do not understand their language unless it is spoken with a high degree of grammatical precision. In regard to the limits of intelligibility each language is different, and in each tribe each individual is different. Some natives are so habituated to hearing their language spoken only by tribesmen that they never learn to understand a white man.

[2] "A Kaingáng Text," *International Journal of American Linguistics*, 8:3-4, p. 172.

[3] An *m* made by touching the upper teeth to the lower lip. A *d* and a *b* and a *g* in which the air is expelled through the nose instead of through the mouth occur in Kaingáng at the end of words, but these also occur in English. Examples: nasally exploded *d* in English ":laden"; nasally exploded *b* in English "grab him" (grab'm); nasally exploded *g* in English "wagon" (in New York City). As a matter of fact the labio-dental *m* also occurs in English in words like "triumph" where the *m* is followed by a labio-dental consonant, but it is extremely difficult for English-speaking people to produce this consonant in other positions.

[4] As in the pronouns *Bbl*, you, and *Mbl*, we.

[5] Where three or four consonants come together at once.

gáng. Thus there is nothing completely strange in the phonetic structure of the language.

The problem of grammar is more difficult. There are two fundamental categories in Kaingáng, the static and the dynamic, and these are expressed by different particles and by changes in the verb. The category of number—singularity and plurality—is also expressed principally in the verb. Present and past time are expressed by identical verbal forms, but the ideas of futurity, contingency and continuity are conveyed by elements that directly follow the verb which is in the active form. There is no subjunctive, but all ideas that would be subjunctive in English are expressed by syntactic forms, i.e. by placing statements in intelligible juxtaposition. There is no sex gender, and there are no concepts of definiteness or indefiniteness. Thus, on the whole, what one has to do in Kaingáng is to satisfy oneself with a much reduced mechanism. As far as morphology is concerned Kaingáng is actually easier to learn than French and German. When one considers the whole battery of case forms in German and the elaborate devices for expressing time—the specific forms and their proper sequence in complex sentences—Kaingáng actually is simple. The categories of the static and dynamic are not foreign to the Indo-European languages, which generally express them in the verb.[6]

The sentence structure of Kaingáng is, on the whole, subject+object+modifier+verb. Subject and object are followed by one of those troublesome formal elements that are so hard to define, and the verb is always followed by the sign of the static or dynamic or by one of the modal particles (time, static or dynamic, continuative). These elements are always the same, and one learns to put them in automatically. Thus, the major change in syntactic form from English is in the position of the verb. But for the student familiar with German the shift of the verb's position should present no difficulties. The picture of sentence structure that I have given here is rather elementary, and there are, of course, a number of modifications; nevertheless, this is the form the beginner learns, and it is not difficult to master.

The only really difficult problem in Kaingáng is one of memory, for one has to memorize the entire content of the language. Yet by recording large numbers of texts one can increase one's knowledge at a great rate.

People frequently ask me how long it took me to learn to talk Kaingáng, as if one had a period of complete ignorance from which one suddenly burst like a butterfly, splendidly articulate. But learning is gradual. Day by day as he watches the people, the student acquires a word here, an idiom

---

[6] In learning Kaingáng one quickly begins to feel the conceptual similarity of their static forms with the verb *to be*, and of their dynamic forms and ours with the transitive verb.

there. Sometimes a single expression gives him a startling insight into a linguistic problem that has been bothering him for weeks, and then instead of crawling he takes a great leap forward. In this way he learns the language and the culture together. He does not wait until he knows the language well before beginning his ethnological work, but picks up the bits of ethnological information he can be sure of, leaving the rest until his developing linguistic facility permits him to penetrate further into the culture.

Glossary

angdjĭdn   The festa of the rattles that is held when the surviving spouse returns from his (or her) widower's (or widow's) isolation.

chôi chí (*chôi*, to grow; *chi*, old)   Grown old; mature. Said of men above thirty-five or forty.

e   I or my. The first person singular pronoun, *éng*, I or my, becomes *e* before *ķ, t, ch,* and *p.*

ëhëdn   A funeral song to drive off the ghost-soul.

eķlą́ (*e*, my; *ķlą*, offspring)   My offspring in the relationship sense. Used by a parent for his own child, and also applied to all the younger members of his own extended family by an older man.

éng   I or my.

éngdjí   My child. For complete explanation see kinship terms, Appendix II.

énglânglé (*éng*, my; *lânglé*, two)   My co-spouse.

ka lę́lê nya (*ka*, in; *lę́lê*, to live; *nya*, continuative)   To live in; to love. The expression denoting the affective relationship between members of the same extended family.

këlą́   Young man; males from ten to thirty-five or forty.

ķlą   Offspring in the relationship sense.

këmê   A cake made from the mealy interior of the trunk of a palm. Anciently made from pounded corn.

ķóiķá   People in the relationship sense; relative.

ķóika hë (*ķóiķá*, people or relative; *hë*, whole, entire, good)   Real people; individuals having the same body paint design. For complete explanation see Appendix II.

ķóinggëgn   Man.

ķóķlá   Ceremonial father. Often used as a courtesy term. The man who treats an infant's umbilical cord ceremonially and who pierces a boy's lip or a girl's thigh.

kóndjáidn A stick ornamented with feathers and used as a dance ornament.

kóplëgn To divine with charcoal.

Kuchágn A supernatural monster.

kumbëdn To divine from insects.

kuplêng The ghost-soul.

lânglé Two; co-spouse.

lu A dance ornament with a basketlike top.

lų Doom.

mang A special possessive form for animals that are owned.

mbâdn Husband. For more complete definition see kinship terms, Appendix II.

mbë Ceremonial mother. The woman who treats one's umbilical cord ceremonially and who assists at the piercing of the lip of a boy and the thigh of a girl.

nê To marry; to sit.

nêklȩ̂ The *nêklȩ̂* is the drinking name.

nungnyên Brother, sister, or cousin. For complete definition see kinship terms, Appendix II.

ndegn To refuse.

nggign A fern with a thorny, woody stem. Used for fermenting beer and in death rituals.

nggïyúdn The supernatural. All supernatural beings are *nggïyúdn*.

nyô̧ Mother. For complete definition see kinship terms, Appendix II.

nyungnyên First person singular of *nungnyên*.

nyungnyȩ̂lȩ̂ Child. A term used only in keening chants. It has about the same feeling as the term *yi*.

plų Wife. For complete explanation see kinship terms, Appendix II.

tai A fruit.

të Woman.

të tagn (*të*, woman; *tagn*, fat, new, desirable) A young woman who has not borne more than one or two children.

thangglïgn Dirty; taboo.

thêyê A projectile shot by a supernatural being. It makes people sick and may be extracted by a shaman.

thô Bitter. Said of beer that has reached the degree of fermentation proper for drinking.

thúgn Enemy.

thúpqaya A widowed person during the period of his (or her) isolation and the festa given on his (or her) return.

tutólo A herb used as a remedy.

úyólo nya tëi. (*úyólo*, tapir; *nya*, food; *tëi*, raw) Tapir's raw food. A herb used frequently as a medicine.

vai Supernaturally dangerous. Said particularly of corpses that will not burn.

vayú Divining by belching.

Vëin A supernatural monster.

waindji To flirt; to have an affair with.

waikayú   Aggressive; quarrelsome; enterprising; brave.

waikó   To have sexual intercourse.

waikómáng   The widow's (or widower's) period of isolation.

wangdjó   The succulent top of the tapir's neck. The mythological name of the Kaingáng. A supernatural monster.

yi   Child in the kinship sense. For complete definition see kinship terms, Appendix II.

Yóin   A supernatural monster.

yóktë   Women having the same body-paint design as a man. For complete explanation see Appendix II.

yókthệ   Guilt; fault; custom.

Yunggí   A supernatural monster.

yúgn   Father; any man much older than the speaker. Often used as a courtesy term. For complete explanation see kinship terms, Appendix II.

Name Index

(d) indicates that the person is deceased. The names of most of the characters in the chapter on Folklore have been omitted.

ABOUT THE AUTHOR

In December 1932, JULES HENRY, fresh from his training as student and teacher under Franz Boas and Ruth Benedict in the Department of Anthropology at Columbia University, travelled to the state of Santa Catarina in the highlands of Southeastern Brazil to begin an intensive study of the primitive Kaingáng people. Establishing his home in the center of their village, he learned their language and observed and partook of their life until January 1934. His fascinating report of Kaingáng life—and death—and the subsequent forming of his ideas about Kaingáng culture resulted in the publication in 1941 of *Jungle People*. It immediately established his reputation as both an ethnographer and a writer, for throughout the book his perceptive observations and stimulating ideas about Kaingáng life and culture are revealed in a warm, appealing, and lively style.

In more recent years, Dr. Henry, as teacher, writer, and consultant to many national research organizations, has secured his position in the vanguard of American anthropologists. He has taught at Columbia University and the University of Chicago, and is at present Professor of Sociology and Anthropology at Washington University. As a writer he attained his most brilliant success with the publication in 1963 of his highly praised *Culture Against Man*.

CARAVELLE EDITIONS

72

A free catalogue of VINTAGE BOOKS will be sent at your request. Write to Vintage Books, 457 Madison Avenue, New York, New York 10022.

V-198	Bardolph, Richard	THE NEGRO VANGUARD
V-42	Beard, Charles A.	THE ECONOMIC BASIS OF POLITICS *and Related Writings*
V-60	Becker, Carl L.	DECLARATION OF INDEPENDENCE
V-17	Becker, Carl L.	FREEDOM AND RESPONSIBILITY IN THE AMERICAN WAY OF LIFE
V-191	Beer, Thomas	THE MAUVE DECADE: *American Life at the End of the 19th Century*
V-199	Berman, H. J. (ed.)	TALKS ON AMERICAN LAW
V-211	Binkley, Wilfred E.	PRESIDENT AND CONGRESS
V-44	Brinton, Crane	THE ANATOMY OF REVOLUTION
V-37	Brogan, D. W.	THE AMERICAN CHARACTER
V-72	Buck, Paul H.	THE ROAD TO REUNION, 1865-1900
V-98	Cash, W. J.	THE MIND OF THE SOUTH
V-190	Donald, David	LINCOLN RECONSIDERED
V-264	Fulbright, J. William	MYTHS AND REALITIES IN AMERICAN FOREIGN POLICY AND DOMESTIC AFFAIRS
V-31	Goldman, Eric F.	RENDEZVOUS WITH DESTINY
V-183	Goldman, Eric F.	THE CRUCIAL DECADE—AND AFTER: *America, 1945-1960*
V-95	Hofstadter, Richard	THE AGE OF REFORM
V-9	Hofstadter, Richard	AMERICAN POLITICAL TRADITION
V-120	Hofstadter, Richard	GREAT ISSUES IN AMERICAN HISTORY, Volume I (1765-1865)
V-121	Hofstadter, Richard	GREAT ISSUES IN AMERICAN HISTORY, Volume II (1864-1957)
V-242	James, C. L. R.	THE BLACK JACOBINS
V-102	Meyers, Marvin	THE JACKSONIAN PERSUASION
V-189	Miers, Earl Schenck	ROBERT E. LEE
V-84	Parkes, Henry B.	THE AMERICAN EXPERIENCE
V-212	Rossiter, Clinton	CONSERVATISM IN AMERICA
V-52	Smith, Henry Nash	VIRGIN LAND
V-253	Stampp, Kenneth	THE PECULIAR INSTITUTION
V-179	Stebbins, Richard P.	U. S. IN WORLD AFFAIRS, 1959
V-204	Stebbins, Richard P.	U. S. IN WORLD AFFAIRS, 1960
V-222	Stebbins, Richard P.	U. S. IN WORLD AFFAIRS, 1961
V-244	Stebbins, Richard P.	U. S. IN WORLD AFFAIRS, 1962
V-110 V-111	Tocqueville, Alexis de	DEMOCRACY IN AMERICA, Volumes I and II
V-103	Trollope, Mrs. Frances	DOMESTIC MANNERS OF THE AMERICANS
V-265	Warren, Robert Penn	LEGACY OF THE CIVIL WAR
V-208	Woodward, C. Vann	BURDEN OF SOUTHERN HISTORY

A free catalogue of VINTAGE BOOKS will be sent at your request. Write to *Vintage Books, 457 Madison Avenue, New York, New York 10022.*